Eco-Cuisine

ECO-CUISINE

An Ecological Approach to Gourmet Vegetarian Cooking

Ron Pickarski, CEC
(formerly Brother Ron Pickarski, OFM)

Photography by Francine Zaslow

TEN SPEED PRESS
Berkeley, California

🕐 TEN SPEED PRESS
PO Box 7123
Berkeley, California 94707

Cover and text design by Sarah Levin
Photographs © 1995 by Francine Zaslow

**Product names mentioned herein may be legally protected trademarks and/or registered
trademarks of their respective companies. It is not our intent to use any of these names generically.**

The author wishes to gratefully acknowledge the following for generously supplying
several of the items which appear in photographs throughout the book:

The Artful Hand Gallery, 36 Copley Place, Boston, MA 02116 (617) 262-9601
(glass plate—photo after page 22)

Annieglass, P.O. Box 8445 Santa Cruz, CA 95061 (800) 347-6133
(glass plates—photo after page 70)

Newton Pottery House, 1021 Boylston St., Newton Highlands, MA 02161 (617) 332-8960
(ceramic plates—photos before page 71 and after page 134)

Chilmark Pottery, 77 Union St., Newton Centre, MA 02159 (617) 332-2311
(ceramic plates—photos before page 135 and before page 231)

Terrafirma Ceramics Inc., 152 West 25th St., New York, NY 10002 (212) 645-7600
(ceramic plate—photo before page 23)

Jubilation, 91 Union St., Newton Centre, MA 02159 (617) 965-0488
(glass plate—photo after page 230)

Francine Zaslow Photography Inc., 27 Drydock Ave, Boston, MA 02210
(plaster casts—photos before page 23, after page 70, after page 134, after page 230, and before page 231)

Library of Congress Cataloging-in-Publication Data
Pickarski, Ron.
Eco-cuisine: an ecological approach to gourmet
vegetarian cooking/Ron Pickarski.
p.   cm.
Includes index.
ISBN 0-89815-635-1
1. Vegetarian cookery.   2. Ecology.   I. Title.
TX837.P5276   1995
641.5'636--dc20   95-18700
CIP

1 2 3 4 5 6 7 8 9 – 00 99 98 97 96 95
Printed in the United States of America

Dedication

St. Francis of Assisi is the patron saint of ecology in the Roman Catholic Church. Having been a Franciscan Friar for 23 years, my heart has a fondness for his love and compassion for Mother Nature. Francis found himself and his God in the quiet of nature and beckons us to our spiritual roots through her. May his spirit and the spirit of all Franciscans live in the spirit of this book.

Acknowledgments

This book was an enjoyable task because I was blessed with a wonderful group of people to work with. My sincere appreciation and thanks to all for making this book a beautiful work of art.

Nancy Loving is a wonderful natural foods cook who brought not only her expertise as a culinarian, but also as an editor and manager. Her dedication to this book is a reflection of her desire to inspire humanity to a healthier dietary lifestyle.

Andrea Hart moved from New Jersey to Boston for two months to do her externship with me as a natural foods chef. She worked in the office with Nancy and with myself in my kitchen during August and September of 1993. Her love of the art was an inspiration. We had a wonderful time developing and testing many of these recipes.

Sal Glynn provided editorial assistance, working tirelessly to give this book a sense of literary identity. Sal contributed far beyond the call of duty and took a personal and professional interest in bringing this book to completion.

Special thanks to Jo Ann Deck and the creative staff of Ten Speed Press for their support of my second book. They pooled a great deal of their resources creating this book.

The color photography was provided by Francine Zaslow, a commercial photographer based in Boston, whose dedication and artistic vision are truly appreciated. Working closely with expert food stylist George Simons, they both did a wonderful job capturing the essence of my art.

I would also like to give sincere thanks to all of my recipe testers, especially Andrea Hart, Cathy Chiara, Freya Dinshaw (and her family, friends, and neighbors), Laura Evers, Jonette and June Nagai, and Cary Bernette, who were all given many recipes to test. The second wave of recipes were tested by Amie Hamlin (and the Binghamton Area Vegetarian Society), Cindy Grogan, Arlene Ciroula, and Maryann Bolles, all of whom provided great assistance.

CONTENTS

Desserts & Dessert Sauces

Dessert Sauces

Beverages

INTRODUCTION

"Couscous and tofu in a cheesecake! That sounds terrible!" This response was from a pastry chef at the 1991 American Culinary Federation convention in Connecticut. Later he dared to attend my presentation with an open mind and try the cheesecake made with tofu, chocolate, and couscous. He enjoyed it so much that he became a believer and invited me as the guest of honor to the first vegetarian dinner ever served to me by professional chefs. One needs to keep that same open mind when approaching such a controversial issue as diet and vegetarianism. It is likened to parachuting out of an airplane at 10,000 feet. If one's mind is open like the parachute, the experience will be wonderful.

Transformation is a slow process. I know from my experience. I gradually weaned myself off meat, dairy, eggs, junk food, and smoking as I transformed my life and diet. I weighed 198 pounds and was not in the best of health. What I did have going for me is an open mind. The greatest barrier to any change are the illusions in one's mind. Reality is what it is, not what we think it is, and illusions can become obstacles to commitment. The belief that if the food is healthy it will not be an enjoyable dining experience is an illusion. Dispelling that illusion with my food is the challenge that inspires me. Yet, there are other levels of inspiration in my love affair with food and they have transformed my love of food into a pure passion. It is my vision to take vegetarian plant-based food and make it a complete cuisine. This challenge fuels my creative talent.

My ambition isn't to have everyone eating a totally plant-based vegetarian diet, but rather to inspire people to consume a plant-based diet as part of their diet because it resonates best with our eco-systems, both internal (bodies) and external (Mother Earth). Every time I create a great recipe or serve a wonderful feast of vegetarian foods to non-vegetarians, it helps create positive dietary transformation.

D.H. Lawrence sums up my passionate love affair with food when he writes: "The essential function of art is moral. Not aesthetic, nor decorative, not pastime and recreation, but moral…a passionate, implicit morality, not didactic. A morality which changes the blood, rather than the mind. Changes the blood first, the mind follows in the wake." In culinary art, the food literally changes our blood by going through a form of transubstantiation (or digestion). It is an illusion to think of food as something that we consume simply for calories and nutrients. Food relates to art, culture, economics, ecology, religion, and society. Food is central to the celebration of life and the soul of humanity's social life. It affects all five senses (touch, smell, taste, sight, and hearing) as an art form. Food is the art form and the plate is the culinarian's canvas. Deepak Chopra calls food recycled energy and our bodies are one step in the process. I call it the life blood of the earth that flows through our bodies in the form of culinary art. Creating that river of energy that transforms our bodies and spirits is what inspires me.

What is Eco-Cuisine?

Ecology is an awareness of the interrelationships between living organisms and their environment. Eco-Cuisine is about the human diet and its relationship to our personal health and the natural environment. We must begin to look at food as a route back to nature and a way to understand our connections with natural cycles. We need to live in harmony with nature and within our biological boundaries that are part of that natural system.

Eco-Cuisine's premise is that vegetarianism should be the foundation of one's dietary lifestyle. Plant-based foods are not only nutritious but are low on the food chain and have a low impact on the environment because they take minimal energy to produce, yet give a maximum return.

Modern cuisine is primarily centered around animal-based foods and their by-products. The major concern of non-vegetarians is what will replace meat in the center of the plate. My transforming of classic cuisine towards plant-based foods need not be misconstrued as creating a pseudo-meat diet. Vegetarianism is a complete and independent diet, not a pseudo-meat diet. Vegetables and herbs are what give animal foods their vibrant flavor profile.

Eco-Cuisine is a dietary approach to ecology, seeking a balance between personal and environmental nutrition. By living in harmony with our environment we nurture it just as it nurtures us. This cooperation with the energies of nature is no more prevalent than in our dietary lifestyle. Diet, like our environment, is dynamic, not static, and constantly changing. Our bodies are in the same constant transition. Our diets must meet our constantly changing biological needs; this is one reason why we should consume seasonal and regional foods because they meet our body's and nature's needs simultaneously.

Eco-Cuisine isn't just about consuming a plant-based diet. Dietary changes alone will not save the environment. We must realize that we did not weave the web of life, but are merely strands in it. What we do to the web, we do to ourselves.

In an ecological diet, humanity is considered part of the eco-system and how humanity best functions within the spectrum of the environment is determined, in part, by one's diet. We are likened to mobile trees needing nutrients from both the soil and sun. My emphasis is on diet because it is one area where we constantly tax the environment. What is the best diet for humanity? It is a high complex carbohydrate, high fiber, low fat, and low protein diet found in grains, vegetables, and legumes. Animal-based foods are generally high in fat and protein, and have no carbohydrates or fiber. The choice is clear.

Changing Your Diet

Diet comes from the Greek word *diatia,* meaning a way of life. The diet must be transformed, not merely changed, and the diet (or specific group of foods) must be applied to the person, not the person to the diet. Christ spoke to the farmers in simple parable form about the sower and the seeds. Forgetting the academics and taking people from where they are is a great starting place for dietary transformation.

My first and only health crisis came when I had an attack of appendicitis. In the first year that my parents had opened their restaurant, I was constantly indulging in hamburgers, French fries, and milk shakes. For three weeks before the attack I was sick every Saturday evening; then one Saturday evening the pain hit and the crisis ended with the removal of my appendix. The Chinese call a crisis, "a dangerous opportunity." Disease is the crisis point of breakdown in our eco-system. At the point of crisis one needs immediate relief. I remembered that painful lesson at the seminary when I weighed in at 198 pounds. There was more than a battle of the bulge going on. Dietary awareness was the beginning of my journey back to health.

My transformation started by a simple reduction of meat in my diet. I made a commitment to replace the unhealthy foods with healthy alternatives over a period of time. Commitment has to be for the right reasons if it is going to attain the right results, so be clear about your motivation. I took no radical approaches and allowed myself to be human, especially in social settings (this is a great way to justify indulging). Shortly after becoming a total vegetarian, I was invited to a Greek restaurant by a Greek Coptic priest. Not knowing that I was vegetarian, the priest insisted that I eat the fish. I did with reluctance at first and didn't really enjoy it because it was not well prepared. But I had cooked shrimp Creole (one of my favorite dishes) for my community that evening before leaving for dinner at the restaurant. Upon returning to the monastery from the Greek restaurant, I promptly sat down to a generous portion of my shrimp Creole and thoroughly enjoyed the meal. It was wonderful and also the last time I have eaten shrimp.

The starting point to transforming your diet is to find the offending foods. Is it the extra bowl of ice cream before bed or potato chips for an afternoon snack that is putting on the weight? Not exercising enough (exercise suppresses one's appetite and helps the body retain its calcium stores)? In ecological nutrition, the universe must get a return for the food it produces, the body must receive a nutritional return from the food ingested to compensate for the energy expended to ingest and digest the food, as well as nurture one's body. An ecological diet addresses the dynamics of ecology from the perspective of human nutrition in getting the greatest nutrient return from the food, and then addresses the ecological approach of food production.

In North Carolina, I gave a lecture on the need to make vegetarianism a part of our dietary lifestyle but not necessarily the absolute diet. A young woman came up to me afterwards and told me how much it meant to her. Her husband said that now he can be vegetarian six days a week and still have his buffalo wings at weekend parties. Americans are generally extremists wanting no fat or full fat. In the seventies the fad was sugar, in the eighties it was cholesterol, and in the nineties the fad is fat. Nutritional density will most likely be the next fad but one that will not falter in a decade because that is what culinary art is all about. Part of learning how to live is learning how to eat.

Conscious Cookery as a Spiritual Path

Every major religion centers part of its ritual around the meal. With Catholicism, it is the Eucharist; in Judaism, there is the Seder meal; and in India, it is the Bandar. From the onset of civilization humanity has seen food as a gift from its creator (God) and Mother Earth. That is why we begin our meals with a prayer of thanks.

A vibrant attitude towards one's life and diet is essential to being healthy. Just being vegetarian isn't going to result in health. A vegetarian can consume white flour, white sugar, margarine (which is worse than butter), and junk foods and still be a vegetarian. Another person can consume a little poached fish with fresh vegetables, whole grains, and fresh fruits and not be a vegetarian. Who would be the healthiest? Health isn't the absence of disease; it's the optimum function of body, mind, and spirit and the free flow of physical energy. Health is a state of balance, and dietary attitudes have a prominent effect on health.

Death is part of life, or a transformation of states of being, not an end of life. I eat a healthy diet so that I can die a healthy death. To die properly, one must be healthy. Death should be the wearing out of one's body, not the premature breakdown of it. There is a vast difference between dying of old age and dying of a chronic disease. Diet is a vehicle to transmute health and teach us how to live. The length of one's life is a gift from God, but the quality of life is a personal responsibility.

Joseph Campbell wrote that for the Native American, hunting was a ritual and not a slaughter. The Native American saw the animal as a divine messenger. Out of respect for the spirit of the animal, the hunter who killed the animal was forbidden to consume its flesh. We sit down to a meal and thank God, and the Native American sits down and thanks the animal. For them, eating the flesh of an animal was a sacred act. The Native American attitude about life is one of respect, in which the taking of life was for food. The tension between love and knowledge is harmoniously solved in the symbol of food. In the preparation and eating of food, human and divine action is required. Matter and spirit are united in the food by which they subsist. When I am in the kitchen, either to create new recipes or cook a dinner, my work becomes a spiritual discipline. Culinary art is my spiritual path, the way I commune with God and humanity through the forces of nature.

Food Quality, Processing, and Packaging

Dietary ecology isn't solely related to eating low on the food chain. Other ecological concerns include the way food is grown, how far it is transported for processing and retail sales, the way the food is processed or refined, the type of packaging, and whether it is recyclable. When natural resources (including food) are not recycled back into nature, this is a broken link in the food chain.

Ecological foods are plant-based foods that are low on the food chain, preferably whole and organic. Organic foods keep food production in the loop of nature, using the natural refuse of the environment to nurture the soil. Organic foods are generally free from chemical fertilizers and insecticides. Whole foods refers to the pristine state that nature produces food. Processed foods are preferred over refined foods; processed foods are still whole foods. Processing breaks down food but doesn't fragment it as in refining foods. For example, peanuts are a whole food, peanut butter is a processed food, and peanut oil is a refined food. The process of refining often causes the loss of nutrients along with the expenditure of energy to refine the food.

Buying locally grown and produced foods is more cost efficient. Food travels an average of 1,300 miles to get to your supermarket and about 25 percent of what we pay for food goes to transportation cost. Fifty percent of the produce consumed in America is grown in California, and it costs $5,000 to ship a load of produce from California to the East Coast.

Food packaging is a major contribution to the pollution problem and may be as devastating as consuming foods high on the food chain. Some of the materials used in packaging are not biodegradable and create another pollution problem. Energy is an issue with packaging. Bring reusable shopping bags (sturdy canvas, or used plastic or paper grocery bags) with you when you go shopping for food. Purchase only packaged foods whose containers have been manufactured with recycled materials and/or are recyclable. The recycle symbol, a circling arrow inside a triangular form, appears on the bottom of the package. Large containers cost less overall than do an equal amount of smaller packages.

The most economical form of packaging is bulk dried foods, then frozen (where only paper is used), and finally canned foods. The British thermal units of energy give us another picture, with fresh white potatoes taking 6,250 BTUs to produce, canned 9,000 BTUs, frozen 14,950 BTUs, and dehydrated (instant) potatoes taking 26,700 BTUs to produce. Even though packaging for dehydrated foods may be inexpensive, the cost of producing the product is expensive (unless the food has been sun-dried). A 16-ounce non-returnable glass bottle requires 6,002 BTUs to produce, while a returnable bottle of the same size requires 7,836 BTUs to produce and can be recycled 10 to 15 times before being retired. It takes twice as much energy to produce aerosol spray cooking oil as to bottle the same amount. As for aseptic packaging, the Aseptic Packaging Council states that an aseptic beverage package is 96 percent beverage and 4 percent packaging material, while a comparable glass bottle is 65 percent beverage and 35 percent packaging. The waste associated with the juice industry would decrease by more than 77 percent, eliminating 800,000 tons of municipal solid waste each year, if recyclable containers were used. If consumers used 5 less disposable aluminum trays a week, 56 million barrels of oil a year would be saved. Packaging is definitely an ecological factor in one's food choices.

Cooking Equipment

There are several ecological factors to consider in buying equipment. The cookware should hold the transferred heat without the continued use of heat. For example, aluminum and copper are great heat conductors that transfer heat quickly and evenly, but once the heat is in the pan, how is it held? Food can cook with ambient heat, but the heat must be confined to the pan to continue the cooking. Pressure cookers are good at holding heat to the point of intense cooking and reduce the escape of heat, amount of cooking time, and energy usage. Kuhn-Rikon manufactures an excellent line of energy efficient cookware. It is designed to hold heat in the pan to continue the cooking process without the constant application of heat.

The key to burner cooking is to match the pot's diameter with that of the burner and to temper the flame to get the maximum heat exchange with maximum energy efficiency. Make sure the pot is the same size or larger than the burner. If the pan is too small, the flame will go past it; if the fire is too high, it will roll the flames over the side of the pot instead of into the base. A flame-tamer will spread flame over a larger surface area, reduce heat intensity, and create an evenly heated surface. It also helps prevent food from sticking to the bottom of the pan. Whenever I cook grains or other foods that absorb the liquid in the pan, I achieve excellent results using this method. Kuhn-Rikon makes an aluminum flame-tamer which collects and holds heat, has excellent heat transfer, and continues to cook the food even after the heat source has been turned off.

Buy equipment that is durable and built to last, like pots made of heavy-gauge metals that have good welds on them and are sturdily assembled. The electric motors in the food processors and other electric appliances should have a warranty, especially if the appliance is multifunctional. High priced items don't indicate that the product is of high quality. Being an informed consumer is the best safeguard to getting a quality item at a reasonable price.

The equipment must be repairable. Some equipment is made in such a manner that it costs less to replace than repair. What is needed is equipment that is easy and inexpensive to repair. Waring blenders have not changed their basic mechanical format over the last 30 years, and when they developed a new bearing system for their new models, they designed it to work in their original models. Their blenders take a tremendous amount of abuse and are easy to repair. Durotherm cookware (by Kuhn-Rikon) is easily repaired. When one of my pressure cookers was damaged, I sent in for replacement parts which were readily sent, and I was able to repair the pressure cooker with ease.

Kitchen equipment should be multifunctional. A food processor should come with a bread dough hook to mix dough, as well as processing equipment to slice vegetables. The KitchenAid mixer can mix doughs and batters, process vegetables, juice vegetables, and grind using various attachments. I value the electrical equipment in my kitchen where it can save time and energy from the culinarian's perspective, but I also enjoy the manual tools requiring the skill of the artist. The blender, food processor, and mixer are the primary electrical tools of my trade.

There is much controversy over microwave ovens and their effect on the food and our bodies. Microwave ovens generate high-frequency electromagnetic waves that alternate in positive and negative directions, causing food molecules to vibrate up to 2.5 billion times per second creating friction heat. A car vibrating at that rate would become red hot, causing the windows to burst, metal to melt, and the tires to disintegrate. In the April 1992 *Journal of Pediatrics,* researchers at Stanford University Medical Center reported that microwaving breast milk just enough to warm it destroyed 98 percent of the liposome activity needed to inhibit bacterial growth. Microwaving regular milk or vegetables was associated with a decline in various hemoglobin levels which could lead to anemia, rheumatism, fever, and thyroid insufficiency. On the other hand, Gertrude Armbruster, a nutritional scientist at Cornell University, found that when certain foods are microwaved, they remain more nutritious than foods that are boiled, baked, grilled, or even steamed using conventional stove tops and ovens. Vegetables microwaved with just a teaspoon of water per serving retained up to 100 percent of their vitamin content. The same vegetables retained only 40 to 60 percent of their nutrients when boiled. My use of the microwave oven is one of moderation. I use it to heat water for tea, reheat herb teas gone cold, and for reheating leftover food. Moderation is the key.

Our relationship with our diet is as dynamic as our relationship with ourselves. Diet is the bench mark of our relationship with our physical being and the starting point in developing a conscious relationship with one's body and one's environment. Radical changes are not the solution. What is needed is an understanding of diet from a practical approach and a gradual transition to a diet in harmony with our bodies.

In *Medical Nemesis,* Ivan Illich states that doctor-created diseases are running rampant but that one disease is worse, and that is poor nutrition. What we need is a prudence in our diet that does not sacrifice the pleasure of the table for nutrition. The health messenger must first embrace the joys of the table as the foundation for any dietary transformation. The healthy diet needs to be inclusive and expansive, as in the concept of diatia, and not exclusive and narrow. There are no bad foods as produced by nature, just bad diets. To raise the quality of our cuisine in America, the aesthetics of food as well as the chemistry of nutrition need to be understood.

A culinary revolution isn't the answer. Dietary transformation is the answer, at least in part, and is a gradual process that encompasses the culture from which it is born. America is a melting pot of cultures, cuisines, and nationalities. We aren't locked into set ethnic dietary styles. Therefore, we are free to evolve our unique version of a healthy diet for the next century. Concerning diet, America remains the New World searching for a New World way of eating and Eco-Cuisine is part of that New World way of eating.

What you have read here is but the tip of the iceberg. It reflects some of the reasons why I cook and consume plant-based foods. America's health is going to be won or lost in the kitchen, not on Capitol Hill. To a great degree, so is our environment.

Whether I am cooking dinner for 600 with a hotel staff, competing in the International Culinary Olympics, or researching the development of a new product, I remain driven by my vision for my art. It is an art form, rich with the history of people in love with their cuisine.

From picnics to weddings, from baptisms to Hanukkah, everyone loves an excuse to get together, and when they do, it is always around food. Cuisine is a fun art. What we need to recognize is that it is also a sacred art form given to us by nature, with an intrinsic value richer than our wildest imagination.

Food has a value in resolving many of the health and environmental crises facing the human race in the twenty-first century and what my plant-based cuisine proposes are some creative options to resolve them. They are based on my personal experience and the enjoyment that I have had in reaching the peak of my health at age 46. G.K. Chesterton said: "The trouble with always trying to preserve the health of the body is that it is so difficult to do without destroying the health of the mind." A healthy attitude is as important as a healthy diet.

Culinary art takes on new direction with each age. With our high-tech society, high-tech food, fast-paced society, and fast-food industry we should see the signs of the times written in our cuisine and seize the opportunity to make a shift to a diet that will both nurture us and our environment. This nurturing diet is what I call Eco-Cuisine.

SELECTING WINES FOR VEGETARIAN CUISINE

Sandy Block, Master of Wine

Since spending a summer traveling through Europe in my late teens, I have always enjoyed a glass of wine with dinner. For years I gave scant thought as to whether the wine I was drinking complemented the food I was eating. It was only after I had received a Master of Arts and began working in restaurants that I learned there were people who would ponder how different wines might taste with their meals. At first this was curious to me; I couldn't see how it mattered and suspected that any interest in the subject was simply an affectation.

To help me perform my restaurant duties better, I began to ask questions about wine and found that most people who were fascinated by wine loved good food as well. They always seemed to have a reason, incomprehensible as it was to me at the time, for selecting one wine over another. Then I discovered that there was a serious literature devoted to discussing which wines to drink with which foods.

About this same time, I began to follow a meatless diet. But what wine would go well with vegetarian cuisine? All of the gastronomic bibles I consulted that spoke in such authoritative tones of the affinity between rack of lamb and Pomerol, or oysters and Chablis, turned strangely mute with regard to alternative cuisine. If anything, the wisdom was to avoid wine with vegetables.

Experience was to prove a valuable teacher. Because there were no arcane guidelines dictating which wines to match with which non-animal protein dishes, I experimented freely. Through trusting my own palate and noting wines that harmonized well with what I ate, I began to find many pleasing combinations.

My first discovery was that wine and food flavors have an effect on one another. It became apparent that wines could change the way food tasted in dramatic ways I could not always foretell. Some wines which were delicious by themselves completely lost their appeal with certain meals. Even more mysterious, there were sour-tasting wines which could lift and enliven the stolid flavors of these very same dishes. I noted with excitement that these transformations had become somewhat predictable; certain combinations of wine and food were satisfying while others were not. Not everyone I knew greeted these findings with enthusiasm. Some expressed complete indifference while other people disagreed with my selections. It struck me as no more startling than knowing that some of us like chocolate and others vanilla. As I read more widely I found that too many wine and food authorities seemed not to grasp this fundamental truth. Instead they conveyed the impression that everyone should like what they like.

Since becoming one of the United States' first certified Masters of Wine in 1992, I have grown increasingly aware of the gulf separating so-called wine experts from the majority of people who find joy in drinking wine with their meals. Arrogance, dogmatism, and poor communication skills compound one another to marginalize many of the wine fraternity's most knowledgeable professionals. Rather than providing information relevant to how other wines taste, writers often simply trumpet their own preferences. Few seem disposed to assist consumers in finding out which wine and food matches would appeal to their palates.

In contrast, wine itself addresses people very directly. Its flavors are open and accessible and there is no secret knowledge required to enjoy a glass. Deeply rooted in our civilization and religions, it has been enjoyed as a salubrious beverage since the Middle Ages. In recent years, a ground swell of scientific evidence has supported the popular and enduring belief that this naturally fermented product of the earth provides many health benefits if enjoyed regularly and in moderation with meals. In addition, wine producers throughout the world have responded where possible to environmental concerns by seeking to grow their grapes organically and with respect for the land.

Most importantly, I believe wine need not be mysterious to the vegetarian just because he or she cannot fall back on the clichés of red wine with meat and white wine with fish in making selections. There are reasons why some wines appeal to people with certain foods. You can learn to predict whether a particular combination will taste delicious to you or not, based mostly on the balance of food flavors and textures that you most enjoy. The key to this understanding involves knowing the most important characteristics of wines, how they originate, and the way they affect various food flavors during a meal. These are subjects clearly beyond the reach of a brief article. Short of that, I can offer a general guide which suggests what may happen to wine and food flavors as they mingle on your palate. Whether you agree or not is an entirely personal matter.

Flavors

Heavily spiced preparations: Sparkling wines or lighter wines with young exuberant fruit flavors (German Riesling, California Chenin Blanc, Beaujolais, lighter Pinot Noirs) will moderate the spice. Highly tannic wines (Barolo, Hermitage, Cabernet Sauvignon, oak-aged Chardonnay) or wines with high alcohol (wines from hot climates such as California or the Rhône Valley) will accentuate the spice.

Mildly spicy dishes: Slightly fuller, more assertively fruity wines (a honeyed demi-sec Vouvray or thick Alsatian Gewürztraminer if not too high in alcohol; richer, earthier Pinot Noir, or medium-bodied Zinfandel) will play up the spice. High tannin or alcohol will exaggerate perceptions of spice and increase these characteristics in the wine.

Salty dishes (miso- and tamari-based sauces): Wines with piercing acidity regardless of sweetness (Loire Valley Sauvignon Blanc, Riesling, Chenin Blanc, Pinot Noir, Barbera, Sangiovese) moderate the salt and become somewhat blander themselves, while wines with high alcohol increase bitterness and pungency.

Dishes whose primary flavors are tart or sour (tomato-based sauces, marinades, vinegar-based salad dressings): Wines with high acidity but no sweetness (Alsatian Riesling, Savennières, Trebbiano, Barbera, Beaujolais) moderate and balance the tartness. Sweet wines reduce the tart flavors dramatically.

Earthy flavored dishes (with mushrooms, root vegetables): More complex wines with bolder flavors and perhaps higher alcohol (Gewürztraminer, Rhône Valley whites, oak-aged Chardonnay, Cabernet Sauvignon, Bordeaux, Châteauneuf-du-Pape) will match the earthiness with their own body and fruit. Lighter, simpler wines from cooler climates allow the flavors of the food to predominate.

Bitter flavors (eggplant, artichokes, nuts): Lighter, smoother wines (Pinot Blanc, Semillon, Loire Valley Rosé) will soften the bitterness while tannic reds (Cabernet, Syrah, Nebbiolo) or bitter white wines (Muscat, Gewürztraminer) accentuate it.

Fruit flavors: Slightly sweet wines bring out the fruit while wines with high tannin sharply elevate the impression of acidity.

Methods of Cooking

Food tastes differently if boiled, broiled, sautéed, or grilled. The cooking method alters the main ingredient's essential flavors and changes the way wines react to it. Grilling an eggplant softens its bitterness, introduces new flavors, and will have a nice match with an assertive wine like California Cabernet Sauvignon or Merlot. Crunchy grains sautéed in oil show different flavors than if they are simply steamed.

The dish's texture or weight is always taken into account. Hearty, rich, full bodied dishes may tend to overpower more delicate wines unless the wine features taut acidity. Try a warmer-climate wine with a velvety or robust constitution. Soft, silken textured preparations invite lighter wines for balance. Because the rough tannins of many traditional red wines are difficult to neutralize unless consumed with animal fat and protein, vegetarians should consider the world's most interesting dry rosés (Tavel, the wines of Provence and Rioja), nouveau-style reds (Italian Novello di Sangiovese, Beaujolais, Australian Shiraz), or softer Merlots (Chile, Argentina, Eastern Europe) to complement fuller dishes because they can provide flavor and fair intensity without coarseness.

Specific Wine Recommendations

Pâté Français: Tokay d'Alsace (White) or cru Beaujolais (Red)
Tofu Cacciatore: California Sauvignon Blanc (White) or Côtes du Rhône (Red)
Seitan Carbonara: Dry Vouvray (White) or Chianti Classico (Red)
Beans in Red Wine Sauce: Alsace Gewürztraminer (White)
    or Oregon Pinot Noir (Red)
Pistachio Polenta: California or Australian Chardonnay (White) or Chinon (Red)
Italian Shepherd's Pie: Sancerre (White) or Tavel (Rosé)
Orange Cranberry Ice Cream Cake: California White Muscat
Hazelnut Cream Cake: Australian Botrytis-affected Semillon
Rainbow Fruit Terrine: Mosel Riesling Auslese
Chocolate Bread Pudding: 10-year-old Tawny Port

A NOTE ON CLASSICAL VEGETARIAN CUISINE

There is argument in the culinary arena that my classical vegetarian (totally plant-based food) is a pseudo-meat diet based on classical cuisine. While a great deal of my culinary creations are original, many are also designed after classical recipes. My cuisine redefines plant-based foods in classical terms. The eating habits and diet of the Western world are in constant change and health concerns are the vital force in this change. Vegetarianism is taking center stage and is beginning to define what will be the cuisine of the twenty-first century. My cuisine introduces and defines classical vegetarian food in the professional culinary arena.

Human beings will always consume meat but will begin to do it with more consciousness and moderation. It is plant-based foods (vegetables, fruits, herbs, and spices) that give meats, poultry, and fish their flavor and attractiveness. Plant-based foods are central to any cuisine. My cuisine places plant-based proteins creatively and strategically into classical foods and then further develops it into an innovative cuisine. Humanity has been eating plant-based foods since shortly after its creation. Classical vegetarian cuisine will eventually become a part of classical cuisine. It is an illusion to believe that vegetarian cuisine isn't classical cuisine when, in fact, part of what we know as classical cuisine is vegetarian. All I am doing is defining it.

The use of classical names for some of my plant-based dishes is but one step toward remaking classical cuisine for the twenty-first century.

Nutritional Analysis

There was a dilemma over the issue of providing a nutritional analysis of the recipes in my first book, *Friendly Foods,* and the issue arose again for my second book, *Eco-Cuisine.* My cuisine is centered around whole foods that are plant-based. By their very nature they are nutritionally dense and need not be analyzed. My cuisine is healthy, gourmet yet simple food that is balanced, cholesterol-free, high in fiber, and loaded with nutrition.

This cuisine is meant to be celebrated for its taste, texture, and appearance. It is simply not necessary to analyze recipes that are naturally nutritious. For those recipes that are on the richer side, save them for special occasions and holidays. The recipes have been designed with nutrition in mind; I don't use lards, butter, eggs, cheeses, or meats in my food. Relax and enjoy the cuisine.

Appetizers

Vorspeisen in German, *antipasto* in Italian, *entradas* in Spanish, or *hors d'oeuvres* in French, appetizers can be the first or second course of a meal depending whether you serve a soup or salad. Appetizers cover a wide variety of foods. In general, many entrée foods can be used for appetizers or vice versa. The purpose of appetizers is to stimulate the appetite, not satisfy it. That is why they are strong-flavored and small in portion size. If using an appetizer with a full dinner, the choice of the appetizer is relative to the whole dinner. When serving a heavy entrée, a lighter appetizer should be served. Generally, I serve either a soup or salad and entrée with an appetizer but that isn't an absolute rule of thumb. If serving all three they must be complementary, well balanced, and not too filling.

Most appetizers are based on animal foods and that is where my appetizers make a wonderful difference—they are plant-based and stimulate the appetite. Pâté Français is a good example. Pâtés are generally made with a great deal of animal fat and spices. Pâté Français consists of the classic pâté seasoning, white beans, and roasted walnuts, which are plant-based with a magnificent flavor and texture. That is Eco-Cuisine rising to the realm of classical cuisine.

The following appetizers represent a marvelous array of unusual flavors, colors, and textures. Pâté Français is perfect for a light menu. Florida Aspic also complements a summer or light menu. Confetti Corn Fritters can garnish the Yellow Pepper Cream Soup. Full meals can be centered around appetizers. The appetizers in this section are well-suited for both appetizer parties and courses in a menu. Indeed, one could easily make a well-balanced appetizer party using the appetizers in this section.

Florida Aspic

YIELD: *4 servings*

TIME: *35 minutes preparation;
30 minutes cooking*

1 cup water

*2 tablespoons each finely diced
red bell pepper, yellow bell
pepper, orange bell pepper,
and green bell pepper*

*2 tablespoons drained, seeded,
and finely diced dill pickle*

*1 tablespoon finely diced
seitan "ham" or tofu "hot
dogs" (optional)*

5 teaspoons agar flakes

1 clove minced garlic

1 teaspoon chopped fresh basil

¾ teaspoon fresh thyme

½ teaspoon orange zest

¼ teaspoon sea salt

⅛ teaspoon white pepper

2 tablespoons lemon juice

*1 tablespoon honey or fruit
juice concentrate*

*1/16 teaspoon liquid hickory
smoke (optional)*

*½ tablespoon arrowroot
powder dissolved in
1 tablespoon cool water*

½ tablespoon chopped chives

*1 recipe Orange Aioli Sauce
(page 157)*

*finely diced red, yellow, orange,
and green peppers for garnish*

This colorful, exciting, and flavorful dish was an Olympic silver medal winner in the 1992 International Culinary Olympics.

In a 2-quart saucepan, bring water to a simmer over medium heat and blanch the bell peppers, pickle, and seitan "ham" for 1 minute. Remove from water and transfer to a plate to cool. Add agar to the water and simmer on low for 7 to 10 minutes or until flakes have dissolved. Add the garlic, basil, thyme, orange zest, salt, pepper, lemon juice, honey, and liquid smoke and bring water back to a simmer over medium heat. Add the arrowroot/water mixture and continue simmering the liquid until it thickens. Remove saucepan from heat and allow to cool until it reaches 110 degrees F. Add the bell peppers, pickle, seitan "ham," and chives to the thickened liquid and stir to combine everything well. Pour mixture into a lightly oiled metal or glass mold, or hollowed-out vegetable, and let set for 20 to 30 minutes or until very firm. Remove aspic from mold, slice, and serve with Orange Aioli Sauce, sprinkling each serving with a garnish of the finely diced mixed peppers.

Smoked Portobello Mushrooms

YIELD: *4 servings*
TIME: *10 minutes preparation;*
  40 minutes cooking

3 tablespoons hickory
  wood chips
3 tablespoons water
4 portobello mushrooms

I enjoy these mushrooms just as they are. Serve them with the Italian Mixed Greens Salad or marinate them for the Italian Bistro Sandwich.

Soak the wood chips in the water for 30 minutes (or spread the wood chips over the bottom of the smoker, sprinkle with the water, and proceed as directed). Clean the portobello mushrooms. Place the soaked chips in the bottom of a stovetop smoker. Place the mushrooms on a rack over the chips and cover. Set the smoker over high heat (preheated if using an electric burner) and smoke the mushrooms for 20 minutes. Remove smoker from heat and set aside, still covered, for another 20 minutes. Serve on toast points or with fresh crusted Italian bread.

VARIATIONS

If a smoker is not available, sauté mushrooms in ½ tablespoon extra virgin olive oil for a few minutes on each side. Towards the end of the sautéing, add ¼ teaspoon liquid hickory smoke and sauté a minute or 2 more on each side. Remove pan from heat and serve as above.

Marinated Smoked Portobello Mushrooms

In a large mixing bowl, combine ½ cup water, ½ cup apple cider vinegar, ½ cup barley malt syrup, ¼ cup extra virgin olive oil, 1 tablespoon minced fresh garlic, 2 teaspoons oregano, 2 teaspoons tarragon, 1 teaspoon rosemary, and ¾ teaspoon sea salt and mix well. Smoke mushrooms as directed, then transfer to the marinade, cover, and refrigerate for 3 days. Or, in a 2-quart saucepan, bring the marinade to a simmer over medium heat. Pour the hot marinade over the smoked mushrooms and use as above.

Pâté Français

YIELD: *12 servings*
TIME: *40 minutes; 1 hour chilling*

Pâté Seasoning Blend

1 tablespoon white pepper
1 tablespoon black pepper
1 tablespoon paprika
1 tablespoon nutmeg
1 tablespoon ginger powder
1 tablespoon dried basil
1 tablespoon whole dried thyme
1 tablespoon marjoram
1 tablespoon allspice
1 tablespoon garlic powder
½ tablespoon clove powder

1 cup walnuts
1 teaspoon extra virgin olive oil
2 cups diced onions
2 cups chopped mushrooms
4 teaspoons Pâté Seasoning Blend
1½ teaspoons sea salt
2 cups cooked navy or garbanzo beans

This pâté is my first attempt to make a classical pâté using only plant-based foods. The classical pâté seasoning blend and roasted walnuts make the white beans into a wonderful pâté. This is a great accompaniment to a salad, as a spread on crackers, or baked and served with green lettuces and breads.

Pâté Seasoning Blend

In a mixing bowl, combine all the ingredients, stir well, and transfer to a covered container. The seasoning blend can be used with many other dishes. Add 1 teaspoon of the blend per pound of protein.

Preheat oven to 325 degrees F. Spread walnuts on a baking sheet and roast for about 15 minutes or until lightly browned and very fragrant. Remove from oven and transfer walnuts to a container to cool slightly. In a 10-inch frying pan, heat the oil and sauté the onions, mushrooms, seasoning blend, salt, and beans over medium heat for 10 minutes. Remove pan from heat. Coarsely chop walnuts. In a food processor, combine all ingredients and process until smooth. Refrigerate in a covered container for 1 hour or until chilled thoroughly. Serve cold or at room temperature. Serve as a dip for crackers by mounding the pâté in the center of a plate, then arranging crackers and garnish around it.

VARIATION: *Baked Pâté Francais*

Preheat oven to 350 degrees F. In a 10-inch frying pan, heat 1 teaspoon of olive oil and sauté ½ cup diced mushrooms and ½ cup chopped onions over medium heat for 5 minutes or until onions are transparent and mushroom liquid is reduced. Add sautéed vegetables to the basic pâté mixture along with 2 tablespoons of arrowroot powder, 2 tablespoons agar flakes, and 1 tablespoon minced parsley. Transfer mixture to a lightly oiled loaf pan, cover pan with plastic wrap, and place in a larger baking pan containing several inches of water. Cover larger pan with aluminum foil and steam bake pâté for 30 minutes. Remove loaf pan and refrigerate for 1 hour or until chilled. Unmold the pâté, slice, and serve with Sauce Renaissance.

Black Olive Tapenade

YIELD: *3 cups*
TIME: *35 minutes*

2 tablespoons extra virgin
    olive oil
4 cups thinly sliced Spanish
    onion
3 cloves minced garlic
1 cup pitted, drained
    Kalamata olives

Tapenade can be used as a topping on any bread, served on sandwiches, salads, side vegetables, or mixed into casseroles.

In a 10-inch frying pan, heat the oil and sauté the onions, garlic, and olives on medium heat for about 5 minutes or until the onions are transparent. In a food processor, add the sautéed mixture and process for 15 to 25 seconds or until the mixture is coarse as in a salsa. Transfer to a container, let cool, and refrigerate until ready to serve.

VARIATION: *Tapenade Focaccia*

Preheat oven to 350 degrees F. Prepare ½ recipe Focaccia Dough (page 99) and roll out to a 12-inch diameter circle, ½ inch thick. Spread ¾ cup tapenade over the surface of the dough and bake for 10 to 15 minutes.

Indian Lentil Purée (Dal)

YIELD: *7 servings*

TIME: *30 minutes preparation;
45 minutes cooking*

2 tablespoons unrefined corn oil
½ cup finely diced onions
2 cloves minced garlic
1 teaspoon turmeric
½ teaspoon ginger powder
*¼ teaspoon cardamom
powder*
¼ teaspoon curry powder
1 cup yellow or red lentils
*½ cup peeled, finely diced
potatoes*
3 cups water
1 teaspoon sea salt
*1 teaspoon minced parsley
and ⅛ teaspoon paprika
for garnish*

Dal is a traditional Indian dish made from peas, beans, or legumes, and is typically served with chapatis. Contrary to popular belief, it is very mild, yet carries a rich flavor. Serve at room temperature as a canapé bread spread, or as a dip with chapatis, pita, or crackers.

In a 2-quart saucepan, heat the oil and sauté the onions, garlic, turmeric, ginger, cardamom, and curry powder over medium heat for about 5 minutes or until the onions are transparent. Add lentils, potatoes, and water to the onion mixture. Simmer covered for 45 minutes (30 minutes for red lentils) or until soft and water has evaporated. Salt to taste, garnish, and serve.

Cauliflower Duxelle on Toast

YIELD: *6 servings*
TIME: *40 minutes*

2 tablespoons canola oil
3 cups finely diced cauliflower
1 cup finely diced shallots or
*   onions*
½ cup finely diced celery
¼ cup finely diced red bell
*   pepper*
4 cloves minced garlic
½ teaspoon ginger powder
½ teaspoon sea salt
½ teaspoon Hungarian
*   paprika*
¼ teaspoon white pepper
⅛ teaspoon nutmeg
¼ cup chopped dried wakame
*   (optional)*
½ cup Chablis or other dry
*   white wine*
1 cup soy milk
¼ cup unbleached white flour
1 tablespoon cashew butter
*   (optional)*
2 tablespoons minced fresh
*   parsley*
12 slices whole grain bread
6 quartered cherry tomatoes
*   for garnish*

This appetizer was developed after a recipe I found in a Chinese cookbook. It is a sophisticated presentation of cauliflower and an appetizer you will remember long after you have tasted it.

In a 10-inch frying pan, heat the oil and sauté the cauliflower, shallots, celery, bell pepper, garlic, ginger, salt, paprika, pepper, and nutmeg over medium heat for about 8 to 10 minutes. Add the wakame pieces along with the wine, then cook down for about 5 minutes, or until the liquid is almost completely evaporated. Mix together the soy milk and flour, then add to the cauliflower mixture. Cook until thickened. Add cashew butter and parsley and stir well. Take slices of whole grain bread and cut off the crusts. Toast on both sides and spread about ¼ cup of the cauliflower mixture evenly on each slice. Cut each slice from corner to corner to create 2 triangles (there are 4 toast points per serving with 2 tablespoons cauliflower mixture on each toast point). Garnish with a wedge of tomato and serve.

Opposite: Florida Aspic (page 17) with Orange Aioli Sauce (page 157) and Tricolor Salsa (page 170)

Mushroom Duxelles

YIELD: *4 servings*
TIME: *30 minutes*

*2 tablespoons extra virgin
    olive oil*
2 cups finely diced mushrooms
*1 cup finely diced Spanish
    onions*
*¼ cup finely diced red bell
    pepper*
2 cloves minced garlic
*½ cup chopped fresh parsley
    (or 2½ tablespoons chopped
    dried parsley)*
*1 teaspoon chopped dried
    cilantro*
1 teaspoon dry, chopped thyme
4 teaspoons tamari
*½ cup plus 2 tablespoons
    unbleached white flour*

This recipe is a version of the classic mushroom duxelle. It can be used as a filling for vegetables or crêpes, or eaten as a spread on bread or crackers.

In a 10-inch frying pan, heat the oil and sauté the mushrooms, onions, bell pepper, garlic, parsley, cilantro, thyme, and tamari for 3 to 5 minutes or until onions are transparent. Stir in flour and sauté for another 5 minutes. Serve as a dip with raw vegetables, or as a spread on breads, canapés, or crackers.

VARIATION: *Mushroom Duxelle Crêpes*
Preheat oven to 375 degrees F. Prepare Savory Crêpes (page 111). Use ¼ cup filling per crêpe and roll up. Place crêpes into a baking dish, brush with water, then cover with a tightly fitting lid. Bake for 15 to 20 minutes. Serve 2 crêpes per portion with either Burgundy Sauce Glaze, Sauce Renaissance, or Roasted Vegetable Sauce.

Opposite: Seitan Pine Nut Crêpes (page 118) with Sauce Renaissance (page 155) and Collard Roll with Fresh Vegetables (page 24)

Collard Roll with Fresh Vegetables

YIELD: *2 servings*
TIME: *45 minutes*

2 cups water
½ teaspoon sea salt
4 large collard leaves, stems
    removed halfway up
    the leaves
1 bowl ice water
1 cup grated carrots
1 cup julienned daikon
1 cup julienned red bell pepper
1 cup julienned yellow squash

This is one of my favorite appetizers and can also be used as a vegetable side dish to a sandwich.

In a 3-quart saucepan, combine water and sea salt and bring to a simmer over medium heat. Briefly blanch the collard leaves in the simmering water until the leaves turn a deep green color. Remove leaves and plunge them into the bowl of ice water. When they are cool, squeeze the excess water from them, then spread out and pat dry with a paper towel. Place collard leaves on a sushi mat, overlapping them so that they cover an 11 x 12-inch square area (you may need to trim them to fit that size). Line ¾ of the collard surface with 4 parallel rows of the carrots, daikon, bell pepper, and yellow squash. Roll the collard leaves around the filling as tightly as possible. Hold the rolled sushi mat vertically over the sink and squeeze it to remove excess liquid. Remove the sushi mat and, using a serrated knife, cut the roll into 8 equal slices. Refrigerate for 30 minutes or until cool and serve.

VARIATION

For a more robust flavor, combine ¼ cup water, 1 tablespoon shoyu, and ½ teaspoon ginger powder in a bowl and brush on the slices of collard roll. Refrigerate for 30 minutes or until cool and serve.

Japanese Tofu with Mirin Sauce

YIELD: *3 servings*
TIME: *30 minutes preparation;*
  45 minutes cooking

Mirin Sauce

¼ cup thinly julienned onion
¼ cup thinly julienned carrot
¼ cup thinly julienned red bell
  pepper
1¼ cups water
1 3-inch piece kombu, soaked
  and cut into strips
1 tablespoon brown rice
  vinegar
4 teaspoons mirin
4 teaspoons tamari
½ teaspoon ginger juice (or ¼
  teaspoon ginger powder)
2 tablespoons arrowroot
  powder dissolved in 2
  tablespoons cool water

¼ cup arrowroot powder
¾ teaspoon sea salt
¾ teaspoon garlic powder
  (optional)
1 cup canola or peanut oil
6 1-ounce slices extra firm tofu,
  drained
3 ounces enoki mushrooms and
  3 scallion flowers for
  garnish

This light appetizer uses the fry poach method, allowing for the development of flavor and eliminating a major portion of the oil used in the cooking process. Serve it along with the Japanese Salad.

Sauce

In a 1-quart saucepan, combine the julienned vegetables, water, kombu, vinegar, mirin, tamari, and ginger and bring to a simmer over medium heat. Cook until the vegetables are soft. Add ¾ of the arrowroot/water mixture to the hot vegetables, stirring constantly to prevent lumping, until it thickens slightly. If it doesn't seem thick enough, add the remaining arrowroot mixture. Remove saucepan from heat and cover to keep warm. Prepare the fried tofu.

Tofu

In a mixing bowl, combine the arrowroot, salt, and garlic. In a 10-inch frying pan, heat the oil to 375 degrees F (the oil should be at least ½ inch deep). Coat the tofu slices in the arrowroot mixture. Fry 3 pieces at a time for 30 seconds on each side. Remove the tofu from the oil and drain on paper towels for 10 seconds. To serve, pour ⅓ cup of the mirin sauce on each of 3 pre-warmed appetizer plates. Transfer 2 tofu slices to each plate. Garnish each plate with a scallion flower and the enoki mushrooms, then serve immediately.

VARIATION

For each serving, pour ⅓ cup of mirin sauce on each plate. Place ¼ cup of cooked brown rice on the sauce, and lay the tofu slices over the rice. Garnish as above and serve immediately.

Papaya Guacamole with Sun-Dried Tomatoes

YIELD: *1 cup*
TIME: *20 minutes preparation;*
   1 hour chilling

2 tablespoons julienned
   sun-dried tomatoes
1 ripe avocado
¼ cup finely diced ripe papaya
2 tablespoons lemon juice
1 teaspoon honey or
   FruitSource syrup
1 clove minced garlic
½ teaspoon minced fresh
   cilantro
⅛ teaspoon sea salt

The avocado is one of my favorite foods and papaya complements it well. Serve this appetizer with salads, sandwiches, or with entrées such as Miami Delight.

Soak the sun-dried tomatoes in warm water for 15 to 20 minutes, then drain and set aside. Peel the avocado, remove the pit, then mash it into a paste (this should yield ½ cup). In a mixing bowl, combine tomatoes, avocado, papaya, lemon juice, honey, garlic, cilantro, and salt and mix well. Cover and refrigerate for at least 1 hour and preferably overnight to develop the flavors. Serve cold with corn chips.

Pesto Bread

YIELD: *1 loaf*
TIME: *20 minutes preparation;*
   1 hour baking

1½ teaspoons active dry yeast
¼ cup warm water
1 teaspoon Sucanat
1½ cups packed fresh basil
6 tablespoons warm water
1 tablespoon extra virgin
   olive oil
2 cups unbleached white flour
2 tablespoons pine nuts
1½ tablespoons soaked, sun-
   dried tomatoes, finely diced
1 teaspoon granulated garlic
½ teaspoon sea salt

This bread was developed for the Italian Bistro Sandwich, but I enjoy it with any soup or salad.

Preheat oven to 375 degrees F. In a small mixing bowl, combine the yeast, the first measure of water, and Sucanat and mix well. Set aside for 5 to 10 minutes or until the yeast is foamy. Rinse, pat dry, and chop the basil leaves. In a blender, combine the basil, second measure of warm water, and oil and blend until smooth. Pour the basil mixture in a large mixing bowl, then add the flour, pine nuts, tomatoes, garlic, and salt. Add the yeast mixture, mix well, then knead into a medium-stiff dough. If the dough is too stiff, add more water to soften it. Roll into a loaf shape and place in a lightly oiled 1-pound loaf pan. Let the dough rise until it has doubled in size or the surface doesn't spring back to a soft touch. Bake for 30 minutes or until crust is golden brown. Remove, let cool slightly, and serve.

Black Bean Cracker Cups with Corn Relish

YIELD: *4 servings*
TIME: *1 hour*

Corn Relish

2 tablespoons apple cider
    vinegar
1 red cabbage leaf
1 tablespoon unrefined corn oil
½ cup fresh or frozen kernel
    corn
¼ cup roasted, diced red bell
    pepper
¼ cup diced Spanish onion
2 teaspoons chopped fresh
    cilantro
1 clove minced garlic
¼ teaspoon sea salt
⅛ teaspoon paprika
2 tablespoons brown rice syrup
    (or 1 tablespoon honey)
1 tablespoon apple cider
    vinegar

Black Bean Cracker Cups

1 cup whole wheat bread flour
½ cup Fantastic Foods Instant
    Black Bean Mix, ground to
    a flour in a coffee grinder
2 tablespoons gluten flour
3 tablespoons tamari
1 tablespoon liquid lecithin
1 teaspoon sesame oil
½ teaspoon black pepper
½ cup water

This appetizer won a silver medal in the 1992 International Culinary Olympics. Serve it with the Anasazi Bean Sandwich Rolls and the Black Bean and Corn Roll. The Cracker Cups may also be filled with Cucumber Cilantro Salsa.

Corn Relish

Rub the vinegar into the cabbage leaf. In a vegetable steamer, steam the cabbage until tender. Drain cabbage, dice (this should yield ¼ cup), and set aside. In a 10-inch frying pan, heat the oil and sauté the corn, bell pepper, onion, cabbage, cilantro, garlic, salt, and paprika over medium heat for 5 minutes. Add the syrup and the second measure of vinegar and sauté for 3 more minutes. Serve hot, or transfer the relish to a covered container, refrigerate for 1 hour or until chilled, and serve cold.

Black Bean Cracker Cups

Preheat oven to 350 degrees F. In a mixing bowl, combine all the ingredients and mix until a stiff dough is formed. On a lightly-floured surface, roll out the dough to ¹⁄₁₆-inch thickness, then cut it into 4-inch squares. Place squares in lightly oiled, 3-inch muffin tins to form cups. Bake cups for about 20 minutes or until they are crisp. Remove tins from oven and cool. Remove cups from tins and fill with Corn Relish.

Saffron Raisin Bread

YIELD: *1 loaf*
TIME: *25 minutes preparation;*
2¾ hours rising and baking

1 cup raisins or dried apricots
1 cup hot water
3 tablespoons honey
¼ cup warm water
1 tablespoon active dry yeast
½ cup warm water
½ teaspoon saffron
2 cups whole wheat bread flour
1¾ cups plus 1 tablespoon
* unbleached white flour*
1 tablespoon canola oil
1½ teaspoons grated lemon
* zest*
1¼ teaspoons sea salt
⅛ teaspoon cardamom

This bread goes well with the Italian Orzo Soup and Curried Vegetable Casserole, and also as an unusual breakfast bread.

Preheat oven to 375 degrees F. In a small mixing bowl, combine the raisins and hot water and let stand for 20 minutes. In another bowl, combine the honey, warm water, and yeast and mix well. Allow the mixture to stand about 5 minutes, or until the yeast is foamy. In a blender, combine the second measure of warm water and saffron and blend at high speed until most of the saffron threads have been ground and only small specks remain. In a large mixing bowl, combine 1 cup of the whole wheat bread flour with 1 cup of the unbleached white flour. Add the proofed yeast, saffron/water mixture, raisins, and raisin-soaking water to the flours and mix until well combined. Cover bowl with a damp cloth and set in a warm place to rise, about 30 minutes. After 30 minutes, mix down the sponge and add the oil, lemon zest, salt, and cardamom. Gradually add the remaining flours to make a smooth and elastic dough. Knead the dough for 5 to 10 minutes. Pour 1 teaspoon of canola oil into another large bowl, place dough inside, then turn it in the oil until it is evenly coated. Cover bowl with damp cloth and set in a warm place to rise, about 30 minutes or until doubled in size.

Punch the dough down and remove from the bowl. Flatten the dough into a rectangle. Starting at the short end of the rectangle, roll it up tightly, sealing the ends and sides when it is finished. Lightly oil a 5 x 10 x 3-inch loaf pan and place the rolled dough inside, seam side down. Cover with the damp cloth, then set aside in a warm place to rise for 45 minutes. When risen, bake loaf for 30 minutes, or until it sounds hollow when you tap on the bottom of the pan. Remove bread from loaf pan and set it on a wire rack to cool.

Confetti Corn Fritters

YIELD: *4 servings*
TIME: *30 minutes*

½ cup yellow corn meal
¼ cup unbleached white flour
2 teaspoons Ener-G Egg Replacer or wheat gluten flour
1 teaspoon baking powder
¾ teaspoon coriander powder
¾ teaspoon curry powder
½ teaspoon sea salt
½ cup water
½ cup finely diced, mixed red, green, and yellow bell peppers
canola or peanut oil for deep-frying

These fritters are excellent with Yellow Pepper Cream Soup. For an appetizer, serve them with Onion Butter.

In a mixing bowl, combine corn meal, flour, egg replacer, baking powder, coriander, curry powder, salt, water, and peppers and mix well. In a 3-quart saucepan or deep-fryer, heat the oil. Form mixture into a dozen 1-inch balls, then spoon into the oil to deep-fry until golden brown. Drain fried fritters on paper towels and serve.

VARIATION: *BBQ Corn Fritters*
Place ¼ cup of BBQ Sauce on a plate for each serving, then top with 3 fritters. Sprinkle with chopped parsley and serve.

"Food is our common ground, a universal experience."
–JAMES BEARD

Wakame Quinoa Dumplings

YIELD: *8 servings*

TIME: *30 minutes preparation;*
40 minutes cooking

Vegetable Stock

1 quart water
1 onion, quartered
1 carrot, cut into large chunks
1 celery stalk, cut into large
chunks
¾ teaspoon sea salt
¼ teaspoon thyme
⅛ teaspoon white pepper
1 bay leaf
1 6-inch piece kombu

Dumpling Mixture

½ cup water
1½ teaspoons agar flakes
¼ cup quinoa, washed and
drained
2 tablespoons finely diced
butternut squash
2 tablespoons finely diced sun-
dried tomato
¹⁄₁₆ teaspoon sea salt
1 teaspoon extra virgin olive oil
¼ cup finely diced onions
2 cloves minced garlic
¼ teaspoon sea salt
1 10½-ounce package extra
firm silken tofu
3 tablespoons unbleached
white flour
2 tablespoons sake or mirin
1½ teaspoons finely chopped
fresh cilantro
2 teaspoons chopped dried
wakame

1 recipe Wakame Au Jus
(page 153)

This is a very light dumpling with a delicate flavor, very similar to a quenelle.

Vegetable Stock

In a large saucepan or stockpot, combine all the stock ingredients and bring to a boil, cover, then reduce heat to low and simmer for 30 minutes. Strain out vegetables and reduce liquid to 1 quart, then return the stock to the saucepan, and bring back to a simmer.

Dumplings

In a 1-quart saucepan (with lid), combine the water and agar and bring to a boil, then reduce to low and simmer for 7 to 10 minutes or until agar has dissolved. Add quinoa, squash, sun-dried tomato, and salt, cover, then return to simmer over medium heat. Reduce heat to low and cook for about 15 minutes or until water is absorbed and quinoa is light and fluffy. In a 10-inch frying pan, heat the oil and sauté onions, garlic, and salt for 5 minutes over medium heat. In a food processor, combine vegetables, tofu, flour, sake, and cilantro and process until smooth. Add wakame and quinoa and process long enough to mix ingredients thoroughly.

Forming and Cooking the Dumplings

Using 2 tablespoons, scoop 2 tablespoons of the tofu mixture into 1 of the spoons. Transfer mixture back and forth between the two spoons to create a smooth, 3-sided, oval shape (or simply drop the mixture, unformed, from the spoon into the simmering stock). Drop each formed dumpling into the stock and poach for 3 minutes after they start to float. Gently remove dumplings from stock and serve hot with Wakame Au Jus.

Soups

Soups are usually taken at the beginning of a meal to warm the stomach and stimulate the digestive juices. They may be classified according to their dominant food group such as grains, beans, vegetables, or fruits. In France, the word *soupe* originally denoted a peasant style soup consisting of chunks of various vegetables in broth. These soups were usually garnished with breads and croutons. In relationship to a dinner, the soup is what Grimod de la Reyniere described so well when he said, "It is to the dinner what a portico or a peristyle is to a building, that is to say, it is not only the first part of it, but it must be devised in such a manner as to set the tone for the whole banquet in the same way as the overture of an opera announces the subject of the work."

How is soup used in a menu? The soup must not only be in balance with the entire meal but also with the season. Winter soups are usually hearty and more warming, as opposed to light summer soups that are more cooling and refreshing, especially when served chilled.

Included in this section are consommés, cream soups, and simple stock soups. My soup section runs the range from the classic Vichyssoise to Portuguese Cream Soup, Roasted Vegetable Consommé, and Boston Seafood Chowder. Then there are unusual soups like the Cold Cucumber Kiwi Soup. All of these soups are sure to please.

From an ecological perspective, soups are a great way to utilize every morsel of scrap foods. I keep vegetable peels for the stock pot, leftover sauerkraut for Kasha Soup, and broccoli stems for Cream of Broccoli Soup. The list goes on. When I was in the seminary, Saturday lunch was usually called the weekly review and included an innovative soup using the remnants of the weekly menu. Soup is the best way to ecologically and economically utilize food. It is the true test of one's creativity and culinary skill.

Mango Crackers

YIELD: *4 servings*
TIME: *25 minutes*

¾ cup unbleached white flour
¼ cup fresh mango purée
1 tablespoon canola oil
¼ teaspoon sea salt
⅛ teaspoon coriander powder

Serve with Cold Cucumber Kiwi Soup or Saffron Millet Soup, Indian Lentil Purée as an appetizer, or with Pineapple Raisin Waldorf Salad.

Preheat oven to 350 degrees F. In a mixing bowl, combine all the ingredients together to form a dough. On a lightly floured surface, roll the dough $1/16$ inch thick and cut it into 3-inch squares. Prick each cracker 3 times with the tines of a fork to prevent puffing during baking. Bake the crackers on a lightly oiled baking sheet for 5 to 8 minutes or until lightly browned and crisp. Remove crackers from oven and transfer to a wire rack to cool.

Cold Cucumber Kiwi Soup

YIELD: *4 servings*
TIME: *20 minutes preparation;*
    2 hours chilling

2 medium peeled, seeded,
    diced cucumbers
2 kiwis, peeled
1½ cups soy or rice milk
¼ cup brown rice miso
2 tablespoons brown rice syrup
¼ cup chopped dried wakame
    pieces, reconstituted in
    water
2 tablespoons chopped fresh
    parsley for garnish

I wanted a cold soup that would be simple yet extraordinary and this is the result. The subtle flavor resulting from the combination of cucumber, kiwi, and miso is delightful.

In a blender, combine ⅔ cup of the diced cucumber, kiwi, soy milk, miso, and syrup and blend until smooth. Transfer mixture to a mixing bowl, add remaining diced cucumber and wakame, then refrigerate for 2 hours or until chilled. Garnish with parsley and serve cold.

Vichyssoise

YIELD: *6 servings*

TIME: *30 minutes preparation;*
*   1 hour cooking; 1 hour*
*   chilling*

6 cups leeks, white part only
*   (about 12 medium leeks)*
1½ cups thinly sliced onions
1 cup peeled, ½-inch cubed
*   potatoes*
3 tablespoons extra virgin
*   olive oil*
1 bay leaf
1 teaspoon sea salt
⅛ teaspoon white pepper
2 cups water
1 tablespoon Vogue Vege Base
1 cup soy milk
chopped chives or parsley
*   for garnish*

Vichyssoise is a cold cream of leek soup, not a potato soup. The potato is used primarily as the thickening agent, not as the main ingredient. The key to making a successful Vichyssoise is to cook the leeks slowly. In this soup, the vegetables make it aromatic, not the seasonings. This soup tastes best when eaten fresh the same day it is made.

Remove the roots from the leeks, quarter, wash well, and slice thinly. In a 2-quart saucepan, combine the leeks, onions, potatoes and oil and stir until all the vegetables are coated with the oil. Add the bay leaf, salt, and pepper, then stir well again. Place the pan on a flame-spreader over medium-low heat, cover, and cook gently for about 45 minutes, stirring occasionally. (It is important that this "sweating" of the vegetables be done slowly, so that they will release their flavor without burning. Using a flame-spreader underneath the pan will help spread the heat and prevent burning.) Add the water and the Vogue Vege Base to the vegetables and cook for another 5 to 10 minutes. Remove the bay leaf, transfer soup to a blender, and blend until smooth. Transfer to a serving bowl, stir in soy milk, and refrigerate for 1 hour or until chilled thoroughly. Garnish with the chopped chives or parsley and serve cold.

Chestnut Soup

YIELD: *3 servings*
TIME: *20 minutes preparation;
    25 minutes cooking*

2 teaspoons canola oil
½ cup diced onion
½ cup peeled, diced carrot
½ cup diced celery
2 cloves minced garlic
¼ teaspoon sea salt
⅛ teaspoon white pepper
2½ cups water
1 cup boiled fresh chestnuts
*2 tablespoons soy milk powder
    (optional)*
2 tablespoons white miso
*1 tablespoon finely chopped
    fresh parsley for garnish*

I enjoy this hearty winter soup, because of my love of chestnuts. I sometimes think of it as a Christmas soup.

In a 2-quart saucepan (with lid), heat the oil and sauté the onion, carrot, celery, garlic, salt, and pepper over medium heat for 5 minutes or until onion is transparent. Add water and chestnuts, then simmer covered for 20 minutes, stirring occasionally. Add soy milk powder and miso, then stir until smooth. Garnish with chopped parsley and serve hot.

Swiss Cucumber Soup

YIELD: *5 servings*

TIME: *20 minutes preparation;
35 minutes cooking*

2 tablespoons unrefined
 corn oil
1 large cucumber (to yield 2½
 cups peeled, seeded, and
 sliced ⅛ inch thick)
1 medium onion, sliced in half
 moons
¼ cup chopped parsley (or 2
 tablespoons dried parsley)
1 clove minced garlic
1 teaspoon dill weed
1 teaspoon sea salt
½ teaspoon tarragon
 (optional)
2 tablespoons arrowroot
 powder or cornstarch
 dissolved in 1¾ cups
 cool water
2 cups soy milk
¼ teaspoon black pepper
5 sprigs fresh dill

This creamy cucumber soup is one of the few cream soups that can be served as a summer soup. The unique flavor is a result of cooking the cucumbers.

In a 2-quart saucepan, heat the oil and sauté the cucumber, onion, parsley, garlic, dill weed, salt, and tarragon for 5 minutes or until the onions and cucumbers are transparent. Pour the arrowroot/water mixture into the saucepan and stir until it thickens. Gradually add the soy milk and continue stirring until smooth and creamy. Simmer for 3 minutes. Add pepper and mix well. Garnish each serving with a sprig of dill and serve hot.

Roasted Vegetable Consommé

YIELD: *6 servings*

TIME: *30 minutes preparation;*
    2 hours cooking

2 unpeeled, quartered onions
2 coarsely chopped carrots
2 coarsely chopped celery stalks
1 large coarsely chopped
    parsnip
¼ coarsely chopped leek
5 cloves garlic
5 quarts water
½ cup tamari or shoyu
¼ cup sliced, dried shiitake
    mushrooms
2½ cups chopped fresh
    mushrooms
1½ teaspoons green
    peppercorns
6 sprigs fresh tarragon
3 bay leaves

The key to making this soup is lightly simmering the vegetables after roasting them. Combined with the herbs, the roasted vegetables impart a rich flavor to the broth that can be served with a summer or winter menu.

Preheat oven to 350 degrees F. Spread the onions, carrots, celery, parsnip, leek, and garlic on a baking sheet and roast for 15 minutes or until golden brown. Remove vegetables and transfer to a large stock pot. Add the water, tamari, mushrooms, peppercorns, tarragon, and bay leaves and simmer slowly for about 2 hours. Remove pot from heat and allow to cool. It should yield about 8½ cups of consommé. If not, continue to reduce it until it yields the desired amount. Strain out the vegetables and serve hot.

Italian Orzo Soup

YIELD: *5 servings*

TIME: *15 minutes preparation;
55 minutes cooking*

1 teaspoon extra virgin olive
oil
1 cup diced onions
2 cloves minced garlic
½ cup diced fresh fennel (or ½
cup diced celery, plus ½
teaspoon fennel powder)
5 cups water
¼ cup whole wheat or regular
orzo
4 teaspoons Vogue Vege Base
2 teaspoons sea salt
¼ teaspoon saffron threads
1 tablespoon chopped fresh
parsley for garnish

This soup goes well with the Italian Bistro Sandwich or the Italian Country Loaf. It is a light, hot soup, perfect for a cold day.

In a 3-quart saucepan, heat the oil and sauté the onions, garlic, and fennel over medium heat for 5 minutes. Add water, orzo, Vogue Vege Base, salt, and saffron, then simmer for 50 minutes. Remove from heat, garnish with parsley, and serve hot.

Boston Seafood Chowder

YIELD: *5 servings*
TIME: *25 minutes preparation;
    25 minutes cooking*

1 tablespoon extra virgin
    olive oil
1 cup finely diced onions
¾ cup peeled, diced potato
½ cup finely diced celery
¼ cup diced red bell pepper
¼ cup chopped, rehydrated
    wakame
1 tablespoon Vogue Vege Base
1 bay leaf
½ teaspoon thyme
¾ teaspoon sea salt
3 tablespoons unbleached
    white flour
5 cups soy milk
1 cup fresh or canned oyster
    mushrooms

Sea vegetables are seafood! I wanted a rich chowder with a cream base that resembled Bean Town's chowder (everyone who loves a great chowder can relate to this desire), but was plant-based. Besides being a tasty and warming soup, this also makes a great pasta sauce. Just double the seasonings and let simmer a little longer for extra richness.

In a 3-quart saucepan, heat the oil and sauté the onions, potato, celery, bell pepper, wakame, Vogue Vege Base, bay leaf, thyme, and salt over medium heat for 10 to 12 minutes, stirring to prevent them from burning (add a little water if necessary). Add flour and stir for 3 minutes or until well blended. Add 1 cup of the soy milk and continue to cook, stirring constantly, until thickened. Add another cup of soy milk and continue stirring until thickened. Add remaining soy milk and mushrooms, then bring the soup to a simmer. Remove from heat and serve immediately.

Kasha Soup

YIELD: *5 servings*

TIME: *25 minutes preparation;
35 minutes cooking*

1 piece kombu, 4–6 inches long
4 cups water
1 tablespoon untoasted
    sesame oil
½ cup peeled, diced potatoes
½ cup peeled, diced carrots
½ cup sliced mushrooms
½ cup shredded or thinly sliced
    cabbage (optional)
1 tablespoon garlic powder
2 teaspoons basil
½ cup kasha, washed and
    drained
½ cup pre-cooked or frozen
    lima beans
½ cup sauerkraut, drained
2 to 4 teaspoons brown rice
    or barley miso
chopped parsley for garnish

Kasha, or roasted buckwheat groats, is featured in this very satisfying and warming winter soup. This soup is in honor of Mary Sciullo, my second mother, who introduced me to this soup on Christmas Eve.

Prepare the kombu by soaking it in the water until reconstituted. Reserve the water, then chop the kombu and set it aside until ready to use. In a 2-quart saucepan, heat the oil and sauté the potatoes, carrots, mushrooms, cabbage, garlic powder, and basil over medium heat for 10 minutes or until done. Add water, kombu, kasha, lima beans, and sauerkraut, then bring to a simmer. Let the soup simmer covered for 5 to 10 minutes, or until the beans (if using frozen) and kasha are cooked. In a small bowl, combine the miso with a small amount of the broth, mix until miso is dissolved, and return to saucepan. For stronger flavor, use the higher measure of the miso. If soup is too thick, add more water. Garnish with chopped parsley and serve hot.

Saffron Millet Soup

YIELD: *6 servings*
TIME: *25 minutes preparation;*
30 minutes cooking

2 tablespoons canola oil
1 cup diced onions
¾ cup peeled, diced carrots
½ cup peeled, diced butternut
squash
½ cup chopped celery
4 cloves minced garlic
4 cups water
½ cup millet, washed and
drained
½ teaspoon ginger powder
¼ teaspoon saffron threads
⅛ teaspoon white pepper
¼ cup white miso
chopped parsley for garnish

The saffron in this recipe adds additional color and a unique and distinctive flavor.

In a 2-quart saucepan, heat the oil and sauté the onions, carrots, squash, celery, and garlic over medium heat for about 5 minutes or until onions are transparent. Add the water, millet, ginger, saffron, and pepper to the sautéed vegetables, then bring to a simmer. Continue to simmer for 20 minutes or until the millet is cooked. In a small bowl, combine the miso with a small amount of the broth, mix until miso is dissolved, and return to saucepan. Garnish with parsley and serve hot.

San Francisco Vegetable Soup

YIELD: *4 servings*
TIME: *25 minutes*

1 teaspoon sesame oil
½ cup sliced onions
½ cup peeled, thinly sliced
carrots
½ cup thinly sliced bok choy
(leaves included)
¼ cup thinly sliced red bell
pepper
1 teaspoon sea salt
3 cups water
1 tablespoon Vogue Vege Base
½ teaspoon granulated garlic
¼ teaspoon ginger powder
¼ cup snow peas, cut into
diagonal strips

There is an elegance in simplicity, and this soup is a perfect example of that idea. It is important to serve this soup immediately after adding the snow peas, as the peas will lose their color if left in the hot broth for too long.

In a 2-quart saucepan, heat the oil and sauté the onions, carrots, bok choy, bell pepper, and salt over medium heat for about 5 minutes or until onions are transparent. Add the water, Vogue Vege Base, garlic, and ginger. Bring the soup to a simmer and cook for another 5 minutes. Add the snow peas and serve hot with whole wheat crackers on the side.

"The fact is that America, unlike France, Italy, China and so on—does not have a national legacy of 'great' cooking that has been handed down from generation to generation. Many of its 'great' dishes are wholly regional."

—CRAIG CLAIBORNE

Southern Peanut Butter Soup

YIELD: *6 servings*
TIME: *30 minutes*

*1 tablespoon peanut or
    sesame oil*
1 cup diced celery
1 cup diced carrots
1 cup diced onions
½ cup diced red bell pepper
4 cloves minced garlic
2 teaspoons sea salt
1 teaspoon thyme
½ teaspoon black pepper
5 cups water
1 cup creamy peanut butter
chopped parsley for garnish

This unusual soup is a favorite with anyone who has tried it. Make sure you use the highest quality peanut butter.

In a 2-quart saucepan, heat the oil and sauté the celery, carrots, onions, bell pepper, garlic, salt, thyme, and pepper over medium heat for about 5 minutes or until onions are transparent. Add the water and peanut butter, then stir with a whisk until the peanut butter is dissolved. Bring to a simmer and cook covered for 10 more minutes over low heat. Garnish with chopped parsley and serve hot.

Little Havana Black Bean Soup

YIELD: *6 servings*

TIME: *20 minutes preparation;*
2 hours cooking

1½ cups uncooked black
beans
6 cups water
1 cup peeled, diced potatoes
1 6-inch piece kombu
2 bay leaves
2 tablespoons canola or
sesame oil
1 cup peeled, finely diced
carrots
1 cup chopped onions
1 cup diced celery
6 cloves minced garlic
1 teaspoon liquid hickory
smoke (optional)
1½ teaspoons sea salt
1½ teaspoons thyme
1 teaspoon rosemary
¾ teaspoon black pepper
½ teaspoon oregano
3 tomatoes
2 tablespoons dark miso
6 tablespoons thinly sliced
scallions or chopped parsley
for garnish

Combined with a salad and Anasazi Bean Sandwich Rolls or Southwestern Double Crust Pizza, this soup makes a fine lunch.

Prepare beans by removing any stones or broken beans, then wash them. Soak beans in 3 cups of water for 6 hours, or preferably overnight. When ready to use, drain the beans, and discard the soaking water. In a 3-quart saucepan, combine the beans, 6 cups of water, potatoes, kombu, and bay leaves and bring to a simmer over medium heat. In a 10-inch frying pan, heat the oil and sauté the carrots, onions, celery, garlic, liquid smoke, salt, thyme, rosemary, pepper, and oregano over medium heat for about 8 minutes or until onions are transparent. Add the sautéed vegetables to the beans and continue simmering for 2 hours or until beans are cooked. Rinse the tomatoes and make a small cut in the skin of each tomato. In a 2-quart saucepan, bring 6 cups of water to a boil, add the tomatoes, and simmer for 2 to 3 minutes, or until the skins begin to pull away. Remove tomatoes immediately and place in a bowl of cold water to cool. Remove loosened skins, then cut each tomato in half and squeeze out the seeds. Chop tomatoes, add to soup, and continue to simmer. In a small bowl, combine the miso with a small amount of the broth, mix until miso is dissolved, and return to saucepan. (For a creamier soup, blend 1½ cups of the soup until smooth, then add back to the soup.) Simmer for 5 minutes longer. Garnish with chopped scallions or parsley and serve hot.

Yellow Pepper Cream Soup

YIELD: *3 servings*
TIME: *30 minutes preparation;*
1 hour cooking

4 yellow bell peppers
1 medium quartered Spanish
onion
1 cup soy milk
2 tablespoons lemon juice
2 tablespoons white miso
1 tablespoon chopped fresh
cilantro
¼ teaspoon fennel powder
3 sprigs fresh cilantro for
garnish

Confetti Corn Fritters, Pesto Bread, and Black Bean Cracker Cups are all excellent companions to this soup.

Preheat oven to 325 degrees F. Wash, dry, halve, and seed the peppers. Rub the skins with oil. Place pepper halves on a baking sheet along with the quartered onion and roast for 30 to 40 minutes or until the pepper skins are soft and begin to shrivel and onion becomes golden brown. Remove vegetables from oven and place the peppers in a brown paper bag to steam for 10 minutes. When cool, remove the loosened skins from the peppers. In a blender, combine the peppers, onion, soy milk, lemon juice, miso, cilantro, and fennel powder and blend until smooth and creamy. Garnish with a sprig of cilantro and serve either hot or chilled.

Cream of Cauliflower Soup

YIELD: *6 servings*

TIME: *25 minutes preparation;*
35 minutes cooking

2 tablespoons extra virgin
olive oil
4 cups chopped cauliflower
2 cups diced onions
1 cup diced celery
½ cup diced carrots
3 cloves minced garlic
1½ teaspoons sea salt
¼ teaspoon nutmeg
1⁄16 teaspoon white pepper
4 cups soy milk
1 cup water
6 tablespoons rolled oat flakes
2 bay leaves
chopped fresh parsley, scallions,
or watercress for garnish

For a simple and tasty meal, serve this soup with Italian Country Loaf and Italian Mixed Greens Salad.

In a 2-quart saucepan, heat the oil and sauté the cauliflower, onions, celery, carrots, garlic, salt, nutmeg, and pepper over medium heat for 10 minutes, stirring occasionally. Add the soy milk (less for a thicker soup), water, oats, and bay leaves to the sautéed vegetables, then bring to a simmer and cook for 20 minutes. Let the soup cool slightly, then remove bay leaves. Transfer soup to a blender and blend well. Reheat soup, garnish with parsley, and serve hot.

Portuguese Cream Soup

YIELD: *8 servings*
TIME: *35 minutes preparation;*
    1 hour cooking

2 tablespoons sesame oil
1 cup peeled, diced carrots
½ cup diced onions
5 tablespoons unbleached
    white flour
3 cups vegetable stock or water
½ cup uncooked brown rice
1 cup tomato juice
2 tablespoons brown rice syrup
    (or 1 tablespoon honey)
2 sprigs chopped parsley
1 clove minced garlic
1 teaspoon basil
¾ teaspoon tarragon
½ teaspoon sea salt
⅛ teaspoon white pepper
5 tomatoes
2 tablespoons barley or
    rice miso
2½ cups soy milk

This wonderfully warming winter soup follows the classic French version.

In a 3-quart saucepan, heat the oil and sauté the carrots and onions over medium heat. Sprinkle the flour 1 tablespoon at a time into the pot, stirring well. Cook for 5 minutes, carefully scraping the bottom of the pan while stirring to prevent sticking and burning. Gradually add the vegetable stock, rice, tomato juice, syrup, parsley, garlic, basil, tarragon, salt, and pepper. Rinse the tomatoes and make a small cut in the skin of each tomato. In a 2-quart saucepan, bring 6 cups of water to a boil, add the tomatoes, and simmer for 2 to 3 minutes, or until the skins begin to pull away. Remove tomatoes immediately and place in a bowl of cold water to cool. Remove loosened skins, then cut each tomato in half and squeeze out the seeds. Chop tomatoes, add (about 2½ cups) to soup, and bring to a simmer. Cook soup covered for 45 to 60 minutes, or until the rice is done. In a small bowl, combine the miso with a small amount of the broth, mix until miso is dissolved, and return to saucepan. Add the soy milk to the soup and stir until heated through. Serve hot.

Cream of Broccoli Soup

YIELD: *4 servings*
TIME: *25 minutes preparation;*
  30 minutes cooking

*1 tablespoon extra virgin
  olive oil*
*3½ cups peeled, chopped
  broccoli stems*
1½ cups chopped onion
¼ cup peeled, chopped carrots
¼ cup chopped celery
1 clove minced garlic
¼ teaspoon dill weed
⅛ teaspoon black pepper
1/16 teaspoon nutmeg
2 cups soy milk
*2 tablespoons kuzu or
  cornstarch dissolved in
  2 tablespoons cool water*
chopped parsley for garnish

This versatile soup can also be used in casseroles or as a pasta sauce.

In a 2-quart saucepan, heat the oil and sauté the broccoli, onion, carrots, celery, garlic, dill weed, pepper, and nutmeg over medium heat for about 10 minutes. Add soy milk, bring to a simmer, and continue to cook for another 10 minutes or until the vegetables are soft. Add kuzu/water mixture to the soup and stir until thickened (if soup is too thick, thin it out by adding a little more soy milk). Garnish with chopped parsley and serve hot.

Cream of Pumpkin Soup

YIELD: *4 servings*
TIME: *15 minutes preparation;*
20 minutes cooking

1½ cups fresh pumpkin (or
1 15-ounce can)
1 tablespoon corn or sesame oil
1 cup diced onions
1 cup diced mushrooms
3 cloves minced garlic
1 teaspoon sea salt
1 teaspoon Vogue Vege Base
1½ cups water
chopped parsley, scallions, or
watercress for garnish

This excellent autumn soup goes well with Vermont Seitan with Chestnuts and Millet Stuffed Squash with Roasted Vegetables.

Peel, seed, and cube the pumpkin. In a vegetable steamer, steam the pumpkin for 20 minutes or until soft. In a 10-inch frying pan, heat the oil and sauté the onions, mushrooms, garlic, salt, and Vogue Vege Base for 8 minutes. In a blender, combine the sautéed and steamed vegetables, then add water and blend until smooth. If desired, add more water and seasoning to taste. Reheat soup, garnish with fresh parsley, and serve hot.

"Things that are supposed to be good for you should keep the secret of their good intentions strictly to themselves."
—BERT GREENE'S GRANDMOTHER

Old-Fashioned Cream of Cabbage Soup

YIELD: *5 servings*
TIME: *20 minutes preparation;*
    45 minutes cooking

2 tablespoons canola oil
2¼ cups shredded green
    cabbage
1½ cups chopped onions
½ cup peeled, diced potatoes
¼ cup chopped celery
1 tablespoon Vogue Vege Base
¾ teaspoon basil
¾ teaspoon sea salt
½ teaspoon caraway seeds
¼ teaspoon tarragon
5 tablespoons unbleached
    white flour
2¼ cups water
1 cup soy milk
¼ cup chopped scallions
    and a sprinkle of
    paprika for garnish

The difference between old-fashioned and modern cream soups is that the old-fashioned ones had chunks of vegetables in them; no Cuisinarts or blenders were available to completely purée the ingredients. As we approach the millennium, what better time to go back to a simpler soup?

In a 2-quart saucepan, heat the oil and sauté the cabbage, onions, potatoes, celery, Vogue Vege Base, basil, salt, caraway seeds, and tarragon over medium heat for about 5 minutes or until onions are transparent. Stir flour into the vegetable mixture and continue to sauté for another 4 to 5 minutes while stirring constantly. Add half the water and continue to stir until thickened. Add remaining water and soy milk and continue to stir until smooth and creamy. Reduce heat to low and cook for another 20 to 25 minutes, stirring periodically to prevent burning. Garnish with scallions and paprika and serve hot.

Salads
& Salad
Dressings

More than any other course or category, salads are considered the most healthy of all foods. This general perception is accurate but can also be misleading. The determining factor is the amount of fat in the salad. Dietitians have discovered that curing the craving for fat may be more difficult than curing the craving for sweets. When there is a craving for fat, people will somehow work it into their diet. Two tablespoons of a typical salad dressing can add 15 to 20 grams of fat to a green leafy salad, putting it on par with a medium order of French fries. No-fat and low-fat dressings neither fulfill the natural need for fat nor do they give any nutritive value to the food.

My response was to create dressings that, while they contain fat, are also loaded with nutrition. Some of the fat comes from nuts, seeds, and tofu which are nutritious foods. Vegetables and fruits also add to the nutritive value of some of the dressings. Because of the increased nutritive value, my salad dressings become a nutritional asset rather than a liability to the salad. Some favorites are the Maple Balsamic Vinaigrette, Creamy Herb Miso Dressing, and Green Goddess Dressing.

In this section I have created a wonderful array of hearty and light salads. Salads are dishes generally made up of plant-based foods such as lettuces and herbs. A variety of plant- or animal-based proteins are often added to them. There are two kinds of salads represented here: plain salads, which consist of fresh raw vegetables and dressings, and mixed combination salads such as Potato Salad or Berlin Bean Salad. Salads like the Berlin Bean Salad and Tempeh Salad are meals in themselves. While the world of salads has become more sophisticated, they remain the symbol of health for everyone. Salads belong in everybody's diet.

Arugula and Smoked Portobello Mushroom Salad

YIELD: *4 servings*
TIME: *25 minutes*

*2 bunches arugula (about
    6 cups)*
8 large radicchio leaves
8 large slices ripe tomato
8 pieces Belgian endive
*4 medium Marinated Smoked
    Portobello Mushrooms
    (page 18)*
1 cup thinly sliced scallions
1 cup salad dressing

This salad is best with either Creamy Herb Miso Dressing, Maple Balsamic Vinaigrette, Cilantro Lime Vinaigrette, or Easy French Dressing.

Wash the greens and either spin dry or shake and drain them. On a salad plate, arrange 2 radicchio leaves to create a pocket, 2 tomato slices at the base of the radicchio leaves, 2 pieces of Belgian endive, and the arugula (divided evenly between the salads) on the radicchio. Thinly slice the smoked and marinated mushrooms, then fan half of each mushroom across each of the tomatoes on each salad plate. Sprinkle scallions on tomatoes. Drizzle ¼ cup of dressing on each salad. Serve cold.

VARIATION
If a smoker is not available, sauté fresh portobello mushrooms in 1 tablespoon olive oil for a few minutes on each side. Towards the end of the sautéing, add ½ teaspoon liquid hickory smoke and sauté a minute or 2 more on each side. Remove the pan from the heat, thinly slice the mushrooms, then refrigerate until needed.

Pineapple Raisin Waldorf Salad

YIELD: *8 servings*
TIME: *40 minutes preparation;*
   1 hour chilling

Dressing

1 10½-ounce package extra
   firm silken tofu
¼ cup soy mayonnaise
3 tablespoons honey or
   FruitSource syrup
1 tablespoon lemon juice
¼ teaspoon nutmeg
¼ teaspoon pure vanilla
   extract

Salad

½ cup walnuts
2 cups diced Red Delicious
   apples
2 cups fresh or canned
   pineapple chunks, drained
1 cup diced celery
½ cup raisins
2 heads of lettuce, shredded
   (or 8 whole leaves of
   lettuce)
8 mint leaves and 4 fanned
   strawberries

This is a variation of the classic Waldorf salad, with the exception of a plant-based dressing. It's one of my favorite salads and I wanted a totally plant-based version of it.

Dressing

In a blender, combine the dressing ingredients and blend until smooth. Check the flavor and adjust seasonings if necessary. Transfer to a covered container and refrigerate until ready to use.

Salad

Preheat oven to 325 degrees F. Spread the walnuts on a baking sheet and roast for about 15 minutes or until lightly browned and very fragrant. Immediately remove from oven and transfer to a container to cool. Once cool, coarsely chop the nuts. In a salad bowl, combine the walnuts, apples, pineapple, celery, and raisins, cover, and refrigerate for 1 hour or until chilled. When ready to serve, combine the dressing with the salad ingredients and arrange the mix on a bed of lettuce, shredded or whole, on each of the serving plates. Slice each strawberry in half, then slice into a fan. Garnish each serving with a mint leaf and fanned strawberry, then serve immediately.

NOTE: Add the dressing to the salad just prior to serving. Adding it far in advance will cause the salad to go limp.

White Bean and Pasta Salad

YIELD: *8 servings*
TIME: *20 minutes preparation;*
20 minutes cooking; 12
hours chilling

6 cups water
1 tablespoon extra virgin olive
oil
½ teaspoon sea salt
2 cups dry whole grain pasta
shells
1½ cups cooked navy beans or
1 15½-ounce can navy
beans, drained
1 cup finely diced onions
1 cup finely diced green bell
peppers
¾ cup peeled, chopped carrots
½ cup diced celery
½ cup diced fresh fennel (or 1
teaspoon fennel powder)

Dressing

½ cup apple cider vinegar
¼ cup extra virgin olive oil
1 teaspoon prepared yellow
mustard
1 teaspoon dill weed
1 teaspoon garlic powder
1 teaspoon sea salt
½ teaspoon black pepper

During the hot summer months, I enjoy this cold salad as a meal in itself. You can leave it in the refrigerator until ready to use, serve on large washed lettuce leaves, and sit down to dinner.

In a 4-quart pot, bring the water to a boil over high heat. Add the oil, salt, and pasta shells, then bring the water back to a simmer and reduce the heat to medium. Stir occasionally with a wooden spoon to prevent the pasta from sticking and cook for about 5 to 10 minutes or al dente. Drain and rinse pasta under cold water until cool. Drain again and set aside. In a salad bowl, add the pasta, beans, onions, bell pepper, carrots, celery, and fennel and mix well. In another bowl, combine the dressing ingredients and mix well. Add ½ cup of the dressing to the salad and mix well. For more flavor add the remaining ¼ cup of dressing. Refrigerate overnight so that the flavors will develop. Serve cold.

VARIATION

Crumble a handful of dry arame and cook it in 2 cups of water for about 10 minutes. Drain and press it as dry as possible. Add the arame or ¼ cup chopped black olives to the cooled pasta along with the beans and vegetables.

Tempeh Salad

YIELD: *5 servings*

TIME: *30 minutes preparation;
15 minutes cooking; 1 hour
chilling*

2 8-ounce packages tempeh,
   plain or with sea vegetables
½ cup water
3 tablespoons barley malt
   syrup or sorghum syrup
2 tablespoons tamari
½ teaspoon coriander powder
   (or 1 teaspoon if a spicier
   flavor is preferred)
¼ cup extra virgin olive oil
2 heads Bibb lettuce
2½ cups peeled, julienned
   daikon
2½ cups peeled, julienned
   carrots
1 bunch fresh watercress
   (about 2½ cups)
2½ sliced tomatoes or 5
   tomato roses (optional)
15 slices cucumber, scored
1 cup Cilantro Lime
   Vinaigrette, Creamy Herb
   Miso Dressing, or Lemon
   Garlic Dressing

The presentation of this salad is as dramatic as the flavors and textures. Served with Wehani Rice Pilaf, this makes a wonderful and easy to prepare meal.

Slice each package of tempeh into 10 equal pieces. In a mixing bowl, combine the water, syrup, tamari, and coriander and set aside. In a 10-inch frying pan, heat half of the olive oil on medium heat. Dip the tempeh pieces into the tamari mixture, then drain. Place 5 of the tempeh slices in the frying pan and fry about 3 minutes per side or until brown. Transfer the tempeh pieces to a plate. Add remaining oil to the hot frying pan and fry the remaining tempeh pieces. Lay a generous bed of lettuce leaves on each of 5 plates. At the top of each plate, arrange the julienned daikon in a half moon pattern between the 10 o'clock and 2 o'clock positions. Overlap the julienned carrots over the daikon, leaving the top half of the daikon exposed. Place the watercress on the remaining exposed areas of lettuce, and fan 4 pieces of tempeh across the watercress. Garnish each plate across the bottom with tomato and cucumber. Refrigerate salads for 1 hour and serve cold with salad dressing.

Salad Argenteuil

YIELD: *6 servings*

TIME: *30 minutes preparation;
1 hour marinating; 1 hour
chilling*

*12 asparagus tips, 2 inches
long*

*⅓ cup Easy French Dressing
(page 71)*

*2 cups peeled, finely diced
potatoes*

*½ cup peeled, finely diced
carrots*

½ cup fresh or frozen peas

⅓ cup soy mayonnaise

¼ teaspoon sea salt

⅛ teaspoon black pepper

*6 cups shredded romaine or
other crisp lettuce*

½ cup crumbled, firm tofu

This salad follows the classic French salad and has a surprising array of flavors and textures. Combined with a sandwich, it makes a great summer lunch.

In a vegetable steamer, steam asparagus tips for 5 minutes or until tender crisp. In a shallow bowl, combine asparagus and Easy French Dressing and let marinate for 1 hour. Steam the potatoes and carrots together for 15 minutes, then add the peas and cook until tender crisp. In a mixing bowl, combine the potatoes, carrots, peas, and soy mayonnaise and toss lightly. Add the salt and pepper and adjust to taste. Arrange vegetables in a mound on a serving dish. Top the mound with marinated asparagus tips. Surround vegetables with the shredded lettuce and crumbled tofu. Refrigerate for 1 hour or until chilled. Serve cold.

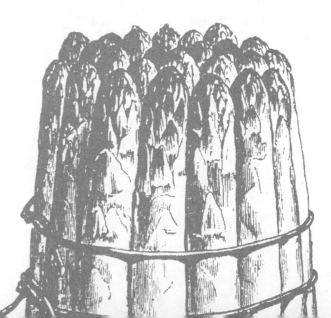

Mediterranean Salad

YIELD: *6 servings*

TIME: *40 minutes preparation;
1 hour chilling*

4 ounces firm tofu, cut in
   ½-inch cubes
¾ cup Easy French Dressing
   (page 71)
1 large head of romaine
   lettuce, washed, dried, and
   torn into small pieces
12 pitted, sliced Kalamata
   olives
½ cup finely chopped tomatoes
6 finely sliced scallions
1 cup finely diced red bell
   peppers
½ cup extra virgin olive oil
1 tablespoon red wine vinegar
1 tablespoon lemon juice
1 teaspoon grated lemon zest
1 clove minced garlic
1 tablespoon chopped Italian
   parsley
¾ teaspoon black pepper
½ teaspoon sea salt

Whenever olive oil, red wine vinegar, olives, and garlic are combined in a salad it has me won over. This salad goes well with any of the pita sandwiches or burgers.

In a mixing bowl, combine the tofu and Easy French Dressing and let marinate for at least one hour in the refrigerator. In a shallow bowl, combine the lettuce, olives, tomatoes, scallions, and bell peppers. In a separate bowl, whisk together the oil, vinegar, lemon juice, lemon zest, garlic, parsley, pepper, and salt. Remove tofu from dressing and pour dressing over the salad ingredients and toss until everything is evenly coated and glistening. Scatter the tofu over top and serve cold.

Asparagus Potato Salad

YIELD: *6 servings*

TIME: *20 minutes preparation;
25 minutes cooking; 1 hour
chilling*

4 cups peeled, diced potatoes
*1 tablespoon extra virgin olive
oil*
1½ cups finely diced onions
½ cups peeled, diced carrots
½ teaspoon sea salt
*1½ cups ½-inch long
asparagus pieces*
2 cups seeded, diced tomatoes
*1 cup Miso Poppy Seed
Dressing (page 80)*

Because this salad holds up so well, it is an excellent choice for a picnic. Serve it with Tempeh Burgers.

In a vegetable steamer, steam potatoes for 20 minutes or until they are soft. Remove the potatoes and transfer to a bowl to cool. In a 10-inch frying pan, heat the oil and sauté the onions, carrots and salt over medium heat for 5 minutes. Add the asparagus and sauté for another 5 minutes. Transfer vegetables to a salad bowl and allow to cool to room temperature. Add the potatoes and tomatoes, then fold in the dressing with a rubber spatula until thoroughly combined. Chill salad for an hour before serving.

Potato Salad

YIELD: *6 servings*

TIME: *20 minutes preparation;
20 minutes cooking; 1 hour
chilling*

4 medium potatoes
¾ cup diced red onions
½ cup diced celery
¼ cup diced pickles
¾ cup soy mayonnaise
1 clove minced garlic
*1 teaspoon yellow prepared
mustard*
¼ teaspoon black pepper
¼ teaspoon sea salt

This is one of my favorite salads, because of my affection for potatoes and it tastes like the potato salad my mother used to make for family picnics. You would never guess that it is a totally plant-based recipe.

In a vegetable steamer, steam the potatoes for about 20 minutes or until they are soft (if they are large, cut them in half to expedite the cooking). Cool, peel, and dice the potatoes. In a salad bowl, combine the potatoes, onions, celery, and pickles. In another bowl, combine the mayonnaise, garlic, mustard, pepper, and salt and mix well. Add mayonnaise mixture to the vegetables and mix gently until well blended. Refrigerate for 1 hour or until chilled and serve.

Mesa Verde Salad

YIELD: *4 servings*

TIME: *15 minutes preparation;*
1 hour chilling

¾ *cup uncooked couscous*

⅔ *cup water*

⅛ *teaspoon sea salt*

¾ *cup peeled, julienned sweet*
potato, butternut squash, or
carrot

¼ *cup julienned zucchini*

¼ *cup julienned yellow squash*

¼ *cup finely diced red bell*
pepper

¼ *cup peeled, finely diced*
cucumber

¼ *cup finely diced red onion*

1 *cup Lemon Garlic Dressing*
(page 78)

¼ *cup aduki beans, cooked*

This salad goes well with the Anasazi Bean Sandwich Rolls and the Black Bean and Corn Roll. Cilantro Lime Vinaigrette or Creamy Herb Miso Dressing may be substituted as the dressing for this salad.

In a 2-quart saucepan (with lid), combine the couscous, water, and salt, then simmer for 3 to 5 minutes, stirring occasionally. Cover and remove from heat. Blanch sweet potato for 90 seconds by plunging into boiling water and cooling quickly in cold water. Blanch the zucchini, yellow squash, and red pepper for 30 seconds each. In a salad bowl, combine the sweet potato, zucchini, yellow squash, red pepper, cucumber, and onion, then pour dressing over and toss. Add beans and couscous and toss again. Refrigerate 1 hour before serving. Serve on a bed of lettuce greens or in hollowed-out tomatoes.

Monastic Salad

YIELD: *6 servings*
TIME: *30 minutes preparation;*
12 hours chilling

Dressing

6 tablespoons extra virgin
olive oil
6 tablespoons apple cider
vinegar
6 tablespoons water
9 cloves minced garlic
1½ tablespoons chopped
parsley
1½ teaspoons basil
1½ teaspoons oregano
1½ teaspoons sea salt
1 teaspoon Sucanat
¼ teaspoon black pepper

3 ripe medium tomatoes,
thinly sliced
½ pound fresh mushrooms,
halved
1½ cups sauerkraut
½ cup diagonally sliced
scallions
green lettuce leaves and black
olives for garnish

This salad is truly monastic—simple, pure, and wonderful.

In a large mixing bowl, combine the dressing ingredients and mix well. Add the tomato slices and mushrooms. Rinse the sauerkraut, lightly squeeze dry, and add with the scallions to the dressing. Cover bowl and refrigerate overnight to marinate the vegetables and develop the flavors. Serve cold on leaves of green lettuce and garnished with black olives.

Berlin Bean Salad

YIELD: *6 servings*

TIME: *25 minutes preparation;
45 minutes cooking*

½ cup uncooked lentils
1 cup water
¼ teaspoon sea salt
4 ounces firm tofu, finely diced
(about 1 cup)
1 cup green beans, cut into
1-inch pieces
¼ cup canola or extra virgin
olive oil
¼ cup apple cider vinegar
2 tablespoons Sucanat
1 teaspoon chopped fresh
parsley
½ teaspoon prepared mustard
¼ teaspoon tarragon
¼ teaspoon sea salt
⅛ teaspoon black pepper
½ cup chopped red onions
¼ cup finely diced red bell
peppers or pimentos
¼ cup pitted and chopped
green olives
lettuce leaves, tomato wedges,
pickles for garnish

Served over the Italian Mixed Greens Salad, this salad is a meal in itself. It also goes well with soup or the Grilled Vegetable Sandwich.

In a 1-quart pot (with lid), combine the lentils and water and cook over medium heat for 30 minutes. Add first measure of salt and cook lentils another 10 to 15 minutes or until they are soft but not mushy (if the water cooks out before the lentils are done, add a little more water to complete the cooking process). In a vegetable steamer, lightly steam the tofu for about 1 minute, then remove and set aside to cool. Steam the green beans until tender crisp, then remove and transfer to a bowl of cold water to stop the cooking. In a mixing bowl, combine the oil, vinegar, Sucanat, parsley, mustard, tarragon, second measure of salt, and pepper and mix until well blended. Add lentils, tofu, green beans, onions, bell pepper, and olives, then mix well and refrigerate overnight to allow the flavors to develop. Serve cold on a crisp lettuce leaf with a tomato wedge and dill pickle wedge as garnish.

Carrot Aspic

YIELD: *8 servings*

TIME: *20 minutes preparation; 15 minutes cooking; 1 hour chilling*

2 tablespoons kuzu or arrowroot powder

2 tablespoons carrot juice

4 cups fresh carrot juice

¼ cup agar flakes

1 teaspoon dill weed

1 teaspoon umeboshi plum paste

cucumber slices and pimiento-stuffed green olives, or fresh dill and scallion flowers for garnish

Fresh carrot juice is highly nutritious and flavorful, and far superior to the canned variety. If possible, make it yourself in a juicer or buy it freshly bottled. This aspic can also be served as a dessert (just omit the dill weed and umeboshi plum paste) that even children will enjoy.

In a small bowl, combine the kuzu and first measure of carrot juice and mix until well dissolved. In a 2-quart saucepan, bring the second measure of carrot juice, agar, and dill weed to a simmer over medium heat, then cook for 7 to 10 minutes or until all of the agar has dissolved. Add the umeboshi paste and stir to dissolve. Whisk the carrot/kuzu mixture into the carrot/agar mixture, stirring vigorously to prevent lumping. Cook on low until thickened. Pour the aspic into 1 large or 8 individual lightly oiled molds. Refrigerate for 1 hour, or until agar is completely set. When ready to serve, unmold the aspic and garnish with cucumber slices and olives or dill and scallion flowers. Serve with Mango Dressing or Tricolor Salsa.

Andalusian Salad

YIELD: *4 servings*
TIME: *30 minutes preparation;*
1 hour chilling

2 cups cooked, chilled long
grain brown rice
6 tablespoons Andalusian
Vinaigrette (page 79)
2 tablespoons finely chopped
fresh parsley
1 tablespoon finely chopped
onion
1 clove minced garlic
1 medium green bell pepper,
julienned
3 medium tomatoes, quartered
2 tablespoons chopped fresh
chervil for garnish
(optional)
½ teaspoon Hungarian
paprika for garnish

This salad follows the classic French version and is perfect with Navy Beans Tarragon or Beans in Red Wine Sauce. Use the Hungarian paprika in this recipe, because it is sweeter than Spanish paprika.

In a mixing bowl, toss the rice gently with the vinaigrette, parsley, onion, and garlic, then arrange the mixture in a mound in the center of a serving dish. Arrange the julienned bell pepper in clusters around the rice, alternating with the quartered tomatoes. Sprinkle with chervil and paprika. Refrigerate for 1 hour or until well chilled. Serve cold.

Italian Mixed Greens Salad

YIELD: *4 servings*
TIME: *25 minutes*

*3 cups mesclun salad mix or
    assorted baby salad greens*
*3 cups spinach leaves, stems
    removed*
*2 cups arugula leaves, stems
    removed*
1½ cups radicchio (optional)
½ cup thinly sliced fresh fennel
*½ cup chiffonade-cut fresh
    basil*
*1 tablespoon fresh thyme
    leaves*
*1 tablespoon fresh marjoram
    leaves*
¾ cup salad dressing

Maple Balsamic Vinaigrette, Cilantro Lime Vinaigrette, or Creamy Herb Miso Dressing complement this salad beautifully.

Wash salad mix, spinach, arugula, and radicchio and either spin dry or shake and drain to remove the water. Transfer to salad bowl and add fennel, basil, thyme, and marjoram and toss to combine well. Pour dressing over the salad ingredients and toss until everything is evenly coated and glistening. Serve chilled.

Roasted Vegetable Terrine

YIELD: *8 servings*

TIME: *50 minutes preparation;*
1 hour cooking; 2 hours
chilling

2 red bell peppers
1 green bell pepper
1 yellow bell pepper
1 medium onion, peeled,
quartered
3 medium carrots, peeled,
sliced lengthwise into
¼-inch thick slices
1 cup water
1 medium sweet potato,
peeled, sliced lengthwise
in ¼-inch thick slices
2 cups water
3 tablespoons agar flakes
½ cup dried cranberries
(optional)
1 teaspoon sea salt
½ teaspoon liquid hickory
smoke (optional)
1 clove minced garlic
2 teaspoons fresh marjoram
leaves
2 teaspoons fresh thyme leaves
2 teaspoons fresh oregano
leaves
1 tablespoon arrowroot
powder dissolved in 2
tablespoons cool water
2 cups chiffonade of romaine
lettuce

Serve Cilantro Fennel Pesto or Creamy Herb Miso Dressing over this wonderful terrine.

Preheat oven to 325 degrees F. Wash, dry, halve, and seed the peppers. Separate the onion layers from each quarter. Rub the pepper skins with olive oil and lightly oil the onions and carrots as well. Place them on a baking sheet and roast in the oven for 15 minutes. Remove the onions and carrots, then set aside. Continue to roast the peppers for another 15 to 25 minutes or until they are soft and the skins begin to shrivel. Remove the peppers from the oven and place them in a brown paper bag to steam for 10 minutes. When cool, remove the loosened skins. Take 1 cup of water and pour as much of it as possible onto the baking sheet while the sheet is still hot (this is called deglazing). Reserve this deglazing liquid, then add it back to the measuring cup, adding more water if necessary, to yield 1 cup of roasted pepper liquid. Set aside. In a vegetable steamer, steam the sweet potato slices for 10 minutes or until soft but not mushy.

To Make the Gelatin

In a 2-quart saucepan, combine the second measure of water and agar and cook on medium heat for about 10 minutes or until agar has dissolved. Add the roasted pepper liquid, cranberries, salt, liquid smoke, garlic, marjoram, thyme, and oregano and continue to simmer for a few minutes. Add the arrowroot/water mixture and stir until thickened. Ladle a small amount of agar mixture (about ¼-inch layer) into the bottom of a lightly oiled 2-quart loaf pan. Place the pan in the freezer for 5 minutes or until agar is set. Cover saucepan containing the remaining agar mixture and set aside until ready to use.

To Assemble the Terrine

Remove loaf pan from freezer. Working as quickly as possible, arrange the sliced sweet potatoes, overlapping the slices if necessary, to cover the entire ¼-inch layer of gelatin, but leaving about ⅛ inch uncovered around all of the sides so that the gelatin will surround the vegetable layers when it is poured over them. Next add a layer of green peppers, followed by the onions, red pepper, carrots, and yellow pepper, repeating the same pattern until you either use up all the vegetables or come to the top of the loaf pan. Ladle the gelatin mixture over the layered vegetables, being sure to completely surround them on the sides of the pan. Gently shake the pan back and forth to disperse the gelatin throughout the vegetables, then with both hands lift up the loaf pan and gently tap the bottom on a flat surface to remove as many air bubbles as possible. Make sure the top layer of vegetables is completely covered with the agar mixture. Place terrine in the refrigerator and chill for 2 hours, or preferably overnight, until agar is completely set.

To Unmold the Terrine

Remove terrine from refrigerator. Wipe the outside of the loaf pan with a hot, moist cloth or towel. Place a plate or platter that can accommodate the length of the pan over it, turn it upside down, and unmold the terrine onto the plate. Slice with a serrated knife into 1-inch thick slices and serve cold or at room temperature. Garnish with romaine lettuce and one of the suggested sauces.

Japanese Salad

YIELD: *4 servings*
TIME: *20 minutes*

2 cups tatsoi, plus 2 cups
*   mizuna (or 4 cups mesclun*
*   salad mix or assorted baby*
*   salad greens)*
2 cups arugula
2 large ripe tomatoes
2 Avocado Nori Rolls
*   (page 98)*
1 recipe Three Flavors
*   Dressing (page 80) or*
*   Cilantro Lime Vinaigrette*
*   (page 72)*

This unique and attractive salad features a combination of salad greens, Avocado Nori Rolls, and a dressing composed of sweet, sour, and salty flavors.

Wash tatsoi and arugula, and either spin dry or shake and drain to remove the water. Transfer to salad bowl and toss to combine well. Slice the tomatoes in half, then slice each half into 6 ¼-inch thick slices. Cut each of the Avocado Nori Rolls into 10 ½-inch thick pieces. On each of 4 salad plates, make a wall of 6 tomato slices by standing them up in a semi-circular pattern, overlapping them slightly, starting at 2 o'clock and ending at 6 o'clock. Arrange the nori roll slices in a similar semi-circular pattern, starting at 6 o'clock and ending at 10 o'clock. Arrange a mound of the greens in the center. Sprinkle the tomatoes, nori roll slices, and greens with the dressing. Serve chilled.

"Be a fearless cook! Try out new ideas and new recipes, but always buy the freshest and finest of ingredients, whatever they may be."

—JULIA CHILD

Whole Wheat Orzo with Cilantro

YIELD: *4 servings*

TIME: *30 minutes preparation;*
2 hours chilling

3 cups water
¼ teaspoon sea salt
1 cup whole wheat orzo
1 cup cooked or canned
  garbanzo beans
¼ cup finely diced red bell
  pepper
¼ cup finely diced orange or
  yellow bell pepper
4 teaspoons chopped fresh
  cilantro
4 teaspoons chopped fresh basil
½ cup Cilantro Fennel Pesto
  (page 166)
¼ cup water
½ teaspoon sea salt

This warm weather salad can be served as an entrée. The pesto is an excellent complement to the garbanzos and orzo.

In a 2-quart saucepan, bring the water and salt to a simmer over medium heat. Add the orzo and continue to simmer for 8 to 10 minutes, or until it is soft but still firm. Drain the orzo, soak in cold water for 5 minutes, then drain again. In a large bowl, mix the orzo together with the beans, bell peppers, cilantro, and basil. In another bowl, combine the pesto, water, and salt, then add to the orzo mixture. Transfer mixture to a covered container and refrigerate for at least 2 hours to allow the flavors to develop. Serve cold.

DRESSINGS

Hazelnut Chantilly Dressing

YIELD: *3¼ cups*
TIME: *15 minutes*

¾ cup water
*½ 10½-ounce package soft
   silken tofu*
1 cup canola oil
½ cup white miso
6 tablespoons hazelnut butter
¼ cup chopped onions
¼ cup apple cider vinegar
2 tablespoons honey
*2 tablespoons chopped fresh
   parsley*
1 tablespoon tamari

Serve with Pineapple Raisin Waldorf Salad for a more savory note. The flavors harmonize better with greens and savory foods.

In a blender, combine all the ingredients and blend until smooth. Transfer to a covered container and refrigerate until ready to use. Serve cold.

Opposite: Japanese Salad (page 68) with Oriental Balsamic Dressing (page 76)

Easy French Dressing

YIELD: *3 cups*
TIME: *20 minutes preparation;*
1 hour chilling

1 cup apple cider vinegar
1 cup canola oil
¼ cup honey
1 medium tomato, peeled,
seeded, minced
2 tablespoons chopped fresh
parsley
2 tablespoons chopped fresh
basil
2 tablespoons Dijon mustard
2 cloves minced garlic
½ teaspoon sea salt

Serve with Italian Mixed Greens Salad, Potato Salad, Whole Wheat Orzo with Cilantro, or any green, leafy salad.

In a mixing bowl, combine all the ingredients and whisk until well blended. Transfer to a covered container and refrigerate for 1 hour. Serve cold.

Opposite: Roasted Vegetable Terrine (page 66) with Cilantro Pesto (page 166)

Sweet Potato Vinaigrette

YIELD: *2½ cups*
TIME: *20 minutes preparation;
20 minutes cooking*

*1 cup peeled, diced sweet
potatoes*
¼ cup apple cider vinegar
¼ cup water
¼ cup orange juice
¼ cup extra virgin olive oil
¼ cup white miso
3 cloves minced garlic
⅛ teaspoon black pepper

Serve with Florida Aspic, Collard Roll with Fresh Vegetables, Mesa Verde Salad, or any mixed green salad.

In a vegetable steamer, steam sweet potatoes for about 15 to 20 minutes or until soft. Remove from steamer and set aside to cool. In a blender, combine the sweet potatoes and remaining ingredients and blend until smooth. Transfer to a covered container and refrigerate until ready to use.

Cilantro Lime Vinaigrette

YIELD: *1¼ cups*
TIME: *15 minutes preparation;
1 hour chilling*

¼ cup extra virgin olive oil
¼ cup apple cider vinegar
¼ cup lime juice
4 teaspoons white miso
*1 tablespoon chopped fresh
cilantro*
*2 teaspoons grated lime zest
(about 2 limes)*
2 cloves minced garlic
1 teaspoon honey
½ teaspoon sea salt

Serve with Mesa Verde Salad or any mixed green salad.

In a blender, combine all the ingredients and blend until smooth. Pour dressing into a covered container and refrigerate for one hour. Serve cold or at room temperature.

Red Pepper Miso Dressing

YIELD: *3¼ cups*
TIME: *20 minutes preparation;*
 50 minutes cooking; 1 hour
 chilling

3 red bell peppers
1½ cups soy mayonnaise
¼ cup lemon juice
2 tablespoons white miso
1 teaspoon black pepper
1 teaspoon mustard powder
1 clove minced garlic
¾ teaspoon ginger powder
¼ teaspoon sea salt

Serve with any mixed green salad. I love roasted red peppers in my salads so the next logical step was to make a dressing out of the peppers.

Preheat oven to 325 degrees F. Wash, dry, halve, and seed the bell peppers. Rub the skins with olive oil. Place the pepper halves on a baking sheet and roast for 30 to 40 minutes or until soft and the skins begin to shrivel. Remove the peppers from the oven and place in a brown paper bag to steam for 10 minutes. When cool, remove the loosened skins. In a blender, purée the roasted peppers without any added liquid. Remove the purée, measure out 1½ cups, and return the measured amount to the blender. Add remaining ingredients and blend until smooth. Transfer to a covered container and refrigerate for 1 hour. Serve cold.

Green Goddess Dressing

YIELD: *4½ cups*
TIME: *20 minutes preparation;*
1 hour chilling

2 ripe avocados
¾ cup apple cider vinegar
¾ cup water
½ cup lemon juice
½ cup canola oil
2 tablespoons honey or
FruitSource syrup
1 tablespoon shoyu
1 bunch chopped fresh parsley
1 bunch scallions (about ¾
cup chopped)
6 cloves minced garlic
1 tablespoon dill weed
1 tablespoon basil
1 teaspoon sea salt
¼ teaspoon cayenne pepper

Serve with any mixed green salad. I had the idea for this dressing at the beginning of my journey into natural foods.

Peel and seed the avocados. In a blender, combine all the ingredients and blend until smooth. Transfer to a covered container and refrigerate for 1 hour. Serve cold.

Mango Dressing

YIELD: *2½ cups*
TIME: *20 minutes preparation;*
   1 hour chilling

1½ cups peeled, seeded mango
6 tablespoons apple cider or
   balsamic vinegar
¼ cup water
3 tablespoons extra virgin
   olive oil
2 tablespoons mirin, honey,
   or FruitSource syrup
6 medium, fresh basil leaves
1 tablespoon fennel powder
2 cloves minced garlic
½ teaspoon ginger powder
½ teaspoon sea salt

Serve with fruit and vegetable salads, cooked vegetables, Florida Aspic, or Seafood Patties. A wonderful balance of fruity, sour, and savory flavors is created in this dressing.

In a blender, combine all the ingredients and blend until smooth. Transfer to a covered container and refrigerate until ready to use. Serve cold.

"The discovery of a new dish does more for the happiness of the human race than the discovery of a star."

—BRILLAT SAVARIN

Orange Walnut Dressing

YIELD: *2 cups*
TIME: *20 minutes preparation;*
2 hours chilling

¼ *cup walnut pieces*
¾ *cup soy mayonnaise*
¼ *cup canola oil*
¼ *cup apple cider vinegar*
2 *tablespoons mirin*
2 *tablespoons anise seeds*
4 *teaspoons grated orange zest*
1 *tablespoon honey,*
 FruitSource syrup, or
 orange juice concentrate
½ *teaspoon sea salt*

Serve with fruit salads and the Pineapple Raisin Waldorf Salad.

Preheat oven to 325 degrees F. Spread the walnut pieces in one layer on a baking sheet and roast for about 15 minutes or until lightly browned and very fragrant. Immediately remove the walnuts and transfer to another container to cool slightly. In a blender, combine the walnuts and remaining ingredients and blend until smooth. Transfer to a covered container and refrigerate for 2 hours or until ready to use. Serve cold or at room temperature.

Oriental Balsamic Dressing

YIELD: *1½ cups*
TIME: *15 minutes preparation;*
1 hour chilling

½ *cup balsamic vinegar*
½ *cup mirin*
½ *cup shoyu*
¼ *cup water*
1 *tablespoon FruitSource*
 syrup or honey
1 *clove minced garlic*
1 *teaspoon fennel powder*

Serve with Roasted Vegetable Terrine, Italian Mixed Greens Salad, Japanese Salad, Tempeh Salad, or any mixed green salad.

In a mixing bowl, combine all the ingredients and whisk until well blended. Transfer to a covered container and refrigerate for 1 hour. Serve cold.

Creamy Herb Miso Dressing

YIELD: *1¼ cups*
TIME: *15 minutes preparation;
4 hours chilling*

½ cup soy milk
¼ cup white miso
¼ cup brown rice vinegar
¼ cup chopped onions
*1 tablespoon chopped fresh
basil*
*1 tablespoon chopped fresh
parsley*
*1 tablespoon chopped fresh
tarragon*
*1 teaspoon FruitSource syrup
or honey*
1 clove minced garlic
*½ teaspoon Dijon or yellow
prepared mustard*
⅛ teaspoon coriander powder

Serve with Arugula and Smoked Portobello Mushroom Salad, Italian Mixed Greens Salad, and Roasted Vegetable Terrine.

In a blender, combine all the ingredients and blend until smooth. Transfer to a covered container and refrigerate for at least 4 hours to allow the flavors to develop. Serve cold or at room temperature.

Cucumber Dill Cream Dressing

YIELD: *2¼ cups*
TIME: *20 minutes*

½ 10½-ounce package extra firm silken tofu
½ cup lemon juice
½ cup peeled, seeded, chopped cucumber
¼ cup water
3 tablespoons white miso
1 tablespoon fresh dill, stemmed
1 teaspoon Dijon or yellow prepared mustard
1 teaspoon FruitSource syrup or honey
1 clove minced garlic

Serve with lighter foods, mixed green salads, and cucumbers.

In a blender, combine all the ingredients and blend until smooth. Transfer to a covered container and refrigerate until ready to use. Serve cold or at room temperature.

Lemon Garlic Dressing

YIELD: *1 cup*
TIME: *15 minutes*

½ cup extra virgin olive oil
½ cup lemon juice
2 cloves minced garlic
1 teaspoon fennel seed powder
1 teaspoon sea salt
½ teaspoon black pepper

Serve with Italian Mixed Greens Salad or any mixed green salad.

In a mixing bowl, combine all the ingredients and whisk until well blended. Use immediately or refrigerate in a tightly sealed jar and shake to blend before serving.

Andalusian Vinaigrette

YIELD: *1⅓ cups*
TIME: *10 minutes preparation;*
12 hours chilling

½ cup extra virgin olive oil
½ cup sherry vinegar
¼ cup water
2 cloves minced garlic
2 teaspoons minced capers
½ teaspoon sea salt
½ teaspoon fennel powder
½ teaspoon cumin powder
½ teaspoon thyme
½ teaspoon oregano
¼ teaspoon rosemary
⅛ teaspoon black pepper

Serve with Andalusian Salad, grain salads, and cooked leafy vegetables such as collards or kale.

In a 1-pint jar (with lid), combine all the ingredients (omit water for stronger flavored dressing), cover, and shake until well blended. Refrigerate overnight to develop the flavors. Serve cold or at room temperature.

Maple Balsamic Vinaigrette

YIELD: *2 cups*
TIME: *10 minutes*

½ cup balsamic vinegar
½ cup red wine
¼ cup maple syrup
3 tablespoons Dijon mustard
1 tablespoon fresh lemon
thyme (or 2 teaspoons fresh
thyme plus 1 teaspoon
lemon zest)
1 clove minced garlic
¼ teaspoon sea salt
½ cup extra virgin olive oil

Serve with Arugula and Smoked Portobello Mushroom Salad, Italian Mixed Greens Salad, Roasted Vegetable Terrine, and steamed greens.

In a mixing bowl, combine the vinegar, wine, maple syrup, mustard, lemon thyme, garlic, and salt and mix well. Slowly whisk in the oil to prevent separation in the dressing. Transfer to a covered container and refrigerate until ready to serve.

Miso Poppy Seed Dressing

YIELD: *2 cups*
TIME: *15 minutes preparation;*
   1 hour chilling

¾ cup sunflower oil
¼ cup apple cider vinegar
¼ cup lemon juice
¼ cup diced onions
¼ cup poppy seeds
¼ cup honey, sorghum, or
   FruitSource syrup
2 tablespoons Dijon mustard
6 cloves minced garlic
2 tablespoons white miso
½ teaspoon celery seed powder
¼ teaspoon sea salt

Serve with Arugula and Smoked Portobello Mushroom Salad, Japanese Salad, or any mixed green salad.

In a blender, combine all the ingredients and blend until smooth. Transfer to a covered container and refrigerate for 1 hour or until ready to use. Serve cold.

Three Flavors Dressing

YIELD: *1 cup*
TIME: *10 minutes*

½ cup mirin
¼ cup tamari
¼ cup balsamic vinegar
1 clove minced garlic
1 teaspoon minced fresh ginger

Serve with Japanese Salad, Collard Roll with Fresh Vegetables, and Avocado Nori Rolls.

In a blender, combine all the ingredients and blend until smooth. Transfer to a covered container and refrigerate until ready to use. Serve cold or at room temperature.

Sandwiches & Others

More than any other food, the sandwich typifies the American desire to eat on the go. A sandwich is generally two slices of bread with any combination of ingredients in between: sliced meats, cheeses, or meat salads. The ecological approach is to use more plant-based proteins between slices of whole grain bread.

The sandwich is more popular in America than in its country of origin, Great Britain. Sandwiches are considered a luncheon item in American households and restaurants, but also for those who don't have the time to sit and eat a full meal. Originally it was named after the notorious gambler in the English court of King George III, John Montagu (1718–1792), the fourth Earl of Sandwich. Montagu was such an avid gambler that during twenty-four-hour betting marathons, he would order slices of meat and bread to sustain him so he could continue to gamble. This substantial snack came to be named after him about 1762, but it was not adopted in America until some time later.

What I have done with my sandwiches is to develop creative and tasty plant-based options to some popular sandwiches. A vegetarian sandwich can be filling or light. I love eating vegetables between slices of bread, especially roasted vegetables. Sandwiches originated as time-saving foods, but lost their ecological integrity; my sandwich cuisine blends the ecological concerns of a plant-based diet with the appeal of mainstream taste. From a natural foods version of the classic Reuben to burgers and creative sandwiches such as the Italian Bistro, I offer you a healthy option to animal-based protein sandwiches.

Grilled Vegetable Sandwich

YIELD: *4 servings*
TIME: *30 minutes preparation;*
 24 hours marinating

Marinade

1 cup barley malt syrup
 (or ½ cup honey)
¾ cup extra virgin olive oil
½ cup water
1 cup apple cider vinegar
2 tablespoons tarragon
4 cloves minced garlic
1 tablespoon basil
1 tablespoon marjoram
1 tablespoon oregano
1½ teaspoons sea salt

Vegetables

8 shallots, halved
4 large mushrooms, halved
2 small onions, ¼-inch thick
 crescents
2 eggplant slices cut lengthwise,
 ¼ inch thick
1 red bell pepper (sliced into
 8 pieces)
1 medium zucchini (cut
 lengthwise into 4 strips)

½ cup soy mayonnaise
8 slices whole grain bread

You don't need to put a protein-rich food between two slices of bread every time you make a sandwich. This light and colorful sandwich is one of my favorites and great on a hot summer day.

In a large mixing bowl, combine the marinade ingredients and mix well. Add the vegetables and let sit for 24 hours. After 24 hours, remove the vegetables from the marinade and grill the vegetables using a stove-top or outdoor grill (depending on the type of vegetable, from 5 to 15 minutes). Grill them over medium heat to prevent the vegetables from burning before they are fully cooked. Remove the vegetables from the grill after they have softened slightly but are still firm. Spread the mayonnaise on the bread and place the vegetables on the mayonnaise while they are still hot. Top the vegetables with the second slice of bread and serve with salad or garnish.

VARIATIONS

Marinate and grill 8 ½-inch thick eggplant slices. For each serving place 2 slices of eggplant between 2 slices of whole grain bread that have been spread with 2 tablespoons of soy mayonnaise.

Add 2 ounces of cooked, sliced tempeh or seitan (page 112) per sandwich.

Italian Bistro Sandwich

YIELD: *2 servings*
TIME: *35 minutes*

1 red bell pepper
¼ cup Red Pepper Pistachio
Butter (page 165)
4 slices Pesto Bread (page 26) or
any whole grain bread
2 Marinated Smoked Portobello
Mushrooms (page 18)

This sandwich takes time in preparing the different elements, but your hard work will provide you with the sandwich of your life. The Earl of Sandwich would have stopped his poker game for this one.

Preheat oven to 325 degrees F. Wash, dry, halve, and seed the pepper, then rub the skins with olive oil. Place the pepper halves on a baking sheet and roast in the oven for 30 to 40 minutes or until they are soft and the skins begin to shrivel. Remove the pepper from the oven and place in a brown paper bag to steam for 10 minutes. When cool, remove the loosened skins, and cut into strips. Spread one tablespoon of pistachio butter on each slice of bread. Slice the marinated mushrooms into strips, make a layer on one slice of bread, then add a layer of roasted pepper strips. Top with the second slice of pesto bread and slice corner to corner. Serve with a salad.

Seitan Reuben Sandwich

YIELD: *4 servings*
TIME: *35 minutes*

½ cup soy mayonnaise
8 slices rye bread
4 thin slices of seitan (page 112),
about 2 ounces each, patted dry
1 cup sauerkraut, drained,
pressed dry
4 slices soy mozzarella cheese,
⅛ inch thick
3 tablespoons unrefined corn oil

This sandwich has been a favorite of mine since culinary school days. I love the added excitement of complex flavors and contrasting textures. The tempeh option is as good as using the seitan.

Spread 1 tablespoon of the soy mayonnaise on each slice of rye bread. Place a slice of seitan on the mayonnaise, then top with sauerkraut, soy cheese, and the top slice of bread. Evenly spread 1 teaspoon of oil on each side of the sandwich. In a 10-inch frying pan, fry the sandwich over medium heat until each side is golden brown (if the seitan and the soy cheese are at room temperature, the sandwich will cook more quickly). Cut the sandwich diagonally and serve hot with blue or yellow natural corn chips.

VARIATION: *Tofu Reuben Sandwich*
Replace seitan with 8 ounces of extra firm tofu and slice into four 2-ounce pieces. Dip tofu into a marinade consisting of ¾ cup tamari and 2 teaspoons water. Sauté the tofu in oil until lightly browned on both sides. Proceed as directed.

VARIATION: *Tempeh Reuben Sandwich*
Replace seitan with 8 ounces of tempeh sliced in half lengthwise, then in half crosswise to make four 2-ounce pieces. Dip tempeh into a marinade consisting of ¾ cup tamari and 2 teaspoons water. Sauté the tempeh in oil until lightly browned on both sides. Proceed as directed.

Seitan Pesto Sandwich

YIELD: *1 serving*
TIME: *15 minutes*

4 ounces commercially
    prepared seitan "ham,"
    or sliced regular seitan
    (page 112)
2 tablespoons Sun-Dried
    Tomato Pesto (page 167)
2 slices whole grain bread
6 arugula leaves
1 slice tomato

I love the combination of pesto and arugula. This sandwich has fast food nutrition, but with flavor and texture.

Press the seitan dry. Spread the pesto on one slice of the bread. Lay the slices of seitan "ham" on the plain slice of bread. Lay the arugula leaves on the seitan, the tomato on the arugula, then the slice of bread with pesto, on the tomato. Slice diagonally and serve.

Tofu Carbonara Sandwich

YIELD: *4 servings*
TIME: *25 minutes*

1 pound firm tofu
½ cup tamari
½ cup water
12 cloves minced garlic
8 drops liquid hickory smoke
   (optional)
¼ cup sesame oil
8 slices whole grain bread
2 cups Carbonara Sauce
   (page 129)
4 teaspoons finely chopped
   parsley

This open-faced sandwich was made for chilly autumn days. The beer and caramelized onions in the sauce enliven the marinated tofu and make an easy, elegant lunch.

Cut the tofu into 8 2-ounce slices. In a shallow bowl, combine the tamari, water, garlic, and liquid smoke and marinate the tofu slices for a few minutes, turning the slices to coat both sides. In a 10-inch frying pan, heat the oil and sauté the tofu over medium heat until golden brown on both sides. Transfer the fried tofu to a paper towel to drain. Toast the bread slices and heat the Carbonara Sauce. Cut 4 slices of bread in half diagonally to form 2 triangles from each slice and leave the other 4 slices whole. For each serving, place a whole slice of bread in the center of a plate and one triangle on either side of it. Pour ¼ cup of the sauce on the bread slices. Split one tofu slice into a triangle to fit the 2 bread triangles. Place a tofu slice on the whole bread slice and the tofu triangles on each bread triangle, then top those with another ¼ cup of sauce and 1 teaspoon chopped parsley. Serve hot or at room temperature.

Tempeh Sandwich Lyonnaise

YIELD: *3 servings*
TIME: *45 minutes*

1 teaspoon extra virgin olive oil
1½ cups sliced onions
2 cloves minced garlic
2 teaspoons white miso
2 teaspoons Dijon mustard

I came across this combination of flavors while studying macrobiotic cooking. The onions, miso, and mustard give a wonderful, savory excitement to tempeh.

In a 10-inch frying pan, heat the first measure of oil and sauté the onion, garlic, miso, Dijon mustard, and salt over medium heat for 8 minutes. Add the ¼ cup of water and simmer the

¼ *teaspoon sea salt*
¼ *cup water*
½ *teaspoon arrowroot powder*
  dissolved in 1 teaspoon cool
  water
12 ounces tempeh
1 tablespoon extra virgin olive
  oil
1 tablespoon low-sodium
  tamari
3 tablespoons water
6 slices whole grain bread

mixture for a few more minutes. Add the arrowroot/water mixture and continue cooking, stirring constantly, until the mixture thickens. Transfer the onion mixture to a bowl and set aside until needed. Wipe frying pan clean with a paper towel and return to the stove. Cut the tempeh into thirds and brush both sides of each piece with 1 teaspoon of olive oil. In a 10-inch frying pan, sauté the tempeh pieces over medium heat on both sides until they are golden. In a small mixing bowl, combine the tamari and water, then add to frying pan and continue to cook, turning the tempeh so that both sides absorb the liquid. Remove tempeh from pan. Place 1 piece of tempeh on each of 3 slices of the whole grain bread. Top each piece of tempeh with one third of the onion mixture, and cover the onions with the remaining slices of bread. Serve hot.

Tempeh Club Sandwich

YIELD: *4 servings*
TIME: *35 minutes*

8 ounces firm tofu
2 tablespoons Vogue Vege Base
½ *teaspoon sea salt*
2 tablespoons sesame or canola
  oil
6 smoked tempeh strips (Fakin
  Bacon)
12 slices whole grain bread
¾ *cup soy mayonnaise*
8 large leaves romaine lettuce
8 medium slices of tomato

This sandwich is reminiscent of the traditional bacon, lettuce, and tomato sandwich, but with less fat and better nutrition.

Slice the tofu into 2-ounce pieces and pat each piece dry. In a shallow bowl, combine the Vogue Vege Base with the salt and dredge the tofu in the Vege Base mixture. In a 10-inch frying pan, heat 1 tablespoon of the oil and sauté the tofu over medium heat for about 4 minutes on each side. Remove from pan and set aside. Wipe frying pan clean with a paper towel. Cut the tempeh strips in half. Brush frying pan lightly with ½ tablespoon of the oil. Heat pan over medium heat and fry the tempeh strips until they are golden brown on each side, brushing pan with the remaining oil before turning the strips over. Remove strips from pan and set aside.

Lay 4 slices of the bread on a flat surface. Starting from the bottom and working upward, spread each slice with 1 tablespoon of the soy mayonnaise. Place 1 leaf of lettuce on

continued…

the mayonnaise, being careful not to let the lettuce hang over the edges of the bread. Place 2 slices of tomato on each lettuce leaf. Place 3 slices of smoked tempeh on the tomatoes. Take 4 more slices of bread and spread each with 1 tablespoon of soy mayonnaise. Place each slice of bread mayonnaise side down on top of the smoked tempeh. Spread another tablespoon of mayonnaise on top of each slice. Place the second leaf of lettuce on each slice of bread. Slice each piece of tofu in half, horizontally, to make 2 thin slices. Lay the 2 slices on each sandwich, overlapping them if necessary to fit on the bread. Spread 1 tablespoon of mayonnaise on each of the remaining 4 slices of bread. Place each slice mayonnaise side down on top of each sandwich. Using a sharp knife cut each sandwich diagonally into 2 triangles or into quarters. Serve each sandwich on a plate garnished with a slice of tomato on lettuce, a black olive, unsalted potato chips, and a fanned dill pickle.

VARIATION
Replace tempeh strips with seitan (page 112) cut into 2-ounce slices or commercially prepared seitan "ham." Assemble sandwich as directed.

Avocado Pita

YIELD: *4 servings*
TIME: *20 minutes*

2 medium ripe avocados
16 medium leaves Boston or Bibb lettuce, whole or shredded
4 large whole grain pita pockets, with top ¼ removed
1 cup Sauce Concassé (page 156)

Pita breads are not only for falafels. This versatile bread can also be used with western sandwiches such as this one made with avocado.

Cut the avocados in half and remove pits. Peel the skins off of each half and slice the avocado. Lay the lettuce on the bottom of each pita pocket. Arrange avocado slices evenly over surface of the lettuce. Spoon Sauce Concassé over all of the avocado and serve cold.

Milwaukee Pita

YIELD: *4 servings*
TIME: *20 minutes*

1 tablespoon sesame oil
¾ cup sliced onions
¾ cup unpeeled, grated red potato
½ cup sauerkraut, rinsed and pressed dry
1 clove minced garlic (or ½ teaspoon garlic powder)
1¼ cups finely chopped seitan (page 112)
1½ teaspoons caraway seeds
½ teaspoon thyme
½ teaspoon sea salt
⅛ teaspoon black pepper
½ teaspoon balsamic vinegar
¼ cup finely diced tomato
2 tablespoons finely chopped fresh parsley
4 small whole grain pita breads

This hearty German filling is loaded with onions, potatoes, and sauerkraut. Seitan and thyme replace the pork used in the original recipe.

In a 10-inch frying pan, heat the oil and sauté the onions, potato, sauerkraut, garlic, seitan, caraway, thyme, salt, and pepper over medium heat for about 10 minutes, stirring occasionally to prevent burning. Add the vinegar during the last 5 minutes of cooking. Finally, add the tomatoes and parsley and mix well. Cut the tops off the pitas and open. Place a heaping ½ cup of filling in each small pocket. Serve while hot.

Southwestern Pita

YIELD: *5 servings*
TIME: *35 minutes*

2 tablespoons unrefined corn
   or canola oil
1½ cups diced onions
¾ cup diced green bell peppers
½ cup peeled and grated carrots
3 cloves minced garlic (or 1½
   teaspoons garlic salt)
2 teaspoons chili powder
1 teaspoon chopped fresh
   cilantro
½ teaspoon thyme
½ teaspoon cumin powder
½ teaspoon sea salt
½ teaspoon black pepper
1 cup fresh or frozen kernel corn
1 cup cooked pinto beans
5 whole grain pita bread halves
5 lettuce leaves
5 tomato slices
2½ ounces jalapeño soy cheese,
   grated (optional)

This sandwich has a robust southwestern flavor with a wonderful blend of vegetables, beans, and grains.

In a 10-inch frying pan, heat the oil and sauté the onions, bell pepper, carrots, garlic, chili powder, cilantro, thyme, cumin, salt, and pepper over medium heat for 5 minutes. Add the corn and the beans and continue to cook until corn and beans are heated through. For each serving, take 1 pita half, open pocket, and put in 1 leaf of lettuce. Place a tomato slice on one side, then ½ cup of filling in the center. Top with cheese and serve hot.

Garbanzo Bean Burger

YIELD: *4 servings*
TIME: *20 minutes preparation;*
15 minutes cooking

1 tablespoon Basil Garlic Olive
   Oil (page 163)
½ cup diced onions
½ cup peeled, grated carrots
2 cloves minced garlic
1½ teaspoons chopped dried
   cilantro
1 teaspoon cumin powder
1 teaspoon celery seed
½ teaspoon sea salt
½ cup walnuts (or ¾ cup
   chopped sunflower seeds)
1½ cups cooked garbanzo beans
   (or 1 15½-ounce can,
   drained)
5 tablespoons gluten flour
2 tablespoons arrowroot
   powder
oil for pan-frying
4 whole grain burger buns

Falafels are one of my favorite foods, so I created a burger version. The texture and flavor are very satisfying.

In a 10-inch frying pan, heat the oil and sauté the onions, carrots, garlic, cilantro, cumin, celery seed, and salt over medium heat until the onions are transparent. Remove pan from heat and set aside. In a blender, place the nuts and blend until half of them are broken down into a coarse meal, with the other half cracked or whole. Transfer nuts to a large mixing bowl and add garbanzo beans to the blender and blend in the same manner as the nuts. Add the processed beans and sautéed vegetables to the mixing bowl, and mix well. In another bowl, combine the gluten and arrowroot flours, then add to the mixing bowl. Mix everything together well until the mixture has enough body to form a patty. If too dry or crumbly, add a small amount of water to help the mixture bind. Form the mixture into 4 burgers. Lightly oil the frying pan and fry the burgers over medium heat for 3 to 4 minutes on each side until lightly browned. Remove burgers from pan and serve immediately on a whole grain bun.

VARIATION

Place two bun halves or bread slices on a plate. Cut each burger in half and place each half onto the bun or bread. Top the burger halves with Burgundy Sauce Glaze, Carbonara Sauce, or Roasted Vegetable Sauce.

Millet Burger

YIELD: *10 servings*

TIME: *1 hour preparation;*
30 minutes cooking

¼ *cup millet, washed and*
drained

½ *cup water*

¾ *cup soy grits*

¾ *cup water*

2 tablespoons sesame oil

½ *cup finely diced onions*

½ *cup sesame seeds*

¼ *cup chopped sunflower seeds*

2 tablespoons tamari

2 cups rolled oats

½ *cup gluten flour*

2 tablespoons whole wheat
pastry flour

2 tablespoons Ener-G Egg
Replacer

1 tablespoon chili powder

1 teaspoon garlic powder

¾ *teaspoon cumin powder*

½ *teaspoon dill weed*

½ *teaspoon thyme*

½ *teaspoon Vegit seasoning salt*

½ *teaspoon sea salt*

This burger was created for the former Renaissance Restaurant in Milwaukee, Wisconsin, where it was a popular item on the menu. Millet also was the favorite grain of Michaelangelo.

In a 1-quart saucepan (with lid), combine the millet with first measure of water, cover, and bring to a simmer over medium heat. Reduce heat to low and cook millet for 25 minutes or until all water is absorbed, checking periodically to make sure that it doesn't burn. Remove saucepan from heat and set aside. In a 2-quart saucepan, combine the soy grits and the second measure of water, cover, and bring to a simmer over medium heat. Cook soy grits until all of the water is absorbed, checking periodically to see when the grits are done. Remove saucepan from heat and set aside. In a 10-inch frying pan, heat the oil and sauté the onions and sesame and sunflower seeds over medium heat for 5 minutes or until the onions are transparent. Add the tamari and cook for 1 minute longer. In a large mixing bowl, combine the rolled oats, flours, egg replacer, chili, garlic, cumin, dill, thyme, Vegit, and salt and mix well. Add the cooked millet, soy grits, and onion mixture and mix until thoroughly combined. Use ⅓ cup of the mixture to form each patty and separate patties with wax paper to keep them from sticking. The burgers can then be frozen for future use or used as needed. To bake, preheat the oven to 350 degrees F. Lightly brush each side of the burgers with oil and place on a baking sheet. Bake for 10 minutes or until golden on the top, then turn over and brown the other side. To pan fry, heat a large frying pan, then add a small amount of canola or sesame oil, and fry burgers until golden. Serve hot on whole grain buns.

Seitan Burger

YIELD: *10 servings*
TIME: *40 minutes preparation;*
20 minutes cooking

¼ *cup pecans*
1 *tablespoon extra virgin*
olive oil
2 *cups chopped onions*
2 *cloves minced garlic*
8 *ounces extra firm tofu*
¼ *cup tamari*
½ *teaspoon thyme*
¼ *teaspoon black pepper*
4 *cups seitan (page 112),*
chopped into ¼-inch pieces
½ *cup whole wheat bread flour*
2 *tablespoons gluten flour*
(or 3 tablespoons Seitan
Quick Mix)

Due to their low fat content, these burgers tend to burn easily when cooked. Cook them over no higher than medium heat and watch them carefully. Serve these burgers with BBQ Sauce, Corn Relish, Onion Butter, or Molé Rojo Sauce.

Preheat oven to 325 degrees F. Spread the pecans on a baking sheet and roast for 15 minutes or until lightly browned and very fragrant. Immediately remove pecans and transfer to a container to cool. Once cool, chop pecans coarsely into ¼-inch pieces and set aside. In a 10-inch frying pan, heat the oil and sauté the onions and garlic over medium heat for 5 minutes or until onions are transparent. In a blender, combine the onion/garlic mixture, tofu, tamari, thyme, and pepper and blend until smooth. In a large mixing bowl, combine the pecans, seitan, and flours and mix well. Add tofu mixture and mix until thoroughly blended. Using ½ cup for each burger, form into patties and separate patties with wax paper to keep them from sticking. The burgers can then be frozen for future use or used as needed. To broil, brush each side of the burgers with a small amount of oil after they begin to cook. To bake, preheat oven to 350 degrees F. Lightly brush each side of the burgers with oil and place on a baking sheet. Bake for 10 minutes or until golden on the top, then turn over and brown the other side. To pan fry, heat a large frying pan, then add a small amount of canola or sesame oil, and fry burgers until golden. Serve hot on whole grain buns.

VARIATION: *Seitan Balls with Pasta*
Preheat oven to 375 degrees F. Form balls by taking ¼ cup of burger mix for each ball and press together firmly. Place the balls on a rack inside a baking pan containing ⅛ inch of water. Cover and steam bake for about 30 minutes. To serve, place 2 or 3 balls on a bed of pasta and top with Roasted Vegetable Sauce or any tomato-based sauce.

Tempeh Burger

YIELD: *2 servings*
TIME: *30 minutes*

Marinade

½ cup water
1 clove minced garlic
2 tablespoons tamari
½ teaspoon sea salt
½ teaspoon coriander powder

1 8-ounce package tempeh,
    cut in half crosswise
1 tablespoon canola oil
¼ cup soy mayonnaise
2 whole grain burger buns
2 tomato slices
2 lettuce leaves

Tempeh is the simplest of burger options. Grilled or sautéed, this burger has an inviting light tamari flavor.

In a large mixing bowl, combine the marinade ingredients and mix well. Dip the tempeh into the marinade and drain briefly on a wire rack until ready to use. In a 10-inch frying pan, heat the oil over medium-high heat and sauté the tempeh for 5 minutes or until golden brown on each side. Remove tempeh from pan and let drain on a paper towel for a few minutes. Place 1 tablespoon of soy mayonnaise on each half of the buns. Cover bottom half of each bun with a lettuce leaf. Place tempeh and tomato slice on the lettuce, then the top bun. Serve hot.

VARIATION
Substitute ¼ cup Red Pepper Pistachio Butter for the mayonnaise.

Anasazi Bean Sandwich Rolls

YIELD: *4 servings*
TIME: *55 minutes preparation;*
    2 hours cooking

1 cup Anasazi beans, uncooked
3 cups water
1 6-inch piece kombu
¼ teaspoon sea salt
2 teaspoons extra virgin olive oil
2 red bell peppers
2 yellow bell peppers

This sandwich won a silver medal in the 1992 International Culinary Olympics and a gold medal in the 1995 Connecticut Chef's Association Culinary Salon. Try it and you'll know why.

Wash beans, then soak in water for 4 hours or overnight. Preheat oven to 325 degrees F. Drain beans and in a 2-quart saucepan, combine the beans, water, and kombu. Bring to a boil and cook covered for 45 minutes. Add salt and cook 15 minutes longer. While the beans are cooking, wash, dry, halve, and seed the red and yellow bell peppers. Rub skins with oil.

Bean Filling

8 ounces extra firm tofu,
*   pressed dry*
2 cups cooked Anasazi beans
3 tablespoons arrowroot
*   powder*
1 tablespoon agar flakes
2 teaspoons paprika
1½ teaspoons sea salt
1½ teaspoons cumin powder
1½ teaspoons chili powder

Assembly

2 pieces of whole wheat flat
*   bread, trimmed to 8½ by 11*
*   inches ("Thin Thin Bread"*
*   by Garden of Eatin' or whole*
*   wheat lahvosh bread by*
*   Cedar Lane) or 6 whole*
*   wheat flour tortillas,*
*   trimmed to 5¼ by 6 inches*
2 green bell peppers, halved,
*   seeded, and sliced lengthwise*
*   into ½-inch strips*
1 recipe Molé Rojo Sauce
*   (page 156)*
1 recipe Cucumber Cilantro
*   Salsa (page 169)*

Place the pepper halves on a baking sheet and roast for 30 to 40 minutes or until soft and skins begin to shrivel. Remove peppers from oven and place in a brown paper bag to steam for 10 minutes. When cool, remove the loosened skins.

Bean Filling

In a blender, combine tofu, 2 cups of cooked beans (reserve rest of beans for rolls), arrowroot, agar, paprika, salt, cumin, and chili and blend until smooth.

Assembling the Rolls

Preheat oven to 325 degrees F. Slice roasted pepper halves lengthwise into thirds. Slice raw green bell pepper lengthwise into ½-inch strips. Moisten a flat table top, then cover with a piece of plastic wrap 12 by 16 inches long. Lay flat bread on wrap horizontally. Spread flatbread with half of the bean filling mixture, leaving 1 inch uncovered at the top, then using half of the peppers, lay strips from left to right, creating bands of yellow, red, and green from the bottom to the top of the flatbread. Sprinkle on half of the beans left over from the bean filling, then beginning with the bottom edge, roll up the flatbread using the plastic wrap to keep roll tight. Moisten top 1 inch to help seal the roll. Wrap roll again in plastic wrap, then in aluminum foil. Repeat procedure for the second roll. Place the foil-wrapped rolls onto a rack inside a deep baking pan. Add water to the pan, keeping the water level below the bottom of the rack. Cover the baking pan with aluminum foil and steam bake for 1 hour. When done baking, remove foil from baking pan and each roll, then let them cool for 15 minutes with the plastic wrap on. Slice roll into 1-inch thick pieces, remove plastic wrap, and serve 4 slices per person with Molé Rojo Sauce and Cucumber Cilantro Salsa.

Black Bean and Corn Roll

YIELD: *2 servings*
TIME: *35 minutes preparation;*
   1 hour 30 minutes cooking

Tofu Mixture

1 10½-ounce package extra
   firm silken tofu
¼ cup chopped sun-dried
   tomatoes
2 tablespoons arrowroot
   powder
2 cloves minced garlic
1½ teaspoons agar flakes (or
   ¼ teaspoon agar powder)
1 teaspoon sea salt

Black Bean Mixture

1 cup Fantastic Foods Instant
   Black Bean Mix
½ cup hot water

For the International Culinary Olympics in 1992, I presented a Southwestern Luncheon plate including these rolls, along with Anasazi Bean Sandwich Rolls, Molé Rojo Sauce, and Corn Relish served in a Black Bean Cracker Cup.

Tofu Mixture

In a blender, combine tofu, tomatoes, arrowroot, garlic, agar, and salt and blend until smooth.

Black Bean Mixture

In a coffee grinder or blender, grind the instant black bean mix until it becomes a powder. In a mixing bowl, combine the water with the powdered bean mix, then add ½ of the tofu mixture and mix until well blended.

Corn Mixture

1¼ cups water
⅛ teaspoon ground saffron
1½ teaspoons agar flakes (or
    ¼ teaspoon agar powder)
½ cup fresh or frozen
    kernel corn
6 tablespoons yellow corn grits
1 clove minced garlic
½ teaspoon cumin powder
½ teaspoon sea salt
¼ teaspoon chili powder

1 package flat bread sheets
    ("Thin Thin Bread" by
    Garden of Eatin' or whole
    wheat lahvosh bread by
    Cedar Lane)
1 recipe Molé Rojo Sauce
    (page 156)

Corn Mixture

In a 2-quart saucepan, combine the water and saffron and bring to a boil over medium heat. Pour the saffron water into a blender and blend for 1 minute to thoroughly dissolve the saffron. Pour blended liquid back into saucepan. Add agar, then cook over medium heat for 7 to 10 minutes or until agar is dissolved. Add the corn, corn grits, garlic, cumin, salt, and chili, then continue to cook the mixture for 10 to 15 minutes or until it is soft and thickened. Add remaining tofu mixture and stir well to combine. Remove saucepan from heat and set aside.

Assembling the Roll

Preheat oven to 325 degrees F. Cut 1 piece of the flat bread into one 8 x 12-inch piece. Moisten a flat surface and lay plastic wrap, overlapping 2 or more pieces if necessary, to make a rectangle 12 x 16 inches. Lay cut piece of bread on plastic wrap. Moisten 1 of the 8-inch wide ends with water. Spread a strip of corn mixture across opposite 8-inch wide end. Spread a strip of black bean/tofu mixture next to strip of corn mixture. Repeat this pattern 3 more times. To roll, start at the end with the filling strips and roll bread tightly around filling, using the moistened end to seal the roll. Wrap the roll tightly with plastic wrap. Cut 2 pieces of aluminum foil slightly larger than length of the roll. Wrap the foil securely around the roll and twist ends to make a tight seal. Place roll on a rack in a large baking pan that has been filled with 2 cups of water and cover the pan. Steam bake roll for 1 hour. Remove pan from oven and let roll cool to room temperature. Unwrap roll, slice, and serve, or remove only the aluminum foil and refrigerate roll until ready to use.

Avocado Nori Roll

YIELD: *4 servings*
TIME: *30 to 40 minutes*

4 sheets sushi nori (toasted)
*4 cups cooked short grain
   brown rice*
*2 teaspoons umeboshi plum
   paste*
*½ cup peeled, julienned carrots,
   steamed*
8 strips red bell pepper
*1 large ripe avocado, peeled,
   pitted, and sliced into strips*

Because of the avocados, sea vegetables, and brown rice, this recipe is a perfect accompaniment to the Japanese Salad. Nori Rolls are also great for brown bag lunches.

For each roll, take 1 sheet of nori and lay it on a bamboo mat. Spread 1 cup of cooked rice on the sheet, leaving ½ inch uncovered at the top of the sheet. Going from left to right, spread ½ teaspoon of the umeboshi plum paste across the bottom edge of the rice. Lay the carrot, red pepper, and avocado strips in a line next to the paste, on the side closest to you. Moisten the uncovered section of the nori. Starting at bottom of sheet, tightly roll nori away from you until you reach the top, wrapping the moistened section around the roll to seal it. Allow it to rest in the mat for a minute, then remove the roll and set it aside until needed. Continue the same procedure for the remaining sheets of nori. To cut, moisten a sharp knife with water and slice each nori roll into 10 equal pieces. Serve cold or at room temperature.

Focaccia Dough

YIELD: *2 12-inch crusts*
TIME: *25 minutes preparation;*
1 hour 45 minutes rising
and baking

1¾ cups lukewarm water
(90 degrees F)
1 teaspoon Sucanat
1½ teaspoons active dry yeast
1¾ cups stone ground whole
wheat bread flour
1½ cups unbleached white flour
2 tablespoons extra virgin
olive oil
½ teaspoon sea salt

This glorified yeast dough goes well with many toppings such as Black Olive Tapenade. It is a creative way to serve bread, especially with salads.

Preheat oven to 350 degrees F. In a small mixing bowl, combine the water, Sucanat, and yeast. Allow mixture to stand 5 to 10 minutes or until yeast is foamy. In a large mixing bowl, combine 1 cup of the whole wheat flour with ¾ cup of the unbleached white flour. Add the proofed yeast to the flours, stir quickly, then add the oil and salt, mixing all together until well combined. Cover bowl with a damp cloth and set in a warm place to rise, about 30 minutes. After 30 minutes, mix down the sponge and add enough of the remaining flours (using the whole wheat flour first) to make a smooth and elastic dough. Knead the dough for 5 to 10 minutes. Pour 1 teaspoon of the oil into a large bowl, place the dough inside, then turn it in the oil until it is evenly coated. Cover bowl with a damp cloth and set aside to rise for about 45 minutes or until doubled in size. Punch the dough down and divide it in half. Roll each half into a 12-inch diameter crust, about ¼ inch thick. Transfer crust to a lightly oiled baking sheet or pizza pan. Brush surface with 1 tablespoon of olive oil. To partially bake the crusts without a topping, prick holes with the tines of a fork across the surface to prevent air bubbles from forming. Bake the crusts for 8 minutes or until the dough is set and does not indent when touched. Partially baked crusts can be frozen for later use or used immediately with a topping and baked according to recipe instructions.

Smoked Portobello Mushroom Focaccia

YIELD: *8 servings*
TIME: *30 minutes*

*1 tablespoon extra virgin
olive oil*
*1½ cups minced Smoked
Portobello Mushrooms
(page 18)*
1½ cups minced onions
3 cloves minced garlic
½ teaspoon sea salt
*1 recipe partially baked
Focaccia Dough (page 99)*
½ cup chiffonade-cut arugula

Few people can resist the winning combination of smoked mushrooms and onions on top of flat bread.

Preheat oven to 350 degrees F. In a 10-inch frying pan, heat the oil and sauté the mushrooms, onions, garlic, and sea salt over medium heat for 10 minutes. Remove pan from heat and spread mixture over focaccia crust, then bake for 15 minutes. Remove focaccia from oven and brush outer crusts with more olive oil while still hot. Garnish with arugula, then cut into wedges or squares and serve.

*"For those who love it, cooking is at once child's play
and adult joy. And cooking done with care is an act
of love."*
—CRAIG CLAIBORNE

Pizza Provençal

YIELD: *6 servings*

TIME: *30 minutes*

1 tablespoon extra virgin olive oil

4 cups sliced mushrooms

3 cloves minced garlic

½ teaspoon sea salt

½ recipe partially baked Focaccia Dough (page 99)

1 tablespoon extra virgin olive oil

1¼ cup Sauce Concassé (page 156)

½ cup chiffonade-cut arugula

½ cup chiffonade-cut basil

The best pizzas are the simplest. Made with Focaccia, this pizza takes little time to prepare, leaving you more time to enjoy it.

Preheat oven to 350 degrees F. In a 10-inch frying pan, heat the first measure of oil and sauté the mushrooms, garlic, and sea salt over medium heat for 5 minutes. Remove pan from heat and set aside. Place the partially baked crust on a lightly oiled baking sheet and brush crust with second measure of oil. Spread the Sauce Concassé evenly over the crust, leaving about 1 inch uncovered around the edges. Sprinkle the arugula and basil over the sauce. Spoon mushroom mixture evenly over the arugula and basil and bake pizza for 7 minutes. Remove from oven, slice, and serve.

VARIATION

After spooning the mushroom mixture over the arugula and basil, evenly distribute ½ cup seeded, diced plum tomatoes. Bake as directed.

Designer Pizza

YIELD: *6 servings*
TIME: *30 minutes preparation;*
50 minutes cooking

3 cups halved, thinly sliced
Spanish onion
¼ teaspoon sea salt
1 tablespoon barley malt or
Sucanat (optional)
½ recipe Focaccia Dough
(page 99)
12 slices eggplant, ¼-inch thick
olive oil for brushing
6 tablespoons Sun-Dried
Tomato Pesto (page 167)
6 slices tomato, ¼ inch thick
¼ teaspoon sea salt
freshly ground black pepper
to taste (optional)
1 tablespoon chiffonade-cut
basil

Pizza as we know it may have originated in the United States, but it had its start as a Sicilian peasant recipe. Here is a plant-based version, highlighted by my Sun-Dried Tomato Pesto.

Preheat oven to 350 degrees F. In a 10-inch frying pan, heat the oil and sauté the onions and salt over medium heat for 7 to 10 minutes. Stir the onions as they brown to prevent them from burning. If the onions start to burn, just add a few tablespoons of water to deglaze the pan. For extra sweetness, add barley malt to the caramelized onions. Remove pan from heat. Roll the focaccia dough into a circle approximately 12 inches in diameter, ½ inch thick. Place on a lightly oiled baking sheet and partially bake for 10 minutes. Remove crust from oven and allow to cool without removing it from the baking sheet. Brush each slice of eggplant with olive oil on both sides. Place slices on another lightly oiled baking sheet and bake for 20 minutes. Remove eggplant slices from oven. Spread pesto in a thin layer over the surface of the pizza crust. Lay eggplant slices in a circular pattern, overlapping them slightly, making 2 rows that cover the surface of the crust. Sprinkle caramelized onions evenly over eggplant slices. Top onions with tomato slices in the same pattern as the eggplant. Sprinkle tomatoes with salt, pepper, and basil. Bake pizza for 15 to 20 minutes. Remove and cut it into wedges or appetizer-sized pieces. Serve hot or at room temperature.

Southwestern Double Crust Pizza

YIELD: *8 servings*

TIME: *1 hour 30 minutes preparation; 2 hours 15 minutes rising and cooking*

Crust

1¾ cups lukewarm water (90 degrees F)

1 teaspoon Sucanat

1½ teaspoons active dry yeast

1¼ cups stone ground whole wheat bread flour

1½ cups unbleached white flour

2 tablespoons extra virgin olive oil

½ teaspoon sea salt

½ cup yellow corn meal

Filling

1 tablespoon canola oil

2 cups sliced onions

2 tomatillos (or 1 green pepper), sliced ¼ inch thick

3 cloves minced garlic

½ teaspoon sea salt

¼ teaspoon cumin powder

1¾ cup refried beans (homemade or canned)

2 medium tomatoes, sliced ¼ inch thick

¼ cup chopped, pitted, black olives

¼ cup chopped, fresh cilantro

1 tablespoon seeded and diced fresh jalapeño pepper (optional)

I love Southwestern cuisine and wanted to create a dish that is similar to an Italian calzone, but with those marvelous southwestern flavors. I think the marriage is a happy one.

Crust

In a small mixing bowl, combine the water, Sucanat, and yeast. Allow mixture to stand 5 to 10 minutes or until yeast is foamy. In a large mixing bowl, combine 1 cup of the whole wheat flour with ¾ cup of the unbleached white flour. Add the proofed yeast to the flours, stir quickly, then add the oil and salt, mixing until well combined. Cover bowl with a damp cloth and set in a warm place to rise, about 30 minutes. After 30 minutes, mix down the sponge and add enough of the remaining flours (using the whole wheat flour and corn meal first) to make a smooth and elastic dough. Knead the dough for 5 to 10 minutes. Pour 1 teaspoon of the oil into a large bowl, place the dough inside, then turn it in the oil until it is evenly coated. Cover bowl with a damp cloth and set aside to rise for about 45 minutes or until doubled in size.

Filling

Preheat oven to 350 degrees F. Divide crust in half and set aside covered with plastic wrap. In a 10-inch frying pan, heat the oil and sauté the onions, tomatillos, garlic, salt, and cumin over medium heat for 5 minutes, stirring constantly to prevent burning (if the vegetables start to burn, stir in a small amount of water). Remove pan from heat and set aside. On a lightly floured flat surface, roll out ½ of the dough into a 12-inch circle, approximately ½ inch thick. Lay the crust on a lightly oiled baking sheet. Spread the refried beans evenly over surface of the crust, leaving about ¾ inch uncovered around the edges. Brush the uncovered edges lightly with water. Next gently spread the onion/tomatillo mixture over refried beans. Top with the tomatoes. Sprinkle the olives over the tomatoes,

continued…

then the cilantro, and finish with jalapeño pepper. Roll out the remaining dough into a circle slightly larger than the first, ¼ inch thick. Gently place it on top of the first crust, press edges to seal, then roll edges inward 1 roll and press to seal tightly. Transfer pizza to a lightly oiled baking sheet and bake for 30 minutes or until crust begins to turn golden brown. Remove pizza from oven, cut into wedges, and serve.

Caramelized Onion Calzone

YIELD: *6 servings*
TIME: *55 minutes preparation;*
45 minutes cooking

1 tablespoon extra virgin
olive oil
4 cups sliced onions
½ teaspoon sea salt
1 cup finely chopped seitan
(page 112)
3 cloves minced garlic
1 teaspoon chopped dried basil
1 tablespoon barley malt syrup
(optional)
2 tablespoons unbleached
white flour
1 recipe Focaccia Dough
(page 99)

With seitan and onions, these superb calzones make great entrées, picnic food, or brown bag lunches. For a satisfying lunch, just add Italian Mixed Greens Salad and Italian Orzo Soup.

In a 10-inch frying pan, heat the oil and sauté the onions and salt over medium heat for 7 to 10 minutes. Stir the onions as they brown to prevent them from burning. If the onions start to burn, just add a few tablespoons of water to deglaze the pan. Add the seitan, garlic, basil, and syrup, then bring to a sizzling temperature. Add the flour and stir well. Sauté another 2 or 3 minutes and remove from heat. Prepare the Focaccia Dough, cut into 6 equal pieces and roll each one out to a 6- or 7-inch round piece. Preheat the oven to 350 degrees F. Fill each round with ½ cup filling, then wet the edges and fold one end over to seal the calzone. Place the calzones on a lightly oiled baking sheet, then bake in the oven for about 10 minutes. Serve immediately, or cool, refrigerate, and use when needed.

Potato Samosas

YIELD: *8 servings*
TIME: *35 minutes preparation;*
1 hour 20 minutes cooking

This recipe has a wonderful, savory Indian flavor. Serve with Saffron Millet Soup, Yellow Pepper Cream Soup, or Curried Vegetable Casserole.

Filling

2 cups peeled, diced potato
1 tablespoon sesame oil
½ cup finely diced onions
¼ cup thinly sliced green beans, tips removed
1 clove minced garlic
¾ teaspoon curry powder
¾ teaspoon cumin powder
½ teaspoon sea salt
¼ teaspoon cardamom powder

Dough

6 tablespoons cold water
1 teaspoon sea salt
1¼ cups unbleached white flour
¼ cup whole wheat pastry flour
¼ cup canola oil

Filling

In a vegetable steamer, steam the potatoes for 10 minutes. Prepare the remaining vegetables. In a 10-inch frying pan, heat the oil and sauté the potatoes, onions, green beans, garlic, curry, cumin, salt, and cardamom over medium heat for about 15 to 20 minutes or until the potatoes are fully cooked. A little water can be added to prevent burning. Transfer mixture to a large mixing bowl and mash a little to bind ingredients together.

Dough

Preheat the oven to 350 degrees F. In a small bowl, combine the water and salt and let sit for a few minutes. In another bowl, combine the flours and mix in the oil until mixture is somewhat lumpy. Add the salted water and mix into a medium stiff dough, adding more water if the dough is too dry. Knead dough for 8 to 10 minutes. Divide dough into 8 equal parts, then roll each part into a 6-inch circle. Cut each circle in half, then place 1 tablespoon of filling in the center of each semi-circle. Fold the dough over the filling and seal the edges by pressing them together. Place the samosas on a lightly oiled baking sheet and bake for 10 to 15 minutes or until golden. Serve hot with a salad.

Entrées

The entrée is the centerpiece of any meal and protein is usually the center of the entrée. The following recipes use seitan, tempeh, tofu, grains, beans, nuts, and seeds for protein in main dishes. Seitan, a "wheat meat" or gluten, was created by Buddhist monks about 500 years ago and is a tasty substitute for meat. Arrowhead Mills of Hereford, Texas, sells my very own Seitan Quick Mix. I recommend its use in my cookbooks because it is easy to use, very satisfying, and a great transitional food for those seeking to become vegetarians. Yet, the entrée doesn't have to be a protein dish, especially when there are concentrated proteins coming from other courses on the menu. This array of entrées is one of my best collections and covers a wide cross section of classic dishes as well as innovative ones. All are plant-based and represent nutritious, balanced ecological main dishes.

My entrées stand out by combining vegetables and plant-based proteins for flavor and texture. I take the bean cuisine of tofu and plain beans to the level of haute cuisine. The focus of ecology in diet is centered around protein issues; we need to consume more plant-based proteins in place of animal-based proteins for the sake of our and Mother Earth's health. The following entrées cover the spectrum of plant-based proteins from seitan and tofu to plain beans, all served in an elegant manner.

Pistachio Polenta

YIELD: *8 servings*

TIME: *30 minutes preparation;*
30 minutes cooking

1 cup pistachio nuts
1 tablespoon extra virgin
olive oil
1 cup finely diced Spanish
onions
1 cup finely diced red bell
peppers
1 cup finely diced celery
3 cloves minced garlic
1 tablespoon minced fresh basil
1 tablespoon fennel seed
powder
1¼ teaspoons sea salt
4 cups water
2 cups yellow corn grits

This could be called a "designer polenta," created with native Italian ingredients. It is one of my favorites because of the wonderful flavor, textures, and colors of this elegant dish. Grilled vegetables make a good complementary side dish.

Preheat the oven to 325 degrees F. Spread the pistachio nuts on a baking sheet and roast them in the oven for 15 minutes or until lightly browned and fragrant. Remove from baking sheet and transfer to a container to cool. In a 3-quart saucepan, heat the oil, and sauté the onions, peppers, celery, garlic, basil, fennel, and salt on medium heat for 8 minutes, then add water and corn grits. Bring to a simmer and let cook until grits are soft. Stir in nuts and either serve hot or pour into a baking dish and let cool until set, slice, and serve.

VARIATION: *Pistachio Polenta with BBQ Tempeh*
Prepare the polenta as directed, then pour the warm polenta into a round pie pan. Prepare 1 recipe of BBQ Tempeh (page 121) and press 16 triangles of tempeh into the surface of the polenta with the base of the triangle facing outside edge of pan, and the points toward the center. Chill polenta until set. Slice with 2 triangles of tempeh per slice and heat polenta slices in a 325 degree F oven for 15 minutes. Top with Tricolor Salsa and sliced black olives.

Grilled Vegetables and Pasta with Thai Peanut Sauce

YIELD: *4 servings*

TIME: *50 minutes preparation;*
  40 minutes cooking

Sauce

1 tablespoon peanut or sesame oil
1 cup diced onions
½ cup peeled, grated carrots
¼ cup diced celery
3 cloves minced garlic
3 tablespoons chopped fresh
  cilantro
2 tablespoons thinly sliced lemon
  grass or fresh lemon juice
1 teaspoon ginger powder
1 teaspoon allspice
¼ teaspoon cayenne pepper
1½ cups water
½ cup creamy peanut butter
3 tablespoons tamari

Vegetables

¾ cup peeled, diagonally cut
  carrots
¾ cup Spanish onion, cut French
  fry–style
1 cup diced red or yellow bell
  pepper
¾ cup cubed eggplant
1 cup seeded, diced zucchini
1 tablespoon sesame oil
½ teaspoon sea salt
½ teaspoon coriander powder

1 8½-ounce package uncooked
  Japanese udon or soba
  noodles, cooked

This sauce is spicier than the African Peanut Sauce. Served over grilled vegetables, the Thai sauce provides a burst of flavor.

Sauce

In a 2-quart saucepan, heat the oil and sauté the onions, carrots, celery, garlic, cilantro, lemon grass, ginger, allspice, and pepper over medium heat for 10 minutes. Add the water, peanut butter, and tamari and whip mixture until peanut butter is dissolved. Simmer for about 15 to 20 minutes or until sauce becomes creamy and will coat the back of a spoon. While the sauce is simmering, cook the vegetables. Transfer the sauce to a blender and blend until smooth.

Vegetables

Preheat broiler. In a vegetable steamer, steam the carrots for 5 minutes or until tender-crisp. Immediately remove them from the steamer and place into a large bowl with the onion, bell pepper, eggplant, and zucchini. Add the oil, salt, and coriander, then toss vegetables until they are completely coated. Spread coated vegetables on a baking sheet and place under the broiler of the oven and broil for 10 to 15 minutes, or until they are lightly browned. Remove pan from oven. Place 1 cup of the cooked noodles on each of 4 plates. Top the pasta with ½ cup of the peanut sauce, then place ¾ cup of the grilled vegetables on top of the sauce. Serve immediately.

Savory Crêpes

YIELD: *6 servings or 12 crêpes*
TIME: *30 minutes*

1 cup unbleached white flour
3 tablespoons gluten flour
2 teaspoons Sucanat
½ teaspoon sea salt
2 tablespoons canola oil
1⅞ cups water

I wanted to make an eggless crêpe and am delighted with the results. These crêpes are best used when fresh, although they can be frozen for later use.

In a mixing bowl, combine flours, Sucanat, and salt until well blended. Add the oil and water, then mix until smooth. Over medium heat, preheat a non-stick crêpe pan and wipe it lightly with an oiled paper towel. Fill a 2-ounce ladle ⅔ full of batter. Pour batter into the crêpe pan, and immediately tilt and rotate the pan to evenly spread the batter over the entire surface. Cook the crêpe for about 3 to 5 minutes until lightly browned. Turn the crêpe over to the other side and cook it for 3 minutes longer. Transfer crêpe to a plate to cool. When all the crêpes have been prepared and stacked on the plate, either use them immediately or cover plate securely with plastic wrap to keep them from drying out until they are needed. Use Italian Pistachio Pilaf, Mushroom Duxelles, Seafood Patties, Seitan Pine Nut Roll, Bulgur Walnut Croquettes, Smoked Mushroom Loaf, or Pecan Nut Loaf as a filling. Preheat oven to 375 F. Use ¼ cup filling per crêpe and roll up. Place crêpes in a baking dish, brush with water, and cover with a tightly fitting lid. Bake for 15 to 20 minutes. Serve 2 or 3 per person.

Seitan Quick Mix

YIELD: *6 servings*
TIME: *15 minutes preparation;*
1 hour 20 minutes cooking

2 cups or 1 12-ounce box
Arrowhead Mills Seitan
Quick Mix
1½ cups water (reduce by ¼
cup if pressure cooking)

Broth

8 cups water
½ cup tamari soy sauce
6⅛-inch thick ginger slices or
1 teaspoon ginger powder
2 6-inch pieces kombu
1 tablespoon sesame oil
(optional)

Traditionally, seitan was made by mixing wheat flour and water, kneading to develop the gluten, then rinsing to remove the starch and bran. The end result was gluten, the protein part of the wheat berry. When cooked in a seasoned broth, the wheat gluten is called seitan or "wheat meat." I have developed a faster method that requires less kneading and no rinsing. It may be simmered in the traditional manner, pressure cooked, or even microwaved.

In a large mixing bowl, place the Seitan Quick Mix, then add the water. Using a large metal spoon, stir this mixture well until a dough (wheat gluten) is formed. Place the gluten onto a table top and knead until thoroughly mixed and elastic (about 5 minutes). Alternately, use a heavy duty mixer, and mix on low speed for 5 minutes using a dough hook. Form the gluten into a log shape approximately 2½ to 3 inches in diameter and 6 to 8 inches long, then let it rest while preparing the broth.

To Simmer

In a 4-quart saucepan (with lid), combine the water, tamari, ginger, kombu, and oil. Cover pan and bring to a simmer on medium heat. Remove lid, place gluten log in simmering broth, and bring broth back to a simmer. Cover pan, reduce heat to low, and cook gluten for 30 minutes or until it is firm all the way to the center of the log. Using tongs or large forks, remove seitan from broth, drain, and place it onto a cutting board. Prepare a large bowl of cold water. Slice the log into 8 equal pieces, then place the slices into the cold water for 2 to 3 minutes (this step causes the seitan to contract and creates a firmer texture). Return slices to the simmering broth, and continue to simmer on low for 60 to 90 minutes or until tender.

To Pressure Cook, Method 1

Follow the instructions above using ¼ cup less water when mixing the dough for this cooking method so that the log will be firmer. In a 4-quart pressure cooker, combine the water, tamari, ginger, kombu, and oil. Place lid on cooker and bring broth to a simmer on medium heat. Slice uncooked gluten log into 6 equal pieces. Remove lid and gently place gluten pieces in simmering broth, then secure lid and bring up to pressure on high heat. Reduce heat to low and pressure cook for 35 minutes. When done, remove cooker from heat and allow pressure to go down.

To Pressure Cook, Method 2

Follow the instructions above using the full measure of water method to mix the dough. In a 4-quart pressure cooker, combine the water, tamari, ginger, kombu, and oil. Place lid on cooker and bring broth to a simmer on medium heat. Place uncooked gluten log into simmering broth, then secure lid and bring up to pressure on high heat. Reduce heat to low and pressure cook for 10 minutes. Immediately remove the cooker from the heat, place into a sink and run cold tap water onto the lid for about 3 minutes to quickly bring the pressure down. Remove lid from cooker, remove seitan log, drain, and slice seitan into 6 equal pieces. Place slices back in the broth, bring back to pressure and cook for another 25 minutes. When done, remove cooker from heat and allow the pressure to go down.

To Microwave

In a 4-quart saucepan (with lid), combine the water, tamari, ginger, kombu, and oil. Cover pan and bring to a simmer on medium heat. Slice uncooked gluten log into 8 equal pieces and flatten each one until ½ inch thick. Gently place the slices in the simmering broth, then simmer covered for 30 minutes. Transfer slices to a microwave-safe baking dish and cover with broth. Cover baking dish with plastic wrap, then microwave

continued…

on high heat for 7½ minutes. Remove dish from microwave, flip each slice over, then cover dish and microwave again on high heat for 7½ minutes. Remove dish from microwave. Although this is a quick cooking method, pressure cooking is preferable and takes the same amount of time.

Serving and Storage

After cooking the gluten using any of the above methods, the seitan is now ready to serve or use as an ingredient in a recipe calling for cooked wheat gluten or seitan. To store for future use, cool the seitan, then place the cooked slices into a container, covered with broth, and refrigerate up to 1 week or freeze until ready to use. After refrigerating seitan for one week, it should be reheated before use or to store for another week. Place the seitan and broth into a saucepan and bring to a boil for 5 minutes, then either use or cool and store as before.

"To be a vegetarian is to disagree—to disagree with the course of things today. Starvation, world hunger, cruelty, waste, wars—we must make a statement against these things. Vegetarianism is my statement and I think it is a strong one."

–ISAAC BASHEVIS SINGER

Vermont Seitan with Chestnuts

YIELD: *6 servings*

TIME: *40 minutes preparation;*
  45 minutes cooking

1 6½-ounce package frozen
  chestnuts (or 1 cup steamed,
  or canned chestnuts)
1 tablespoon sesame oil
2 cups diced onions
1 tablespoon sesame oil
1½ cups sliced mushrooms
1½ cups thinly sliced seitan
  (page 112)
1 cup finely diced onions
½ cup peeled, finely diced
  carrots
½ cup finely diced red bell
  pepper
½ cup finely diced celery
3 cloves minced garlic
1½ cups red wine
2 tablespoons dark miso
¼ cup maple syrup
2 tablespoons unbleached
  white flour
1 tablespoon sesame oil
½ cup chopped fresh parsley

Chestnuts, New England Indian summers, and fall vegetable harvests are the inspirations behind this superb dish. The savory maple syrup, seitan, and fresh vegetables will make your palate tingle.

Preheat oven to 350 degrees F and take the chestnuts out to thaw. In a 10-inch frying pan, heat the oil and sauté the onions for 5 minutes or until they turn brown and sweet, then set aside. Place chestnuts on a baking sheet and roast for 15 to 30 minutes or until they are lightly browned. Remove chestnuts, cool slightly, then cut in half. Reheat frying pan, heat second measure of oil and sauté mushrooms, seitan, onions, carrots, peppers, celery, and garlic for 5 minutes. Dissolve miso in ¼ cup of red wine. Add miso/wine mixture to sautéing vegetables with remainder of the wine and maple syrup, then continue to cook until liquid is reduced by about half. Mix the white flour with the third measure of oil and add to the sautéed vegetable mixture while stirring constantly. When thickened, add the roasted chestnuts, caramelized onions, and ¼ cup parsley, then mix well. Serve over cooked grain or pasta or by itself. Garnish with remaining parsley.

Seitan Pine Nut Roll

YIELD: *8 servings*

TIME: *1 hour 40 minutes preparation; 30 minutes cooking*

1½ cups ground seitan
    (page 112)
1 tablespoon extra virgin
    olive oil
1 cup finely diced onions
½ cup finely diced red bell
    peppers
3 cloves minced garlic
1 teaspoon sea salt
1 teaspoon thyme
1 teaspoon marjoram
½ cup soy grits
1 cup water
1 cup pine nuts
3 tablespoons nutritional yeast
¼ cup unbleached white flour
¼ cup gluten flour
¼ cup minced fresh parsley
2 tablespoons liquid lecithin
1 teaspoon liquid hickory
    smoke (optional)
½ cup whole grain
    bread crumbs

This recipe won a gold medal in the 1995 Connecticut Chef's Association Culinary Salon. It makes a great stuffing for vegetables and filling for crêpes, or can be served as a casserole or burger.

Grind the seitan in a ¼-inch grinder or in a food processor. In a 10-inch frying pan, heat the oil and sauté the onions, bell pepper, garlic, salt, thyme, and marjoram on medium for 5 minutes. Add the ground seitan, soy grits, water, pine nuts, and nutritional yeast, then let simmer for about 10 minutes or until the water is reduced. Mix the two flours together and add to mixture along with the parsley, stirring well. Add the liquid lecithin and liquid smoke, then continue to mix until evenly dispersed. Add the bread crumbs and mix in evenly. All ingredients must be cooked until "dry" or else the roll may be too loose. If the mixture seems too moist, mix together 1 tablespoon each unbleached white flour and gluten flour, then add to the mixture to help bind it together. At this point, the pine nut mixture may be formed into a roll and steam baked, or put in a container and placed in the refrigerator or freezer for later use.

To Steam Bake

Preheat the oven to 350 degrees F. In a food processor, place the pine nut mixture and process for 30 seconds to increase the binding qualities. Lay out a sheet of plastic wrap, 12 x 14 inches long, on a flat surface and spoon mixture down the center to create a roll 2 inches in diameter. Using the plastic wrap, roll the mixture into a firm log shape, twisting the ends to seal. Squeeze or press the roll together to be sure it is very firm. Wrap the roll in a sheet of aluminum foil. Place a wire rack inside a large baking pan filled with several inches of water. Lay the foil-wrapped roll on rack and cover pan with more aluminum foil. Steam bake for 30 minutes, then slice, and serve with Roasted Vegetable Sauce, Burgundy Sauce Glaze, Sauce Concassé, or Sauce Renaissance.

To Bake as a Loaf

Preheat oven to 350 degrees F. Lightly oil a loaf pan, then press the mixture into it. Cover loaf pan with foil, then bake for 30 to 35 minutes or until loaf reaches an internal temperature of 150 to 160 degrees. Remove loaf from oven, let cool, and slice. Serve cold or hot with Roasted Vegetable Sauce, Burgundy Sauce Glaze, Sauce Concassé, or Sauce Renaissance.

VARIATIONS: *Seitan Pine Nut Roll with Tofu Pâté*

Make roll as directed above with the uncooked pine nut mixture and use the plastic wrap to help form it. Roll 1 recipe Tofu Pâté Base Mix (page 144) out between two pieces of plastic wrap the same size as that used for the Pine Nut Roll. Remove plastic from nut roll, then lay roll on layer of tofu pâté. Wrap tofu around nut roll, then wrap that roll in aluminum foil and steam bake as above for 30 minutes. Unwrap and let cool for 3 minutes before serving.

Seitan Pine Nut Stuffed Vegetables

Preheat oven to 350 degrees F. Fill each half of a seeded winter squash and slightly mound on top. Place on a rack inside a deep baking dish with 1 inch of water in the bottom, then cover the dish with lid or foil. Steam bake in the oven for 1 hour.

Seitan Pine Nut Stuffed Mushrooms

Preheat oven to 350 degrees F. Stuff 4 large portobello mushroom caps with filling and slightly mound on top. Place on a rack inside a baking dish with ¼ inch of water in the bottom, then cover the dish with lid or foil. Steam bake in the oven for 25 minutes.

continued...

Seitan Pine Nut Crêpes

Preheat oven to 375 degrees F. Prepare 1 recipe Savory Crêpes (page 111) and fill each crêpe with ¼ cup of the filling and roll up. Place crêpes into a baking dish, brush them with water, then cover with a tightly fitting lid. Bake for 15 to 20 minutes. Serve 2 crêpes per portion with Fresh Basil Sauce, Sauce Renaissance, or Roasted Vegetable Sauce.

Jewish Seitan Roast

YIELD: *7 servings*
TIME: *30 minutes preparation;*
   1 hour cooking

1½ cups celery chunks
1½ cups onion chunks
2½ cups peeled carrot chunks
1¾ pounds cooked seitan
   (page 112)
3 cups seitan cooking broth
   (page 112)
½ cup unbleached white flour
¼ cup canola oil

Miso Demi-Glace

2 tablespoons dark miso
2 tablespoons barley malt
2 tablespoons water

This recipe was developed at Valentina's Corner Restaurant in North Miami for a Jewish meal. I also served a non-dairy creamy horseradish, which confounded the Jewish community because they don't mix meat and dairy at a meal.

Preheat oven to 375 degrees F. Mix celery, onion, and carrot chunks together, then place in a large baking pan. Slice seitan 1 inch thick and lay slices over vegetables. Mix ingredients for demi-glace together. Pour broth over seitan slices and brush seitan with demi-glace. Cover pan with aluminum foil and bake for 1 hour. Remove pan from oven and transfer seitan slices to a serving platter (vegetables can be served on the same platter). To make a gravy from the seitan broth, mix the unbleached white flour with the oil in a bowl until it forms a smooth paste. In a 2-quart saucepan, pour broth and bring to a simmer over medium heat. Whisk in oil/flour mixture a little at a time to prevent lumping, then stir constantly until the mixture becomes smooth. Remove gravy from heat and use as desired.

Golumpke

YIELD: *3 servings*
TIME: *45 minutes preparation;*
  30 minutes cooking

1 cup brown basmati rice,
  washed and drained
2 cups water
¹⁄₁₆ teaspoon sea salt
9 large whole green cabbage
  leaves (blanched, frozen
  overnight and thawed
  to soften)

Filling

2 tablespoons unrefined corn oil
1½ cups finely diced onions
1 cup finely diced celery
½ cup peeled, finely diced
  carrots
2 teaspoons granulated garlic
½ teaspoon sea salt
½ teaspoon black pepper
2 cups cooked brown basmati
  rice
1 packed cup ground seitan
  (page 112)
1 cup tomato purée or
  tomato sauce

A Polish favorite, I had to create a vegetarian version to celebrate Polish vegetarian cuisine. This savory and well-textured dish has all the attributes of honest, filling, peasant food.

Preheat oven to 375 degrees F. In a 2-quart saucepan (with lid), bring rice, water, and salt to a simmer over medium heat. Cook rice on low heat covered for 45 minutes or until all of the water is absorbed. When done, remove the saucepan from the heat and set aside until needed. In a 10-inch frying pan, heat the oil and sauté the onions, celery, carrots, garlic, salt, and pepper over medium heat until onions are transparent. Add cooked rice and ground seitan to vegetables, then stir to mix well. Continue to cook the mixture until it is heated through. Remove pan from the heat. Place about ⅓ cup of the filling per cabbage leaf. Roll the leaves, folding in both sides as you roll, and place them in a lightly oiled baking pan, seam sides down. Pour the tomato purée or sauce evenly over the rolls. Cover the pan with aluminum foil and bake for 25 to 30 minutes. Remove pan from oven and transfer the rolls and sauce to a serving platter. Serve hot.

BBQ Seitan

YIELD: *4 servings*
TIME: *30 minutes preparation;*
 1 hour 30 minutes cooking

1¼ pounds (about 8 2½-ounce
 pieces) uncooked seitan
 (page 112)
2 tablespoons canola oil
4 6-inch strips kombu, soaked
2 cups BBQ Sauce (page 151)
3½ cups water

Braising and then baking the seitan is what makes this dish so wonderful.

Preheat oven to 350 degrees F. Flatten the seitan pieces to ⅛ inch thick. In a 10-inch frying pan, heat the oil and fry the seitan pieces over medium heat for a few minutes on each side until they are lightly browned. Cut the soaked kombu strips into a total of 16 pieces. Line the bottom of a 9-inch square baking dish with ½ the kombu. Place a piece of seitan on each piece of kombu, overlapping seitan if necessary to make an even layer. Place remaining kombu pieces on top of seitan. Pour BBQ Sauce over them, spreading with a spoon to cover most of the surface. Gently add enough water so that the seitan pieces are almost floating. Cover pan with aluminum foil and bake for 1½ hours. After the first 30 minutes, check water level in the pan and add more water if necessary to keep seitan very moist. Be careful not to add too much water or the sauce will become too watery. When done, remove pan from oven and transfer seitan to serving platter. Serve hot or at room temperature.

BBQ Tempeh

YIELD: *4 servings*
TIME: *30 minutes*

*½ teaspoon liquid hickory
    smoke (optional)*
1½ cups BBQ Sauce (page 151)
2 8-ounce packages tempeh
½ cup water
2 tablespoons tamari
*1½ tablespoons barley
    malt syrup*
½ teaspoon coriander powder
3 tablespoons sesame oil

What's good for seitan is also good for tempeh. This recipe is another way to introduce disbelieving friends and family to the joys of vegetarian cuisine.

Stir the liquid smoke into the BBQ sauce. Cut each tempeh cake into 8 triangles, then slice each triangle in half horizontally to reduce width. Place tempeh into a baking pan and pour BBQ sauce over them, making sure tempeh is covered, and set aside. In a mixing bowl, combine the water, tamari, barley malt, and coriander. In a 10-inch frying pan, heat a small amount of oil over medium heat. Remove the tempeh from the BBQ sauce, shake off any excess sauce, then dip them into the tamari mixture, and again shake off the excess. Sauté the triangles until they are brown on both sides, adding more of the oil as necessary. Place 2 to 4 tablespoons of the BBQ sauce on each plate and fan the tempeh over the sauce. Serve with either corn bread or polenta.

Eggless Frittata

YIELD: *3 servings*
TIME: *20 minutes preparation;*
  1 hour 10 minutes cooking

1 pound extra firm tofu
¼ cup water
1 tablespoon arrowroot powder
2 teaspoons nutritional yeast
1½ teaspoons agar flakes (or
  ¼ teaspoon agar powder)
⅛ teaspoon turmeric
1 cup peeled, cubed potatoes
2 teaspoons extra virgin
  olive oil
½ cup diced onions
½ cup seeded, cubed zucchini
½ cup diced red bell pepper
¼ cup peeled, seeded, and diced
  tomatoes (optional)
2 cloves minced garlic
1 teaspoon sea salt
½ teaspoon fennel seed powder
½ teaspoon rosemary powder
⅛ teaspoon white pepper

The appearance and texture of this dish is similar to a quiche and has an interesting array of flavors. This entrée is best served with a salad and soup.

Preheat oven to 350 degrees F. In a blender, combine tofu, water, arrowroot, yeast, agar, and turmeric and blend until smooth. Steam potatoes in a vegetable steamer until they are cooked through but are still firm enough to retain their shape. Remove potatoes from steamer and set aside. In a 10-inch frying pan, heat the oil and sauté the onions, zucchini, bell pepper, tomatoes, garlic, and salt on medium heat for 2 minutes. Add the fennel, rosemary, and pepper and stir to combine them well. Pour mixture into a lightly oiled 8 x 8 x 2-inch baking dish and cover dish securely with aluminum foil. Place baking dish into a larger pan filled with several inches of water. Bake the frittata for 45 minutes, or until it is puffed up. Remove pans from oven and serve hot, cold, or at room temperature.

Miami Delight

YIELD: *4 servings*

TIME: *30 minutes preparation; 30 minutes cooking*

8 plum tomatoes, rubbed with olive oil

6 garlic cloves, peeled and rubbed with olive oil

3 cups peeled, seeded, diced mango

2 cups peeled, seeded, diced avocado

4 halved, seeded, diced plum tomatoes

2 tablespoons chopped fresh cilantro

2 tablespoons peeled, minced fresh ginger

1 teaspoon sea salt

¼ cup lime juice

¼ cup mirin

2 tablespoons white miso

2 tablespoons cashew butter

1 pound tofu, cut into 8 triangles

A dinner served by Father Jim Murphy of St. Patrick's Catholic Parish in Miami Beach inspired this dish. It is an elegant and sophisticated presentation of tofu and the fruits of Florida.

Preheat oven to 300 degrees F. Place the 8 plum tomatoes and the garlic cloves on a baking sheet and roast them for 20 to 30 minutes. Meanwhile, combine the diced mango, avocado, and tomatoes in a bowl, then set aside. Remove the roasted vegetables from oven and increase temperature to 350 degrees F. In a blender, combine the roasted vegetables and blend until smooth. In a large mixing bowl, pour mixture from blender and add the diced mangoes, avocados, tomatoes, cilantro, ginger, and salt, then mix everything well. In a small bowl, blend the lime juice, mirin, miso, and cashew butter into a glaze. Spread the glaze evenly over the 8 tofu triangles, place in a covered baking pan and bake them for 8 to 10 minutes or until heated through. Remove pan from oven. Pour ½ cup of the mango-avocado sauce on each of 4 plates. Lay 2 baked tofu triangles on top of the sauce on each plate. Drizzle remaining sauce over tofu pieces.

Seafood Patties

YIELD: *4 servings*

TIME: *20 minutes preparation; 20 minutes cooking*

1 tablespoon canola oil
½ cup finely diced carrots
½ cup finely chopped scallions
1 pound firm tofu, drained, patted dry, and crushed
2 tablespoons arrowroot or cornstarch
2 tablespoons chopped dried wakame
5 teaspoons Lemon Herb salt-free seasoning powder
¾ teaspoon sea salt
1 tablespoon agar flakes or ¾ teaspoon agar powder

These patties contain no seafood, but have the same delicate flavor. Serve them with Saffron Sauce, Yellow Pepper Sauce, or use in Tofu Bonne Femme.

In a 10-inch frying pan, heat the oil and sauté the carrots over medium heat for 5 minutes. Add the scallions, stir well, and remove pan from heat. In a food processor, combine the carrots, scallions, tofu, arrowroot, wakame, Lemon Herb, salt, and agar and process mixture into a paste. Use ½ cup of the paste to form each patty.

NOTE: In place of Lemon Herb salt-free seasoning, combine 1 tablespoon white wine, 1 teaspoon fresh lemon zest, ½ teaspoon granulated garlic, and ½ teaspoon dry tarragon leaves.

To Bake

Preheat oven to 350 degrees F. Place the patties in a lightly oiled baking pan, and set that pan into a larger one filled with several inches of water. Cover larger pan and steam bake patties for 25 to 30 minutes. Remove pans from oven and serve patties hot.

To Steam

Lay a piece of plastic wrap on a flat surface, place the patties on the plastic wrap, then cover with another sheet of plastic wrap, sealing the edges. With a spatula or by hand, transfer the patties to a stainless steel or bamboo steamer and cover. Steam for about 10 to 15 minutes, then transfer to a plate and allow to cool for 1 minute before serving.

These patties can be served with any cream sauce, primavera, à la king, or velouté sauce. Do not use a brown sauce with this recipe as the flavor will be too strong and overpower the delicate nature of the patties.

VARIATIONS: *Seafood Crêpes*

Preheat oven to 375 degrees F. Prepare Savory Crêpes (page 111). Use ¼ cup uncooked filling per crêpe and roll up. Place crêpes into a baking dish, brush them with water, then cover with a tightly fitting lid. Bake for about 25 minutes. Serve 2 or 3 crêpes per portion with Carbonara Sauce, Sardaline Sauce, Saffron Sauce, Quick Espagnole Sauce, or Roasted Vegetable Sauce.

Stromboli

YIELD: *6 servings*

TIME: *30 minutes preparation;*
45 minutes cooking

Filling

2 tablespoons extra virgin
olive oil
2 cups diced red bell pepper
1 cup sliced onions
4 cloves minced garlic (or 2
teaspoons garlic powder)
1 tablespoon finely chopped
fresh parsley
2 teaspoons nutritional yeast
1 teaspoon chopped fresh basil
½ teaspoon black pepper
½ teaspoon sea salt
½ 10½-ounce package
silken tofu
2 tablespoons arrowroot
powder or cornstarch
1 teaspoon fennel seed powder

Dough

½ cup warm water
1 teaspoon active dry yeast
1 teaspoon Sucanat
1½ cups unbleached white flour
1 cup whole wheat bread flour
2 tablespoons gluten flour
¼ teaspoon sea salt
1 tablespoon extra virgin
olive oil
1 cup warm water

This is a great food for brown bagging because it can be eaten cold. Be sure to refrigerate it before taking it on the road, as the tofu can spoil if left in a warm area for too long.

Filling

In a 10-inch frying pan, heat the oil and sauté the bell pepper, onions, garlic, parsley, yeast, basil, pepper, and salt over medium heat for 4 to 5 minutes, stirring constantly to ensure even cooking (if necessary, add a few tablespoons of water to keep the vegetables and spices from sticking). In a blender, combine the tofu, arrowroot, and fennel seeds and blend until smooth. Add the tofu mixture to the sautéed vegetables and continue to cook for 4 minutes over low heat. Remove pan from heat and set aside while you make the dough.

Dough

In a small mixing bowl, combine the water, yeast, and Sucanat, stir well, and allow to sit about 3 to 5 minutes or until yeast becomes foamy. In a large mixing bowl, combine the white, wheat, and gluten flours and salt and mix well. Add the oil to flours, but do not mix it into the dry ingredients. Add the proofed yeast and the warm water to the flours and mix to form a stiff dough. Turn dough out onto flat working surface and knead briefly. Using your hands, roll dough into a long even 8-inch roll and divide into 6 equal pieces. On a lightly floured surface, roll each piece into a 6-inch circle.

Assembling the Stromboli

Preheat oven to 400 degrees F. Place ⅓ cup of the filling in the center of each circle. Lightly wet the edges, fold the circles in half, and seal the edges tightly. Place the stromboli on a lightly oiled baking sheet and bake for about 15 minutes or until dough begins to lightly brown. Stromboli can be served as a main course or as a luncheon sandwich.

VARIATION
Replace the tofu with 1 cup cooked navy beans and prepare as directed.

Tofu Bonne Femme

YIELD: *4 servings*

TIME: *20 minutes preparation;
20 minutes cooking*

*2 teaspoons extra virgin
olive oil*

1 cup diced onions

*1 cup peeled, thinly sliced
carrots*

1 cup diagonally cut celery

*½ cup diced red bell pepper or
canned pimento*

8 sliced mushrooms

*2 cloves minced garlic or ½
teaspoon garlic powder*

*2 tablespoons chopped fresh
basil or 2 teaspoons
dried basil*

1½ cups soy milk

½ cup water

2 bay leaves

*2 tablespoons chopped dried
wakame, soaked*

2 teaspoons sea salt

1 pound extra firm tofu

*¼ cup kuzu or cornstarch
dissolved in ¼ cup cool
water*

½ cup white wine

*½ cup half-moon sliced
zucchini*

*2 cups cooked brown rice
or pasta*

*finely chopped parsley
for garnish*

In culinary terms, "Bonne Femme" refers to a method of cooking called poaching, which is one of the many beautiful ways of preparing foods. When making the sauce, it is important to watch it carefully to prevent it from burning. Do not add the wine until after the soy milk has thickened or the milk will curdle. This versatile recipe can be used as an entrée or an appetizer.

In a 10-inch frying pan (with lid), heat the oil and sauté the onions, carrots, celery, bell pepper, mushrooms, garlic, and basil over medium heat for about 3 minutes. Add the soy milk, water, bay leaves, wakame, and salt to the sautéed vegetables, then bring it to a simmer. Dice the tofu and place into the simmering broth, making sure it is covered by the liquid. Cover and simmer for 5 minutes. Pour the kuzu/water mixture into the heated liquid, stirring constantly until the sauce thickens. Add the wine and zucchini, then let simmer for at least 3 minutes. (The wine will thin down the sauce, which will have become very thick after the addition of the kuzu. If for some reason the sauce becomes too thin after adding the wine, make another kuzu/water mixture and add it, a little at a time, until the desired consistency is reached.) Remove bay leaves before serving. To serve, place 1½ cups of the Tofu Bonne Femme over ½ cup of cooked brown rice or pasta and garnish with finely chopped parsley.

Tofu Cacciatore

YIELD: *4 servings*
TIME: *20 minutes preparation;*
  25 minutes cooking

1 pound firm tofu, cut into
  8 2-ounce slices
¼ cup Vogue Vege Base
1 tablespoon tamari
3 tablespoons extra virgin
  olive oil
2 cups diced onions
1 cup quartered mushrooms
1 cup diced green bell pepper
4 cloves minced garlic or 2
  teaspoons garlic powder
2 teaspoons oregano
2 teaspoons basil
1½ teaspoons sea salt
1 teaspoon whole rosemary
  leaves
¼ teaspoon black pepper
1½ cups water
1 cup tomato paste
½ cup Burgundy wine
1 tablespoon Vogue Vege Base
3 tablespoons unbleached white
  flour mixed with ½ cup
  water

This is a plant-based version of chicken cacciatore, a favorite dish of mine before I became a vegetarian. I enjoy this dish over rice or pasta, with a glass of dry Italian red wine.

Cut each of the 8 slices of tofu into 4 pieces. In a mixing bowl, toss the tofu with the Vogue Vege Base. Add the tamari and toss again until all of the pieces are coated. In a 10-inch frying pan, heat the oil and sauté the tofu pieces over medium heat until they are a light golden brown on both sides. Remove the tofu pieces and drain on paper towels. With the remaining oil in the frying pan, sauté the onions, mushrooms, bell pepper, garlic, oregano, basil, salt, rosemary, and pepper over medium heat for 5 minutes, stirring occasionally. To the sautéed vegetables, add the water, tomato paste, wine, and second measure of Vogue Vege Base. Stir the flour/water mixture into the vegetables and cook over medium heat about 3 minutes or until the mixture thickens. Add the sautéed tofu and stir to blend it with the sauce mixture. Continue to cook over medium-low heat for 5 to 10 minutes. Serve hot over brown rice or pasta.

Tofu Carbonara

YIELD: *4 servings*
TIME: *30 minutes*

Carbonara Sauce

*2 tablespoons extra virgin
    olive oil*
2 cups sliced onions
1 clove minced garlic
⅛ teaspoon sea salt
*2 tablespoons unbleached
    white flour*
1 tablespoon tamari
½ cup dark stout (beer)

Tofu

1 pound extra firm tofu
*2 tablespoons gluten flour
    combined with 2 tablespoons
    unbleached white flour*
*¾ cup whole grain bread
    crumbs*
½ teaspoon sea salt
2 teaspoons basil
1 teaspoon rosemary powder
1 teaspoon paprika
*2 tablespoons extra virgin
    olive oil*

Sauce is the magic element in any cuisine because it enhances the flavor of the food. The wonderful flavors of caramelized onions and beer in this sauce combine to give this tofu dish a bit of flair. The sauce can be used in many dishes such as beans to give them a dynamic touch.

Sauce

In a 10-inch frying pan, heat the oil and sauté the onions, garlic, and salt over medium heat until the onions are lightly browned. Add the flour and continue to cook for 3 to 4 minutes longer. Add the tamari and 2 tablespoons of the stout, then cook until thick and smooth. Add the remaining stout, and simmer slowly over low heat for about 20 to 30 minutes.

Tofu

Slice the tofu lengthwise into 4 slices, then cut each one diagonally into triangles. In a shallow bowl, combine the gluten flour with the white flour. In another shallow bowl, combine the bread crumbs, salt, basil, rosemary, and paprika. Dip each triangle into water, then dredge in gluten/white flour mixture. Wet dredged slices with water, then dip in bread crumb mixture, coating all sides thoroughly. In a 10-inch frying pan, heat the oil over medium heat and sauté tofu triangles until they are golden on both sides, about 3 to 4 minutes per side. Remove from pan and serve hot with ¼ cup of the Carbonara Sauce per serving.

VARIATIONS
Replace Carbonara Sauce with Quick Supreme Sauce, Roasted Vegetable Sauce, or Sardaline Sauce.

Tofu Fricassée

YIELD: *3 servings*
TIME: *20 minutes preparation;*
20 minutes cooking

1 tablespoon unrefined corn oil
½ cup diced onions
1 cup peeled carrots, thinly
sliced in half moons
½ cup diced red bell pepper
8 ounces extra firm, cubed tofu
½ cup diagonally cut celery
½ cup diced green bell pepper
2 tablespoons sherry
2 tablespoons Vogue Vege Base
½ teaspoon sea salt
⅛ teaspoon white pepper
½ cup fresh or frozen peas
2 cups preheated Quick
Supreme Sauce (page 152)

Originating in France, fricassée is similar to a creamed stew. The sauce is what makes this a spectacular, lively dish. It is great over pasta, rice, or mashed potatoes.

In a 10-inch frying pan, heat the oil and sauté the onions, carrots, and red bell pepper over medium heat for 5 minutes, stirring occasionally. Add the tofu, celery, green bell pepper, sherry, Vogue Vege Base, salt, and pepper, then continue to sauté for another 8 minutes or until the vegetables are tender-crisp. Add the peas and Quick Supreme Sauce to the sautéed ingredients and mix well. Serve hot over pasta, rice, couscous, whole grains, or baked potato. Broccoli florets make a great vegetable accompaniment.

NOTE: The celery and green bell peppers can be divided in half, using the first half of each for the sauté and adding the second half with the sauce. By doing so, the half reserved for the sauce will retain a bright color, while the sautéed half will impart a richer flavor.

VARIATION
Hollow out small round loaves of whole grain bread and serve the fricassée in each as an individual portion.

Italian Shepherd's Pie

YIELD: *6 servings*
TIME: *40 minutes preparation;*
    3 hours cooking

1 cup uncooked garbanzo beans
3 cups water
1 6-inch piece kombu

Topping

3 cups peeled, cubed potatoes
¼ cup soy milk
1 tablespoon Cilantro Pesto
    (page 166)
½ teaspoon sea salt

Filling

¾ cup pistachios
2 tablespoons extra virgin
    olive oil
1 cup diced onions
1 cup peeled, diced carrots
1 cup diced red bell pepper
1 cup diced green bell pepper
1 cup diced celery
6 cloves minced garlic
¼ cup chopped fresh basil
2 tablespoons fresh marjoram
    leaves
2 tablespoons fresh thyme leaves
2 teaspoons fennel seed powder
2 teaspoons sea salt
¼ cup unbleached white flour
cilantro leaves and ground
    pistachios for garnish

Pesto, potatoes, and pistachios—who could ask for more? This is one of my favorite recipes because of its unique combination of my favorite foods.

Wash and sort the garbanzos. Soak the beans for 8 hours or flash-soak by placing them in a pot with 1 quart of boiling water and let stand covered for 1 hour. Drain the water and place beans into a 3-quart pot with 3 cups of fresh water and the kombu strip. Bring beans to a boil over high heat, then lower heat and simmer for 2 hours or until they are soft. Drain beans, finely dice the kombu, and set aside.

NOTE: To save time, pressure cook the beans with 2 cups of water and kombu for 1 hour.

Topping

In a 2-quart pot, boil the potatoes in salted water to cover until the potatoes are soft. Drain the potatoes, then place in a mixer with soy milk, Cilantro Pesto, and salt. Blend well, then set aside until ready to use.

Filling

Preheat oven to 325 degrees F. Spread pistachios on a baking sheet and roast for about 15 minutes, or until lightly browned and very fragrant. Remove nuts immediately from oven and transfer to a container to cool. In a 3-quart pot, heat the oil and sauté onions, carrots, red bell pepper, ½ cup green pepper, ½ cup celery, and garlic over low heat for about 15 minutes. Add garbanzo beans, diced kombu, basil, marjoram, thyme, fennel, salt, pistachios, and remaining celery and green peppers and sauté for 2 minutes longer. Add flour and stir until thickened.

continued…

To Bake

Transfer filling to a lightly oiled 2-quart baking dish 9½ x 7½ x 3 inches. Cover the top with the potatoes and smooth them with a rubber spatula until flat and even. Cover with foil and bake for 30 minutes. Remove from oven, garnish with cilantro leaves and ground pistachios, and serve hot.

Millet Stuffed Squash with Roasted Vegetables

YIELD: *4 servings*
TIME: *1 hour preparation;*
  30 minutes cooking

2 small buttercup or acorn
  squashes
1 tablespoon tamari
1 tablespoon barley malt syrup
½ cup millet, washed and
  drained
1¼ cups water
2 tablespoons white miso
2 tablespoons water
¼ teaspoon ginger powder
½ cup cooked aduki beans,
  drained
2 tablespoons red wine
1 tablespoon maple syrup
1 tablespoon pecan butter
  (or ¼ cup pecans ground
  into 2 tablespoons meal)
1 tablespoon tamari
½ cup peeled, diced parsnips
½ cup peeled, diced carrots
½ cup diced portobello
  mushrooms

This hearty autumn entrée is a meal in itself. I love squash and millet and the combination is heaven on earth to my palate.

Preheat oven to 350 degrees F. Wash, halve, and seed the squashes, then place on a lightly oiled baking sheet. Mix the tamari and barley malt syrup together and rub it onto the squash halves. Bake squashes covered for 25 to 40 minutes or until they are soft but firm, then remove and set aside. In a 2-quart pan with a lid, add water and millet, bring to a boil, then simmer covered on medium heat until cooked, about 30 minutes. In a large mixing bowl, combine the miso, water, and ginger and mix well. Add the beans and cooked millet and mix well. Gently press ½ cup of this mixture into each half of the squash. Cover the stuffed squash with foil and set aside. In a small mixing bowl, combine the red wine, maple syrup, pecan butter, and tamari into a glaze. In a baking pan, place the parsnips, carrots, and mushrooms, pour the glaze over them, and roast in oven uncovered for 35 minutes. During the last 10 minutes, place the covered stuffed squash back in the oven to reheat. To serve, cut the filled squash halves into four quarters each (crisscross through the center with buttercup squash or slice lengthwise with acorn squash). Fill the center of each plate with roasted vegetables, then lay 4 squash quarters on top with the wedges touching at the center.

Garbanzos and Millet with African Peanut Sauce

YIELD: *8 servings*

TIME: *8 hours soaking; 30 minutes preparation; 2 hours 15 minutes cooking*

1 cup uncooked garbanzo beans
3 cups water
1 6-inch piece kombu (optional)
1 cup millet, washed and drained
1 cup diced sweet potatoes
2½ cups water
¼ teaspoon sea salt

Sauce

2 tablespoons peanut or sesame oil
1 cup diced onions
9 cloves minced garlic
¼ cup chopped cilantro
1½ teaspoons cumin powder
½ cup plus 2 tablespoons creamy peanut butter
¾ cup water
3 tablespoons tamari
¼ cup fresh lime juice (about 2 limes)

½ cup chopped fresh parsley
½ cup finely diced red bell pepper

This recipe takes off in the opposite direction of the Grilled Vegetables and Pasta with Thai Peanut Sauce recipe. The sauce is more mild to compensate for the gentle flavor of the millet.

Wash and sort the garbanzos. Soak the beans for 8 hours or flash-soak by placing them in a pot with 1 quart of boiling water and let stand covered for 1 hour. Drain the water and place the beans into a 3-quart pot with 3 cups of fresh water and the kombu strip. Bring the beans to a boil over high heat, then lower the heat and simmer until they are soft, about 2 hours. Meanwhile, in a 2-quart saucepan, bring the millet, sweet potatoes, water, and salt to a simmer over medium heat. Cover and cook the millet until all of the water is absorbed, about 30 minutes. Remove the millet and sweet potatoes from heat and set aside. When the garbanzos are done, remove from heat, discard the kombu strip (or reserve for another use), and drain the beans.

In a 10-inch frying pan, heat the oil and sauté the onions, garlic, cilantro, and cumin over medium heat for 5 minutes. Transfer the mixture to a blender, add the remaining peanut sauce ingredients and blend until smooth. Add the garbanzos, then cook the sauce and beans over medium heat for 10 minutes. Remove the cover from the millet, fluff it with a fork, and transfer it to a serving platter. Pour the peanut-garbanzo sauce over the millet. Sprinkle with the chopped parsley and diced red bell pepper, then serve hot.

Garbanzos Vesuvius

YIELD: *4 servings*

TIME: *40 minutes preparation;*
1 hour cooking

4 russet potatoes

2 tablespoons extra virgin
olive oil

½ teaspoon paprika

½ teaspoon sea salt

2 tablespoons extra virgin
olive oil

2 cups diced onions

6 cloves minced garlic

4 teaspoons thyme

1 teaspoon sea salt

⅛ teaspoon ground black pepper

3 cups cooked garbanzos (or 2
15-ounce cans), drained

1½ cups white wine

½ cup water

½ cup diced celery

4 teaspoons Vogue Vege Base

2 tablespoons arrowroot powder
dissolved in 2 tablespoons cool
water

6 tablespoons chopped fresh
parsley

2 tablespoons extra virgin
olive oil

4 cups sliced onions

4 cups sliced leeks

2 cups sliced fennel (optional)

4 cloves minced garlic

¼ teaspoon sea salt

2 tablespoons chopped fresh
parsley for garnish

This dish, along with Navy Beans Tarragon and Beans in Red Wine Sauce, follows in the tradition of classic French dishes. All three take bean cuisine to another exciting culinary level.

Wash and quarter the potatoes, but do not peel. Blanch the potatoes by dropping them into boiling water and simmering for 12 minutes. Preheat oven to 375 degrees F. Mix together the oil, paprika, and salt, then rub on the potatoes. Bake potatoes in the oven for 40 minutes, then set aside. In a 2-quart saucepan, heat the oil and sauté the onions, garlic, thyme, salt, and pepper on medium heat for 7 minutes or until the onions become translucent. Add the beans, wine, water, celery, and Vogue Vege Base. Bring to a simmer and add arrowroot/water mixture. Add the first measure of the chopped parsley to the bean mixture and mix well. Set aside. In a 10-inch frying pan, heat the oil and sauté the onions, leeks, fennel, garlic, and salt on medium heat for 5 minutes or until the onions become translucent. For each serving, place 1¼ cups of the bean mixture in the center of the plate and garnish around it with the onion/leek mixture. Place a quarter wedge of baked potato on top of the bean mixture at 3, 6, 9, and 12 o'clock on the plate. Garnish the top of each entrée with parsley and serve hot.

Opposite: Italian Country Loaf (page 142) with Sauce Concassé (page 156), Pesto Mashed Potatoes (page 197) and Sautéed Arame and Vegetables (page 183)

Navy Beans Tarragon

YIELD: *3 servings*
TIME: *20 minutes preparation;*
20 minutes cooking

1 tablespoon extra virgin
olive oil
1 cup finely diced onions
1 cup quartered mushrooms
1 cup thinly sliced scallions
1 cup thinly slicked leeks
¾ teaspoon dry tarragon leaves
1½ cups cooked navy beans
(or 1 15-ounce can)
½ cup white wine
¼ cup soy milk powder
4½ teaspoons dark miso
1 tablespoon fresh lemon juice
3 tablespoons thinly sliced
scallions for garnish
3 tablespoons finely diced red
bell pepper for garnish

Taken from the classic French dish, this recipe can be served with any pasta or grain.

In a 10-inch frying pan, heat the oil and sauté the onions, mushrooms, scallions, leeks, and tarragon over medium heat for 5 minutes or until onions are transparent. Add beans and stir in. In a mixing bowl, combine the white wine, milk powder, dark miso, and fresh lemon juice and mix together until smooth. Add this mixture to the sautéed vegetables and simmer gently for five minutes. Serve over a cooked pasta or grain and garnish with scallions and red bell pepper.

Opposite: American Bounty (page 140) with Roasted Vegetable Sauce (page 160) and Wild Rice and Cabbage Pilaf (page 191)

Beans in Red Wine Sauce

YIELD: *6 servings*

TIME: *25 minutes preparation;*
30 minutes cooking

2 tablespoons extra virgin
  olive oil
2 cups diced Spanish onions
2 cups diced mushrooms
1 cup peeled, finely diced carrot
6 cloves minced garlic
2 tablespoons Vogue Vege Base
2 bay leaves
1 teaspoon thyme
½ teaspoon sea salt
⅛ teaspoon ground black
  pepper
2 tablespoons dark miso
2 cups water
2 cups red wine
3½ cups cooked navy beans,
  drained (or 2 15½-ounce
  cans)
3⅓ tablespoons arrowroot
  powder or cornstarch
  dissolved in ¼ cup cool
  water

This version of the French Coq Au Vin shows how easily a classical vegetarian dish can be created.

In a 2-quart pot, heat the oil and sauté the onions, mushrooms, carrot, garlic, Vogue Vege Base, bay leaves, thyme, salt, and pepper on medium heat for 5 minutes, adding a small amount of water if the vegetables stick to the pan. Dissolve miso in a small amount of the water, then add the red wine, remaining water, dissolved miso, and cooked beans. Bring beans and vegetables to a simmer, add arrowroot/water mixture, and mix well. Cook on low heat for a few minutes or until thickened. Remove bay leaves and serve over mashed potatoes, rice, or wide noodles.

Vegetable Paella

YIELD: *8 servings*

TIME: *20 minutes preparation;
1 hour 10 minutes cooking*

1 green bell pepper
4 cups water
¼ cup Vogue Vege Base
¾ teaspoon saffron threads
¼ cup extra virgin olive oil
1 cup chopped onion
3 cloves minced garlic
2 sliced scallions
2 teaspoons sea salt
1 peeled, seeded, and chopped
    tomato
1½ cups short grain brown rice,
    washed and drained
½ cup frozen lima beans
½ cup white wine
4 ounces coarsely chopped fresh
    oyster mushrooms
3 tablespoons lemon juice
2 tablespoons dry, chopped
    wakame
1 sprig fresh rosemary
1 bay leaf
½ cup green string beans, cut
    into pieces about 1 inch long
¼ cup fresh or frozen peas
2 tablespoons chopped parsley
6 wedges or slices of lemon
    for garnish

This exciting and somewhat wild version of traditional Spanish paella is a meal in itself, not just another pilaf with a pretty name.

Preheat oven to 325 degrees F. Wash, dry, halve, and seed pepper. Rub skins with oil. Place on a baking sheet and roast for 30 to 40 minutes or until they are soft and skins begin to shrivel. Remove peppers and place in a brown paper bag to steam for 10 minutes. When cool, remove loosened skins, and dice.

In a 2-quart saucepan, combine the water, Vogue Vege Base, and saffron threads and bring to a simmer over medium heat. Once simmering, reduce heat to low and cover saucepan; the broth will need to be simmering when it is added to the paella later on. In a 12-inch frying pan or paella pan, heat the oil and sauté the onions, garlic, scallions, and salt for 3 minutes over medium heat. Add the tomato and roasted bell pepper, then sauté for 3 minutes longer. Stir in the brown rice and thoroughly coat it with the oil and vegetable juices. Add 3½ cups of the simmering broth, along with the lima beans, wine, mushrooms, lemon juice, wakame, rosemary, and bay leaf. Stir briefly to evenly distribute the ingredients. Simmer the mixture uncovered for 5 minutes. Cover the pan (if using a paella pan, cover it tightly with aluminum foil), and reduce the heat to low. Cook the rice for about 40 to 45 minutes or until done, checking periodically to make sure that there is enough liquid and that the bottom is not burning (if no more liquid remains but the rice is not completely done, add the remaining broth, cover the pan, and continue to cook the rice over low heat until the broth is absorbed and the rice is done). Scatter the green string beans over the top of the rice during the last 5 minutes of cooking. When the rice is completely cooked, remove the pan from the heat, then scatter peas over the top of the paella. Allow pan to sit covered for 5 to 10 minutes. Remove cover and bay leaf, sprinkle paella with chopped parsley, garnish with the lemon wedges or slices, and serve immediately.

Curried Vegetable Casserole

YIELD: *4 servings*

TIME: *30 minutes preparation;*
1 hour 10 minutes cooking

1 cup brown or white
basmati rice
2 cups water
¹⁄₁₆ teaspoon sea salt
1½ cups half moon-cut carrots
1 cup water
1 cup coconut milk
1 tablespoon sesame oil
1 cup diced onion
1 cup broccoli florets
¾ cup diced red bell pepper
½ cup diced celery
1 tablespoon curry powder
¾ teaspoon sea salt
¼ teaspoon cumin powder
¼ teaspoon black pepper
⅛ teaspoon nutmeg
1 cup cooked (or canned)
garbanzo beans
¾ cup Curried Dijon Topping
(page 171)

Americans are divided between those who hate curry and those who can't get enough of this spicy, savory food. This recipe makes a great main dish for people like me who love curry.

Preheat oven to 325 degrees F. In a 2-quart saucepan (with lid), combine rice, water, and salt, then bring it to a simmer over medium heat. Reduce the heat to medium-low and cook covered for about 45 minutes or until all the water is absorbed. Remove the saucepan from the heat. In another saucepan, combine the carrots, 1 cup of water, and a pinch of sea salt. Bring to a simmer over medium heat, cooking the carrots until they are soft. Drain and transfer to a blender, then add the coconut milk and blend until smooth. In a 10-inch frying pan, heat the oil and sauté the onion, broccoli, bell pepper, celery, curry, salt, cumin, pepper, and nutmeg over medium heat for 5 minutes. Combine the sautéed vegetables and beans with cooked rice, then pour the mixture into a 2-quart casserole. Top with the Curried Dijon Topping, then bake it in the oven for 20 to 30 minutes. Remove casserole from oven and serve hot.

English Curry Stir-Fry

YIELD: *4 servings*
TIME: *30 minutes*

1½ cups soy milk
1 cup brown rice syrup
6 tablespoons arrowroot powder
2 tablespoons curry powder
1 teaspoon coriander powder
1 teaspoon garlic powder
½ teaspoon sea salt (optional)
1 8-ounce package somen
    noodles
1 tablespoon canola oil
2 cups diced onion
2 cups diced red bell pepper
1 cup peeled, diagonally cut
    carrots
unsweetened, toasted coconut
    for garnish

English curry is milder and sweeter than Indian curry. It's simple to make this dish equivalent to an Indian curry—just double the amounts of the spices and add ¼ teaspoon cayenne.

In a 1-quart bottle, combine the soy milk, syrup, arrowroot, curry, coriander, garlic, and salt. Seal tightly, shake well to blend, then set aside until needed. In a 2-quart saucepan, cook noodles in boiling water until they are done, drain, and rinse under cold running water. Set noodles aside. In a 10-inch frying pan, heat the oil and sauté the onion, bell pepper, and carrots over medium heat for approximately 5 minutes, or until they are half-cooked. Add noodles and continue to sauté for a few more minutes until noodles are heated through. Shake the bottled curry sauce until the arrowroot is well blended. Pour sauce over the sautéed vegetables and noodles and stir until the sauce thickens. Transfer the sauté to a warmed plate and serve garnished with a sprinkling of toasted, unsweetened coconut.

VARIATIONS

Add 1 cup cooked and sliced seitan to sautéed vegetables and proceed with recipe as directed.

Add 1 cup cubed firm tofu to the sautéed vegetables and proceed with the recipe as directed.

American Bounty

YIELD: *10 servings*
TIME: *45 minutes preparation;*
    1 hour 45 minutes cooking

Barley Loaf

*¾ cup barley, washed and
    drained*
*1½ cups water or vegetable
    stock*
⅛ teaspoon sea salt
*1 tablespoon unrefined corn or
    extra virgin olive oil*
¾ cup finely diced onions
*¾ cup peeled, finely diced
    carrots*
*¾ cup finely diced red bell
    pepper*
*¾ cup fresh or frozen kernel
    corn*
*2 cloves minced garlic (or ½
    teaspoon garlic powder)*
*2 packed teaspoons minced
    cilantro*
*1 teaspoon chopped fresh basil
    (or ½ teaspoon dried basil)*
1 teaspoon sea salt
⅛ teaspoon black pepper
8 ounces extra firm tofu, rinsed
*2 tablespoons arrowroot
    powder*
*2 tablespoons agar flakes (or 1
    teaspoon agar powder)*
2 tablespoons water

Barley and corn, symbols of America's bounty, are wonderfully combined with cilantro, spices, and fresh vegetables to give this taste and texture. This dish won a silver medal in the 1992 International Culinary Olympics. For a fancier version, try the Corn Polenta Wrap for either loaf or roll shapes. Roasted Vegetable Sauce is a great addition to this dish.

Barley Loaf

Place the barley, water, and salt in a 2-quart saucepan (with lid). Bring to a boil, then simmer covered over medium-low heat for 1 hour (30 minutes for pearled barley). Remove the saucepan from the heat and transfer the barley to a large bowl. In a 10-inch frying pan, heat the oil and sauté the onions, carrots, bell pepper, corn, garlic, cilantro, basil, salt, and pepper over medium heat for 6 minutes. Meanwhile, boil the tofu for 5 minutes, drain, then place tofu, arrowroot, agar, and water into a food processor and blend until smooth. In a mixing bowl, combine tofu mixture, sautéed vegetables, and barley and blend well.

Corn Polenta Wrap

In a 2-quart saucepan (with lid), combine the water, salt, and saffron. Bring water to a boil then add corn grits and stir. Cover, reduce the heat to medium, and simmer for about 10 minutes or until mixture is soft. In a food processor, combine tofu, arrowroot, agar, garlic, and cilantro and blend until smooth. In a mixing bowl, combine tofu mixture with warm corn grits and blend well.

Corn Polenta Wrap

1 cup water
2 teaspoons sea salt
½ teaspoon saffron
¾ cup yellow corn grits
*1 10½-ounce package extra
   firm silken tofu*
2 tablespoons arrowroot powder
*2 tablespoons agar flakes (or 1
   teaspoon agar powder)*
1 clove minced garlic
*1 teaspoon chopped fresh
   cilantro*

Assembling the Roll

Preheat oven to 350 degrees F. Lay down a piece of plastic wrap 18 inches long on a flat surface and spoon barley-tofu mixture down the center to create a roll 13 x 7 inches. Using the plastic wrap, roll the mixture into a log shape 3 inches in diameter. Set aside. Lay down another piece of plastic wrap 18 inches long and spread corn mixture out evenly across the plastic wrap to cover a rectangular area 13 x 7 inches. Remove plastic wrap from barley-tofu roll and place in the center of the corn mixture rectangle, bringing up the sides of plastic wrap to encase roll. Wrap the corn-covered roll tightly in the plastic wrap, wrap in foil, and place on a wire rack inside a large baking pan filled with an inch of water. Cover the pan with aluminum foil and bake for 45 minutes or until the internal temperature is 160 degrees F. Remove pan from oven and set roll aside for 10 minutes. Remove foil and slice the roll with a serrated bread knife into ¼-inch to ½-inch thick slices. Remove plastic from each slice and serve with Roasted Vegetable Sauce.

VARIATION: *American Bounty Loaf*

Preheat oven to 375 degrees F and prepare polenta mixture as directed. Line a loaf pan with a sheet of parchment paper. Oil the paper and press a ½-inch layer of the corn polenta mixture onto all sides of the pan. Gently press the center full with the barley-tofu mixture. Top the loaf with the remaining corn polenta mixture. Cover with another oiled piece of parchment paper. Place the loaf pan in a larger baking pan filled with 1 inch of water. Cover the large pan with aluminum foil and bake it in the oven for 1 hour and 15 minutes, or until the internal temperature reaches 160 degrees F. Remove loaf pan from the oven and allow it to cool and set. Take loaf out of pan and remove parchment paper. Using a serrated bread knife, slice the loaf into 8 pieces, 1 inch thick. Serve with Roasted Vegetable Sauce.

Italian Country Loaf

YIELD: *4 servings*

TIME: *35 minutes preparation;*
1 hour 45 minutes cooking

1 red bell pepper
½ yellow bell pepper
½ teaspoon olive oil
¼ cup pistachios
¾ pound extra firm tofu
2 tablespoons arrowroot
   powder
4 cloves minced garlic
2 tablespoons agar flakes (or 1
   teaspoon agar powder)
½ teaspoon sea salt
½ tablespoon extra virgin
   olive oil
2 teaspoons extra virgin
   olive oil
½ cup chopped onions
½ cup chopped fresh fennel (or
   ½ cup diced celery plus 1
   teaspoon fennel powder)
2 packed tablespoons chopped
   fresh basil
¼ teaspoon sea salt

Tuscany is the home of contemporary cuisine and the following recipe reflects the Tuscan's careful blending of flavors to create a new sensation for the palate. Pistachio nuts, red bell peppers, and fennel give the dish a beautiful color, flavor, and texture. Serve hot with a vegetable sauce, such as Quick Supreme Sauce, Sauce Renaissance, or Wakame Au Jus, for an elegant dinner or cold with a salad for a summer's luncheon.

Preheat oven to 325 degrees F. Wash, dry, halve, and seed peppers. Rub skins with the first measure of oil. Place on a baking sheet and roast for 30 to 40 minutes or until they are soft and skins begin to shrivel. Remove peppers and place in a brown paper bag to steam for 10 minutes. When cool, remove loosened skins, and dice into 1-inch pieces. Spread pistachios on a baking sheet and roast for about 15 minutes, or until lightly browned and very fragrant. Remove immediately from baking sheet and transfer to a container to cool.

Reduce the oven temperature to 300 degrees F. Rinse the tofu, then press it dry. In a food processor, combine the tofu, arrowroot, garlic, agar, and salt and process until smooth. Add the second measure of oil and process again briefly until the oil is completely blended. Transfer the mixture to a large bowl. In a 10-inch frying pan, heat the third measure of oil and sauté the onions for 5 minutes over medium heat until transparent, then add the fennel and sauté for about 4 minutes longer. To the tofu mixture, add the sautéed vegetables, bell peppers, pistachio nuts, basil, and salt, then combine well.

Lightly wet a flat surface with water and lay 2 pieces of plastic wrap down, overlapping each other in the middle, to form 1 large piece about 2 feet long and 1½ feet wide. Arrange the tofu mixture down the edge of the plastic wrap closest to you to form a log about 4 inches in diameter and about 10 inches long. Carefully roll the loaf in the plastic wrap, working away from you, until you reach the end. Twist both ends securely closed. Cover the roll with 1 layer of aluminum foil. Add 1 inch of water to the bottom of a large roasting pan. Insert a wire rack in the pan, and place loaf on rack. Cover pan and place in oven. Steam bake for 1 hour or until loaf reaches an internal temperature of 150 to 160 degrees F. Remove pan from oven, take loaf out of pan and set aside to cool, preferably overnight in the refrigerator. When ready to use, remove loaf from foil and plastic wrap, slice and serve.

"Food is not matter but the heart of matter, the flesh and blood of rock and water, earth and sun. Food is not a commodity which price can capture, but exacting effort, carefully sustained, the life work of countless beings. With this cooking I enter the heart of matter, I enter the intimate activity which makes dreams materialize."

—EDWARD ESPE BROWN

Smoked Mushroom Loaf

YIELD: *6 servings*
TIME: *45 minutes preparation;*
1 hour 15 minutes cooking

Tofu Pâté Base Mix

1½ pounds extra firm tofu
3 tablespoons arrowroot powder
1 tablespoon extra virgin olive oil
3 cloves minced garlic
1 tablespoon nutritional yeast
1 tablespoon agar flakes
1 teaspoon sea salt

Mushroom Duxelles

1 tablespoon extra virgin olive oil
1 cup finely diced onions
½ cup peeled, finely diced carrots
3 cloves minced garlic
1 teaspoon sea salt
1½ teaspoons thyme
2 cups finely diced Smoked
*   Portobello Mushrooms*
*   (page 18)*
½ cup chopped, roasted walnuts
3 tablespoons unbleached white
*   flour*
2 tablespoons minced fresh
*   parsley*

Red Cabbage Center

2 cups water
2 tablespoons apple cider
*   vinegar*
4 cups thinly sliced red cabbage
¼ cup Tofu Pâté Base Mix

This is another silver medal winner from the 1992 International Culinary Olympics and one of my favorite dishes because I love smoked mushrooms. The loaf has superb flavor, texture, and is surprisingly light. Take the extra time to smoke the mushrooms instead of using liquid smoke.

Tofu Pâté Base Mix

In a food processor, combine tofu, arrowroot, oil, garlic, yeast, agar, and salt and process for about 2 to 3 minutes or until mixture is smooth. Transfer to a container and refrigerate until ready to use.

Mushroom Duxelles

In a 10-inch frying pan, heat the oil and sauté the onions, carrots, garlic, salt, and thyme over medium heat for 5 minutes. Add the mushrooms and continue sautéing for another 5 minutes. Add the walnuts, flour, and parsley, then sauté until the mixture is thickened. Remove pan from heat and set aside to cool.

Red Cabbage Center

In a 2-quart saucepan, combine the water and vinegar and bring to a simmer over medium heat. Blanch the cabbage in the simmering vinegar water for about 6 to 10 seconds. Remove cabbage, blot dry to remove excess liquid, then finely chop. In a mixing bowl, add ¼ cup of the Tofu Pâté to the cabbage and mix well. Set aside.

Assembling the Loaf

Preheat the oven to 400 degrees F. Lightly oil a loaf pan. Set aside ¼ of the Tofu Pâté Base Mix. Line loaf pan with plastic wrap, leaving several inches on both sides to cover the top later. Line the sides and bottom of the loaf pan with a ⅛-inch thick layer of Tofu Pâté. Gently press in the Mushroom Duxelle filling, making a V-shaped indentation lengthwise down the center. To this area, add the cabbage/tofu mixture and gently press into place. Cover top with remaining Tofu Pâté. Fold plastic wrap flaps over the top of the loaf. Place loaf pan into a deeper baking pan filled with 1 inch of water. Cover pan with foil and steam bake loaf for about 35 minutes, or until interior temperature of loaf reaches 150 degrees F. Remove pan from oven and set aside to cool. To serve, remove loaf from pan and cut into 1-inch thick slices. If serving the entire loaf, remove the plastic wrap before slicing. To serve only a few slices, leave the plastic wrap on the loaf, and remove from each slice. Serve with Sauce Renaissance, Sardaline Sauce, or Quick Supreme Sauce.

VARIATION: *Smoked Mushroom Crêpes*

Preheat oven to 375 degrees F. Prepare Savory Crêpes (page 111). Add 1 teaspoon liquid hickory smoke to Tofu Pâté Base and mix well. Use ¼ cup filling per crêpe and roll up. Place crêpes in a baking dish, brush them with water, then cover with a tightly fitting lid. Bake for about 20 minutes. Serve while hot, 2 or 3 crêpes per portion, with Burgundy Sauce Glaze, Sauce Renaissance, or Roasted Vegetable Sauce.

Wild Rice and Corn Loaf

YIELD: *8 servings*

TIME: *30 minutes preparation;*
1 hour 15 minutes cooking

1½ cups water
¾ cup wild rice, washed and
    drained
¹⁄₁₆ teaspoon sea salt
¾ pound firm tofu
2 tablespoons arrowroot powder
2 tablespoons agar flakes
3 cloves minced garlic
½ teaspoon sea salt
½ tablespoon extra virgin
    olive oil
1 tablespoon canola oil
¾ cup diced onions
2 teaspoons chopped dried
    cilantro
1½ teaspoons thyme
1 teaspoon sea salt
1½ cups fresh or frozen
    kernel corn
¾ cup diced celery
2 tablespoons minced fresh
    parsley

Grains are the staple of the human diet. With tofu added to boost the amount of protein, this loaf can be enjoyed with Roasted Vegetable Sauce and salad as a complete dinner.

Preheat oven to 350 degrees F. In a 2-quart saucepan, combine the water, rice, and salt and bring to a boil. Reduce heat to low, cover, and simmer for about 45 minutes or until rice is soft. Remove saucepan from heat and fluff rice. In a food processor, combine the tofu, arrowroot, agar, garlic, and salt and process until smooth. Add the olive oil, then process again briefly until the oil is completely blended. Transfer the mixture to a large mixing bowl. In a 10-inch frying pan, heat the canola oil and sauté the onions, cilantro, thyme, and salt over medium heat for 5 minutes. Towards the end of the 5 minutes, add the corn, celery, and parsley. Remove vegetables from heat and combine in mixing bowl with tofu mixture. Add cooked rice and mix by hand until well blended.

To Make a Loaf

Line a loaf pan with plastic wrap, press the filling into it, and cover the top with more plastic wrap. Place loaf pan into a larger baking pan filled with 1 inch of water, then cover and bake for 1 hour, or until interior temperature of loaf reaches 160 degrees F. Remove pan from oven and cool for 30 to 45 minutes to allow loaf to set. Unmold loaf onto a serving plate and remove plastic wrap. Using a serrated bread knife, cut the loaf into 1-inch thick slices and serve.

To Make a Roll

Lightly wet a flat surface with water and lay a piece of plastic wrap down, about 15 inches long and 12 inches wide. Arrange tofu mixture down the edge of the plastic wrap closest to you to form a log about 3 inches in diameter and about 7½ inches long. Carefully roll the log in the plastic wrap, working away from you, until you reach the end. Twist both ends securely closed. Cover roll with 1 layer of aluminum foil. Add 1 inch of water to the bottom of a large roasting pan. Insert a wire rack in the pan, and place tofu roll on it. Cover pan and steam bake for 1 hour. Remove pan from oven, take out tofu roll, and set aside to cool overnight in the refrigerator. When ready to use, remove loaf from aluminum foil and plastic wrap, slice and serve.

Pecan Nut Loaf

YIELD: *8 servings*

TIME: *30 minutes preparation;*
   1 hour cooking

2 6-inch pieces kombu
2½ pounds extra firm tofu,
   pressed dry then crumbled
1½ cups finely diced onions
¾ cup finely chopped fresh
   parsley (or ¼ cup dried
   parsley)
6 tablespoons dark miso
½ cup whole wheat bread flour
   mixed with 3 tablespoons
   gluten flour
½ cup ground pecans
2 tablespoons Dijon mustard
1 tablespoon garlic powder
1 teaspoon thyme
¼ teaspoon black pepper

This loaf is bursting with flavor and is a filling entrée for those in a transitional diet to vegetarianism. It makes a great sandwich as well as an entrée.

Preheat oven to 375 degrees F. In a 2-quart saucepan, cook the kombu in 4 cups of water over medium heat for 20 minutes. Drain and chop the kombu into ½-inch pieces. In a large mixing bowl, combine the tofu, onions, parsley, miso, flour, ground pecans, mustard, garlic, thyme, and pepper and mix together until well blended. Oil a 1-pound loaf pan, then line it with parchment paper. Firmly press the tofu mixture into the pan. Bake for 1 hour or until thoroughly cooked. Remove pan from oven and let loaf stand for 10 minutes to cool slightly. Remove loaf from pan and slice and serve hot.

VARIATION: *Pecan Nut Crêpes*

Preheat oven to 375 degrees F. Prepare Savory Crêpes (page 111). Use ¼ cup uncooked filling per crêpe and roll it up. Place the crêpes into a baking dish, brush them with water, then cover with a tightly fitting lid. Bake about 20 minutes. Serve 2 or 3 crêpes per portion with Carbonara Sauce, Fresh Basil Sauce, Saffron Sauce, or Roasted Vegetable Sauce.

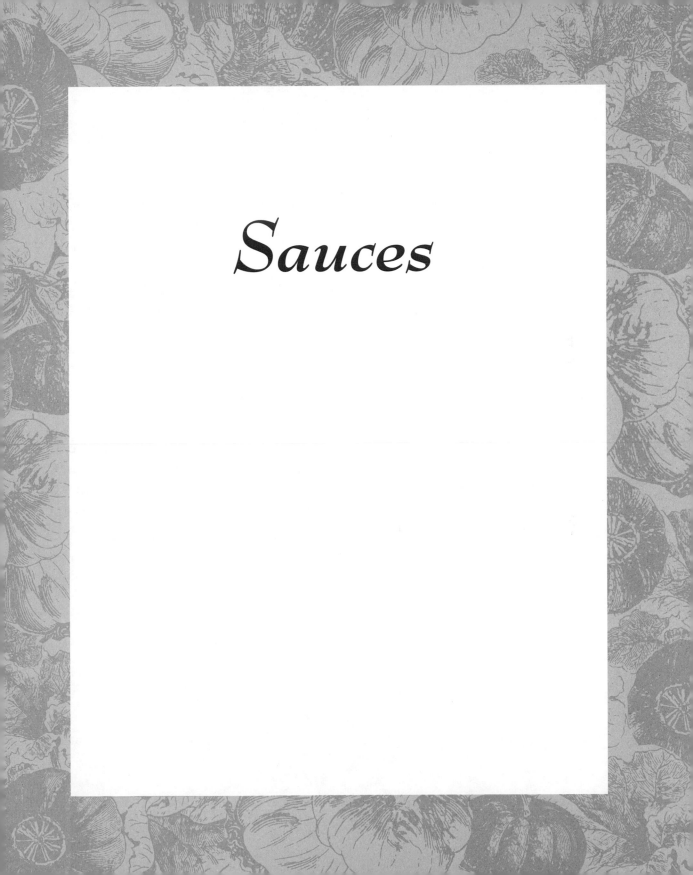

Sauces

"Sauce" means a condiment, relish, or dressing that is used as a topping for food. Stemming from the old Roman salsum, it originally meant a salty brine that was used to preserve perishable food. Modern day sauces have evolved to include salty, bitter, sweet, sour, or piquant flavors and are used with appetizers, entrées, and desserts.

The saucier is the maestro of the professional kitchen. He or she orchestrates the food with different sauces. The sauces are meant to accompany the foods they are being served with and not stand apart from them. It must be suitable to the food and not a mandatory addition that the diner wishes to scrape off.

My sauces are vegetable based and carry the richness and delicate flavors of traditional sauces. Many of my sauces, such as the Yellow Pepper Sauce and Carbonara Sauce, use whole foods in their ingredients, which makes them nutritionally superior to animal-protein based sauces. Coupled with the wonderful flavors and even textures of such sauces as the Sauce Renaissance, one can understand why these eco-friendly sauces are at the forefront of the new plant-based cuisine. Wakame Au Jus, Sauce Renaissance, Espagnole Sauce, and Roasted Vegetable Sauce complement many of the entrées in this book. These wonderful vegetarian sauces will delight and satisfy even the fussiest of gourmets.

BBQ Sauce

YIELD: *4½ cups*
TIME: *1 hour 40 minutes*

2 tablespoons canola oil
½ cup minced onion
3 cloves minced garlic
¼ cup dark miso
*¾ cup plus 1 tablespoon lemon
 juice or apple cider vinegar*
*2 cups tomato purée (or 1 cup
 tomato paste mixed with
 1 cup water)*
¾ cup barley malt syrup
½ cup brown rice syrup
¼ cup tamari
*3 tablespoons blackstrap
 molasses*
1 tablespoon chili powder
1 tablespoon BBQ Spice
2¼ teaspoons black pepper
*1½ teaspoons dry mustard
 powder*
*¼ teaspoon liquid hickory
 smoke (optional)*

One Saturday morning at the Unicorn Village Restaurant in Aventura, Florida, after making many versions of this sauce, I finally came up with a winner. Its rich and robust flavor ranks it with the best of sauces.

In a 3-quart saucepan, sauté the onions and garlic in the oil over medium heat for 5 minutes or until the onions are transparent. In a small bowl, combine the miso and lemon juice and mix well. Add the miso/lemon juice mixture and remaining ingredients to the sautéed vegetables and stir until well blended. Simmer the sauce for 1 hour. Remove sauce from heat and either transfer to a covered container and refrigerate until needed, or use immediately.

Fresh Basil Sauce

YIELD: *1½ cups*
TIME: *30 minutes*

*1½ cups soy milk (or 1½ cups
    water and ¼ cup soy milk
    powder)*
1 cup fresh basil leaves
3 cloves minced garlic
2 teaspoons Vogue Vege Base
¾ teaspoon sea salt
1 tablespoon extra virgin olive oil
*2 tablespoons unbleached
    white flour*

This light sauce has a consistency between an au jus and a cream sauce. It goes very well with delicately flavored dishes such as Pistachio Polenta, Savory Crêpes, Pecan Nut Loaf, and Italian Country Loaf.

In a blender, combine milk, basil, garlic, Vogue Vege Base, and salt and blend for 2 minutes. Pour the mixture into a 2-quart saucepan and bring it to a simmer over medium heat. In a small bowl, combine the oil and flour and mix together into a paste. Add oil/flour mixture to simmering sauce, whisking constantly to prevent lumps from forming. Return sauce to a simmer, remove saucepan from heat, and serve.

Quick Supreme Sauce

YIELD: *2¼ cups*
TIME: *30 minutes*

2 tablespoons canola oil
¼ cup unbleached white flour
2 cups soy milk
1 cup water
*3 tablespoons plus 2 teaspoons
    Vogue Vege Base*
1½ teaspoons granulated garlic
1 teaspoon sea salt
1/16 teaspoon white pepper
1/16 teaspoon nutmeg

Don't serve Bulgur Walnut Croquettes, Millet Stuffed Squash with Roasted Vegetables, Italian Country Loaf, Pecan Nut Loaf, and Wild Rice and Corn Loaf without this sauce!

In a mixing bowl, combine oil and flour until they form a paste (this will be the roux for the sauce). In a 2-quart saucepan, bring remaining ingredients to a simmer over medium heat. Add roux and stir until well blended and sauce is smooth. Cook the sauce over medium-low heat for 15 or 20 minutes, stirring frequently to prevent burning. Remove pan from heat and serve.

Wakame Au Jus

YIELD: *1 cup*
TIME: *15 minutes preparation;
30 minutes cooking*

*3 to 4 medium zucchini
¼ cup vegetable stock
1 tablespoon Vogue Vege Base
¼ teaspoon garlic powder
⅛ teaspoon sea salt
2 tablespoons soaked wakame,
deveined and chopped into
¼-inch pieces (or 1
tablespoon dry, chopped
wakame)*

This light sauce goes well with delicately flavored dishes, especially Wakame Quinoa Dumplings, Italian Country Loaf, and Seafood Patties.

Put zucchini through a juicer to get ¾ cup zucchini juice. (Or chop 2 medium zucchinis and place into a blender with ¼ cup water, blend until smooth, and strain through a fine mesh strainer lined with cheesecloth. Twist and squeeze cheesecloth to extract as much liquid as possible.). In a mixing bowl, combine the juice, stock, Vogue Vege Base, garlic powder, salt, and wakame, mix well and let sit for 30 minutes. Strain and serve uncooked, or warm over low heat and serve.

Saffron Sauce

YIELD: *1 cup*
TIME: *30 minutes preparation;
20 minutes cooking*

*1 teaspoon extra virgin olive oil
¼ cup finely diced onions
¼ cup skinned, seeded, and finely
diced plum tomatoes
1 tablespoon minced shallot
1 clove minced garlic
¾ cup white wine (not too dry)
or semi-sweet sherry
1 tablespoon arame sea vegetable
1 teaspoon saffron threads
¼ teaspoon sea salt
¾ cup Quick Supreme Sauce
(page 152)*

This sauce goes well with Wild Rice and Corn Loaf, American Bounty, and Pecan Nut Loaf. It is also good over plain cooked grains with steamed vegetables.

In a 2-quart saucepan, heat the oil and sauté the onions, tomatoes, shallots, and garlic over medium heat for 5 minutes or until onions are transparent. Add the wine, arame, saffron, and salt, then simmer until the mixture is reduced by ¼ cup. Stir in Quick Supreme Sauce and continue to simmer another few minutes. Remove saucepan from heat and serve either hot or at room temperature.

Yellow Pepper Sauce

YIELD: *1½ cups*
TIME: *10 minutes preparation;*
65 minutes cooking

1 yellow bell pepper
¼ cup extra virgin olive oil
3 tablespoons lemon juice
2 tablespoons white miso
2 tablespoons water
½ 10½-ounce package extra
firm silken tofu
⅛ teaspoon sea salt

To make Italian Country Loaf, Seafood Patties, Savory Crêpes, or Wakame Quinoa Dumplings even more special, serve them with this sauce.

Preheat oven to 325 degrees F. Wash, dry, halve, and seed the bell pepper. Rub skins with oil. Place pepper halves on a baking sheet and roast for 30 to 40 minutes, until they are soft and the skins begin to shrivel. Remove pepper from oven and place in a brown paper bag to steam for 10 minutes. When cool, remove the loosened skins. In a blender, combine bell pepper with remaining oil and ingredients and blend until smooth. Transfer sauce into a 1-quart saucepan, heat over low heat for about 5 minutes, and serve.

Sardaline Sauce

YIELD: *2¼ cups*
TIME: *25 minutes*

1 tablespoon canola oil
2 tablespoons unbleached
white flour
1 cup hot water
2½ teaspoons Vogue Vege Base
1 cup soy milk
¾ teaspoon sea salt
⅛ teaspoon white pepper
1 tablespoon drained capers
2 teaspoons caper juice

This sauce has a superb taste, an excellent consistency, and goes well with Savory Crêpes, Pecan Nut Loaf, and Wild Rice and Corn Loaf.

In a mixing bowl, combine oil and flour until they form a paste (this will be the roux for the sauce). In another bowl, combine the water and Vogue Vege Base, mix well, and let stand for 5 minutes. In a 2-quart saucepan, combine water/Vogue Vege Base mixture, soy milk, salt, and pepper and bring to a simmer over medium heat. Add roux and stir constantly until it thickens. Add capers and caper juice. Remove saucepan from heat and serve either hot or at room temperature.

Sauce Renaissance

YIELD: *3 cups*
TIME: *15 minutes preparation;*
55 minutes cooking

2 red bell peppers
1 yellow bell pepper
½ cup roasted pepper juice
⅛ teaspoon saffron threads
1 tablespoon extra virgin
olive oil
½ cup diced onion
¼ cup diced fennel (or 1
teaspoon fennel seed powder
and ¼ cup diced celery)
3 tablespoons chopped
fresh basil
3 cloves minced garlic
1¼ teaspoons Italian herb
blend (1 part each dried
basil, marjoram, oregano,
and thyme)
1¼ teaspoons fresh marjoram
1 teaspoon fresh oregano
1 teaspoon fresh thyme
¾ teaspoon sea salt

Roasted red bell peppers, fennel, and garlic make this a superb sauce for many dishes. The sauce has a very delicate, savory-sweet flavor that goes well with lightly seasoned foods.

Preheat oven to 325 degrees F. Wash, dry, halve, and seed the bell peppers. Rub skins with olive oil. Place pepper halves on a baking sheet and roast for 30 to 40 minutes, until they are soft and the skins begin to shrivel. Remove peppers from oven and place in a brown paper bag to steam for 10 minutes. When cool, remove the loosened skins. To collect the roasted pepper juice, take ½ cup of water and pour on baking sheet while sheet is still hot. Collect liquid in a measuring cup to make ½ cup. In a blender, add the roasted peppers, juice, and saffron, then blend until smooth.

In a 10-inch frying pan, heat the oil and sauté the onion, fennel, basil, garlic, Italian herb blend, marjoram, oregano, thyme, salt, and saffron over medium-low heat for 10 minutes or until the onions are transparent. Add the roasted pepper purée to the sauté mixture and bring to a simmer. Cover and let the flavors blend for 15 minutes before serving, or refrigerate until needed.

Molé Rojo Sauce

YIELD: *1 cup*
TIME: *20 minutes preparation;
    50 minutes cooking*

1 red bell pepper
1 small tomato
1 clove minced garlic
¼ cup water
1 tablespoon molé paste
1 teaspoon paprika
½ teaspoon cumin powder
½ teaspoon sea salt

Spice up any burger or sandwich with this robust sauce.

Preheat oven to 325 degrees F. Wash, dry, halve, and seed the bell pepper. Rub skins with olive oil. Place pepper halves on a baking sheet and roast for 30 to 40 minutes, until they are soft and the skins begin to shrivel. Remove pepper from oven and place in a brown paper bag to steam for 10 minutes. When cool, remove the loosened skins. Blanch, seed, and chop the tomato. In a blender, combine the tomato and roasted pepper with the remaining ingredients and blend until smooth. Transfer mixture to a 1-quart saucepan, heat and serve.

VARIATION
In place of molé paste, mix together 1 tablespoon soybean (hatcho) miso, 1 teaspoon cumin powder, 1 teaspoon coriander powder, and 1 teaspoon unsweetened cocoa powder. Omit paprika and salt and follow above directions.

Sauce Concassé

YIELD: *2 cups*
TIME: *25 minutes preparation;
    1 hour 10 minutes cooking*

1 tablespoon extra virgin olive oil
1 cup finely diced onions
5 cloves minced garlic
½ teaspoon sea salt
*3½ cups fresh tomatoes,
    blanched, peeled, seeded,
    and chopped (about 5
    medium tomatoes)*
¼ cup dry sherry
2 tablespoons chopped fresh basil

This sauce is superb when made with fresh, vine-ripened tomatoes. Serve with Italian Shepherd's Pie, Pecan Nut Loaf, Pistachio Polenta, and Savory Crêpes.

In a 2-quart saucepan, heat the oil and sauté the onions, garlic, and salt over medium-low heat for 10 minutes or until onions are transparent. Add the tomatoes, sherry, and basil, and mix well. Cook mixture uncovered until it reduces down to half the original amount, about 45 minutes to 1 hour. Serve hot or refrigerate in a covered container until needed.

Burgundy Sauce Glaze

YIELD: *1 cup*
TIME: *15 minutes*

⅔ cup red burgundy wine
2 tablespoons barley malt syrup
4 teaspoons tamari
1 clove minced garlic
2 teaspoons arrowroot powder
3 tablespoons cool water

Try this sauce with Garbanzo Bean or Millet Burgers, Breaded Vegetables, or Seitan Pine Nut Roll.

In a 1-quart saucepan, combine the wine, syrup, tamari, and garlic and bring to a simmer. In a small bowl, combine the arrowroot and water and mix until well dissolved. Remove pan from heat, whip in the arrowroot mixture, then return to heat and cook on medium heat for 2 minutes or until thickened. Serve immediately or reheat when ready to use.

Orange Aioli Sauce

YIELD: *2 cups*
TIME: *10 minutes preparation;*
1 hour chilling

1 10½-ounce package extra
firm silken tofu
6 tablespoons frozen orange
juice concentrate
4½ teaspoons yellow prepared
mustard
2 tablespoons extra virgin
olive oil
1 tablespoon apple cider vinegar
2 cloves minced garlic

Serve with Florida Aspic, Avocado Nori Roll, or with any burger.

In a blender, combine all ingredients and blend until smooth. Refrigerate for 1 hour and serve cold.

Quick Espagnole Sauce

YIELD: *4½ cups*
TIME: *20 minutes preparation;*
50 minutes cooking

¼ cup sesame oil
1 cup diced onions
1 cup diced carrots
1 cup diced celery
4 cloves garlic
2 teaspoons basil
2 teaspoons thyme
½ cup unbleached white flour
4¼ cups water
½ cup red wine
½ cup tomato paste
3 tablespoons Bernard Jensen's
Quick Sip or 1 extra
tablespoon tamari
2 tablespoons tamari

This all-purpose sauce is great with stir-fried vegetables, Pecan Nut Loaf, Wild Rice and Corn Loaf, Smoked Mushroom Loaf, American Bounty, and Italian Shepherd's Pie.

In a 2-quart saucepan (with lid), heat the oil and sauté the onions, carrots, celery, garlic, basil, and thyme over high heat, stirring constantly to prevent them from burning. Continue sautéing for about 6 to 12 minutes, or until vegetables are lightly browned. Add flour and stir vigorously until flour is absorbed into the oil. Cook for another minute and add half of the water. When the mixture thickens, stir in remaining water, wine, tomato paste, Quick Sip, and tamari. Stir until mixture becomes smooth. Cover and simmer over low heat for 30 minutes. Remove pan from heat and strain sauce through a mesh strainer. Serve hot or at room temperature.

All good things come by grace and grace comes by art and art doesn't come easy.

Lima Purée Blanc

YIELD: *1½ cups*
TIME: *15 minutes preparation;*
65 minutes cooking

1 yellow bell pepper
2 tablespoons extra virgin
    olive oil
¼ cup chopped Spanish onion
1 clove minced garlic
1 tablespoon white miso
½ cup cooked or frozen lima
    beans
¼ cup white wine
¼ cup water
2 tablespoons lemon juice

The splendid flavor of this sauce has delicate citrus under-tones, making it a perfect choice for Bulgur Walnut Croquettes, Pistachio Polenta, Seafood Patties, Savory Crêpes, and American Bounty.

Preheat oven to 325 degrees F. Wash, dry, halve, and seed the bell pepper. Rub skins with oil. Place pepper halves on a baking sheet and roast for 30 to 40 minutes, until they are soft and the skins begin to shrivel. Remove pepper from oven and place in a brown paper bag to steam for 10 minutes. When cool, remove the loosened skins. In a 10-inch frying pan, heat the oil and sauté the onions, garlic, and white miso in the remaining oil over medium heat for 5 minutes or until onions are transparent. Add the roasted pepper and the remaining ingredients, then simmer for 8 minutes or until the beans are heated through (if using precooked beans) or cooked through (if using frozen beans). Transfer mixture to a blender and blend until smooth. Serve hot or at room temperature as a sauce or dip for raw vegetables and crackers.

Roasted Vegetable Sauce

YIELD: *1½ cups*
TIME: *45 minutes preparation;
40 minutes cooking*

¾ *cup chopped mushrooms*
¾ *cup chopped onions*
½ *cup peeled, chopped carrots*
3 *cloves minced garlic*
2 *tablespoons extra virgin
olive oil*
2 *tablespoons unbleached
white flour*
2 *bay leaves*
1 *tablespoon savory*
1 *teaspoon paprika*
⅛ *teaspoon black pepper*
⅛ *teaspoon sea salt*
1 *cup water*
1 *cup red wine*
2 *tablespoons tamari*
2 *tablespoons tomato paste
dissolved in 2 tablespoons
water*

This sauce is a superb complement to the American Bounty, as well as Anasazi Bean Sandwich Roll and Jewish Seitan Roast.

Preheat oven to 325 degrees F. In a baking pan, toss vegetables in oil to evenly coat them. Spread the vegetables out, then roast for 20 to 30 minutes or until lightly browned. Add flour and mix into vegetables until well blended. Transfer vegetables to a 2-quart saucepan. Add seasonings, water, wine, tamari, and tomato paste, then bring to a simmer over medium heat. Cover and cook for about 3 minutes. Strain sauce through a mesh strainer, pressing the mixture with the back of a ladle to extract all of the liquid. Discard vegetables, heat sauce, and serve.

Condiments

Technically, condiments are aromatic substances that are added to foods to improve their flavor which usually involve culinary preparation before usage. However, when added during cooking they are referred to as seasonings; when added after cooking they are simply called condiments. This latter definition applies to this section and is the way I refer to condiments, even though the terms are interchangeable in modern culinary terminology. The following condiments are designed to support the recipes in this cookbook but can be used to enhance other recipes as well.

In this section I have focused on the fat issue and specifically created some positive options to butter and high fat spreads. The fat issue is important because animal-based fats are energy inefficient (high on the food chain) and high in cholesterol and saturated fat (poor nutrition). Animal-based fats don't reflect an ecological diet. My savory vegetable nut butter spreads are as tasty as they are nutritious. I created a Red Pepper Pistachio Butter for my Italian Bistro Sandwich, pestos for salads and mashed potatoes, and a Cucumber Cilantro Salsa for the Anasazi Bean Sandwich Rolls.

Basil Garlic Olive Oil

YIELD: *1½ cups*
TIME: *10 minutes preparation;*
7 days refrigeration

½ cup extra virgin olive oil
26 medium to large, fresh,
whole basil leaves
1 cup extra virgin olive oil
4 cloves garlic, peeled and
halved

This flavored oil is best in cold foods, since the herbs are heat-infused. Use in salad dressings, and to grill, roast, or sauté vegetables. It's also good in cold pasta salads, and hot pasta dishes or pilafs.

In a 1-quart saucepan, combine the first measure of oil and basil and bring to a simmer, then remove saucepan from heat and set aside to cool completely. When oil is cool, add remaining oil and garlic and pour into a bottle. Refrigerate for a minimum of 1 week. The flavors of this oil will peak after 1 month.

NOTE: The garlic should not be cooked in the oil as its flavor will become bitter.

Onion Butter

YIELD: *1½ cups*
TIME: *15 minutes preparation;*
3 to 4 hours cooking

1 tablespoon corn or extra
virgin olive oil
9 cups sliced Spanish onions
1 teaspoon sea salt (or 2
tablespoons white miso)

This surprising butter is great with Confetti Corn Fritters, and on any bread, canapés, sandwiches, beans, grains, or vegetables.

In a large saucepan or stock pot, heat the oil and sauté the onions and salt over medium heat until the onions are transparent, stirring them frequently. Turn down the heat to very low and continue to gently sauté the onions uncovered, stirring and turning them occasionally, for approximately 3 to 4 hours or until onions reduce down to a purée consistency. Remove saucepan from heat and transfer onions to a container. The onions can be used immediately while they are still hot, cooled to room temperature, or transferred to a covered container and refrigerated until ready to serve.

VARIATION: *Tahini Onion Butter*
In a blender, combine the onion purée with ¾ cup sesame tahini and ¼ cup white miso and blend until smooth.

Almond Squash Butter

YIELD: *2 cups*
TIME: *30 minutes; 3 hours chilling*

2 cups butternut squash
½ cup almond butter
¼ cup sweet white miso (or 1 teaspoon sea salt)
1 tablespoon maple syrup or honey

When I eat a food rich in fat, I also want it rich in flavor and nutrition. Blending nut butters with puréed vegetables proved to be a winning combination. Enjoy this butter on breads, pancakes, or even French toast.

Peel, seed, and cut the squash into ½-inch cubes. In a vegetable steamer, steam the squash for 15 minutes or until soft. In a blender, combine squash, almond butter, miso, and syrup and blend until mixture is smooth and creamy. Transfer to a container and refrigerate for about three hours or overnight to allow the flavors to develop.

VARIATION
Substitute hazelnut butter for the almond butter.

Carrot Pine Nut Butter

YIELD: *1¼ cups*
TIME: *20 minutes*

½ cup pine nuts
1 cup chopped carrots, steamed soft
3 tablespoons water
3 tablespoons extra virgin olive oil
2 tablespoons white miso
1 teaspoon nutritional yeast
1 teaspoon fresh dill

I use this butter almost exclusively as a spread on bread. It is nutritionally superior to butter or margarine.

Preheat oven to 325 degrees F. Spread pine nuts on a baking sheet and roast for about 10 minutes or until lightly browned. Remove pine nuts and transfer to a container to cool. In a blender, combine pine nuts, carrots, water, oil, miso, yeast, and dill and blend until smooth. Serve chilled or at room temperature on breads, crackers, or sandwiches.

Greek Potato Garlic Butter

YIELD: *1½ cups*
TIME: *30 minutes*

2 cups peeled, chopped potatoes
7 cloves garlic
2 tablespoons extra virgin olive oil
¾ teaspoon sea salt

I had the idea for this recipe while dining at one of Chicago's Greek restaurants. A similar butter was served with the bread and provided the inspiration for this recipe.

In a vegetable steamer, steam the potatoes for 15 minutes or until soft. In a blender, combine potatoes, garlic, oil, and salt and blend until smooth. Serve chilled or at room temperature.

Red Pepper Pistachio Butter

YIELD: *1¼ cups*
TIME: *25 minutes preparation;*
40 minutes cooking

2 red bell peppers
2 teaspoons extra virgin olive oil
½ cup pistachio butter
¾ teaspoon sea salt
½ teaspoon fennel seed powder

The fennel, roasted red bell peppers, and pistachio butter make an unusual and delicious spread for your best home-made bread, crackers, or with raw vegetables.

Preheat oven to 325 degrees F. Wash, dry, halve, and seed bell peppers. Rub the skins with oil. Place peppers on a baking sheet and roast for 30 to 40 minutes or until soft and the skins begin to shrivel. Remove from oven and place in a brown paper bag to steam for 10 minutes. When cool, remove loosened skins. In a blender, place roasted peppers and blend until smooth. Add pistachio butter, salt, and fennel, then blend until smooth. Transfer to a container and refrigerate until ready to use.

Walnut Applesauce Butter

YIELD: *2 cups*
TIME: *10 minutes preparation;*
  1 hour chilling

1 cup whole walnuts
1½ cups unsweetened
  applesauce
¼ cup golden or dark raisins

This butter is based on a traditional Jewish recipe which is spread on unleavened breads during Passover. It also makes a great topping for toast, French toast, pancakes, or waffles.

In a blender, place walnuts and grind into a fine meal (this should yield ½ cup). Add applesauce and raisins to the walnut meal, then blend well. Transfer to a container and refrigerate for 1 hour or until chilled.

Cilantro Pesto

YIELD: *1 cup*
TIME: *20 minutes preparation;*
  15 minutes cooking

18 cloves garlic
1 tablespoon extra virgin
  olive oil
1 cup (packed) fresh cilantro
  leaves
1 cup (packed) fresh parsley
½ cup (packed) fresh basil
¼ cup pine nuts
6 tablespoons extra virgin
  olive oil
½ teaspoon sea salt

A plate of cooked pasta or vegetables comes to life with a few tablespoons of pesto mixed in.

Preheat oven to 325 degrees F. Rub the garlic cloves with the first measure of oil. Place on a baking sheet and roast for 15 to 20 minutes, or until lightly browned. Remove sheet from oven and transfer garlic to a container to cool. Wash, dry, and stem the cilantro, parsley, and basil. In a blender, combine roasted garlic, cilantro, parsley, basil, pine nuts, second measure of oil, and salt and blend until smooth. Transfer to a covered container and refrigerate or freeze until ready to use.

VARIATION: *Cilantro Fennel Pesto*
Add 2 teaspoons fennel seed powder to the above ingredients and proceed as directed.

Spinach Basil Pesto

YIELD: *1¾ cup*
TIME: *40 minutes*

24 cloves garlic
*1 tablespoon extra virgin
    olive oil*
½ cup pine nuts
4 cups fresh spinach
1 cup fresh basil
*¼ cup sun-dried tomatoes
    (optional)*
¼ cup water
*3 tablespoons extra virgin
    olive oil*
¾ teaspoon sea salt
*2 tablespoons soy parmesan
    cheese (optional)*

This pesto is made for special guests and your best homemade pasta.

Preheat oven to 325 degrees F. Rub garlic cloves with first measure of oil. Place cloves on a baking sheet and roast for 15 to 20 minutes or until lightly browned. Remove from oven and transfer to a container to cool. Spread pine nuts on a baking sheet and roast for about 15 minutes or until lightly browned. Remove from oven and transfer to another container to cool. Wash, dry, and stem the spinach and basil. In a blender, combine garlic, pine nuts, spinach, basil, tomatoes, water, second measure of oil, salt, and cheese and blend until smooth. Transfer to a container and refrigerate until ready to use.

Sun-Dried Tomato Pesto

YIELD: *1 cup*
TIME: *15 minutes*

¾ cup fresh basil leaves
½ cup sun-dried tomatoes
¾ cup hot water
¼ cup extra virgin olive oil
1 teaspoon sea salt

There are many ways to enjoy this pesto. Spread it on an Italian Bistro Sandwich, Grilled Vegetable Sandwich, or Seitan Pesto Sandwich. For a pasta sauce, use ¼ cup of pesto per serving, and add cooked vegetables, seitan, or tempeh.

Wash, dry, and stem basil. In a small mixing bowl, soak tomatoes in the water for 15 minutes, then drain and reserve the water. In a blender, combine basil, tomatoes, water, oil, and salt and blend until smooth. Transfer to a container and refrigerate until ready to serve.

Cranberry Relish

YIELD: *1½ cups*
TIME: *40 minutes preparation and cooking; 1 hour chilling*

1 cup water
1 cup chopped dried, sweetened cranberries
1 teaspoon canola oil
½ cup diced onion
¼ cup diced yellow bell pepper
1 tablespoon finely chopped orange zest
¼ cup frozen orange juice concentrate
¼ cup frozen cranberry juice concentrate
¼ cup chopped golden or dark seedless raisins
¼ teaspoon sea salt
2 tablespoons arrowroot powder dissolved in ¼ cup cool water
1½ teaspoons finely minced fresh parsley

Cranberries are not only for the holidays! They can be enjoyed all year long with this relish. Serve it with burgers, sandwiches, and any savory entrée.

In a 1-quart saucepan (with lid), heat the water to boiling, then add the cranberries and remove from heat. Cover and soak the berries for 7 minutes, then drain and set aside. In a 10-inch frying pan, heat the oil and sauté the onions, bell pepper, and zest on medium heat for 5 minutes or until onions are transparent. Add both frozen juice concentrates, raisins, cranberries, and salt to the sautéed vegetables, then bring to a simmer. Add arrowroot/water mixture and stir constantly until thickened. Add the parsley, then transfer the relish to a covered container and refrigerate for 1 hour or until well chilled.

Cucumber Cilantro Salsa

YIELD: *2 cups*
TIME: *25 minutes preparation;*
1 hour chilling

1 tablespoon extra virgin
    olive oil
2 tablespoons apple cider
    vinegar
1 tablespoon brown rice syrup
2 cloves minced garlic
⅛ teaspoon paprika
⅛ teaspoon sea salt
1 medium diced red onion
½ cup peeled, seeded, diced
    cucumber
¼ seeded, diced orange bell
    pepper
1 tablespoon chopped fresh
    cilantro
1 tablespoon diced sun-dried
    tomato

Serve this salsa with Anasazi Bean Sandwich Rolls, Black Bean and Corn Roll, and as a filling for the Black Bean Cracker Cups.

In a 1-quart saucepan, combine oil, vinegar, syrup, garlic, paprika, and salt and bring to a boil. Remove from heat and set aside. Add onion, cucumber, bell pepper, cilantro, and tomato and mix well. Transfer to a covered container and refrigerate for 1 hour or until well chilled. Serve cold.

"My friends were of differing faiths and all came, originally, from different regions of the country. We had hardly any culinary traditions in common. Eating always filled us with a sense of adventure and discovery."
—MADHUR JAFFREY

Tricolor Salsa

YIELD: *1 cup*
TIME: *30 minutes; 1 hour chilling*

1 teaspoon extra virgin olive oil
½ cup diced Spanish onions
1 clove minced garlic
¼ teaspoon sea salt
¼ cup finely diced red bell pepper
¼ cup finely diced yellow bell pepper
¼ cup finely diced orange bell pepper
¼ cup water
¼ cup apple cider vinegar
1 tablespoon honey or FruitSource syrup
2 teaspoons chopped fresh cilantro
1½ teaspoons arrowroot dissolved in 1 tablespoon cool water
¼ cup peeled, seeded, and finely diced papaya

This salsa goes well with any of the burgers. Serve it as you would a pickle relish with the Anasazi Bean Sandwich Roll, Black Bean and Corn Roll, or as a filling for Black Bean Cracker Cups.

In a 10-inch frying pan, heat the oil and sauté the onions, garlic, and salt over medium heat for 5 minutes or until onions are transparent. Add the bell peppers, water, vinegar, honey, and cilantro. Bring ingredients to a simmer, then add the arrowroot/water mixture, and cook until thickened, stirring constantly. Remove pan from heat and add papaya. Let the salsa cool completely, then transfer to a covered container and refrigerate for 1 hour or until chilled. Serve either cold or at room temperature with chips.

Curried Dijon Topping

YIELD: *5 cups*
TIME: *10 minutes preparation;*
55 minutes cooking

1½ cups unsweetened coconut
⅔ cup whole almonds
½ cup extra virgin olive oil
3 cloves minced garlic
3 tablespoons curry powder
2 teaspoons sea salt
1 teaspoon Hungarian paprika
1 cup white wine
1 cup whole grain bread
crumbs
½ cup minced fresh parsley

This is a savory topping which may be used on Curried Vegetable Casserole, English Curry Stir-Fry, or Garbanzos and Millet with African Peanut Sauce.

Preheat oven to 325 degrees F. Spread coconut on a baking sheet and toast in oven for about 5 to 10 minutes or until lightly browned. Remove coconut and transfer to a container to cool. Spread almonds on baking sheet and roast for about 15 to 20 minutes or until lightly browned and very fragrant. Remove almonds and transfer to another container to cool. In a blender, place cooled coconut, finely grind and set aside, then grind cooled nuts into a meal and set aside. In a 10-inch frying pan, heat oil and sauté the coconut, almond meal, garlic, curry, salt, and paprika over medium heat for 5 minutes. Add the wine and reduce until no liquid remains. Add bread crumbs and parsley, then continue to sauté for 3 minutes longer. Remove pan from heat and cool. Transfer mixture to a container and refrigerate until ready to use.

Miso Demi-Glace

YIELD: *6 tablespoons*
TIME: *10 minutes*

2 tablespoons dark miso
2 tablespoons tamari
1 tablespoon barley malt syrup
1 tablespoon water

Three tablespoons of this demi-glace will give a more robust flavor to any savory sauce. Since the sodium content of this recipe is rather high, it is best not to add salt to the sauce until after adding the demi-glace.

In a mixing bowl, combine miso, tamari, syrup, and water and beat with a whisk until well blended. Drizzle on top of American Bounty, Pecan Nut Loaf, or Wild Rice and Corn Loaf.

Vegetable Side Dishes

The word "vegetarian" comes from the Latin vegetus, meaning whole, energetic, and full of life. In the ecological diet, vegetables are the most efficient transporter of Earth's energy into our bodies. Animals and sea life draw their energy from vegetation. Vegetables that grow beneath the earth (root vegetables) draw energy from the earth, and vegetables that grow above the earth draw energy from both the sun and the earth. Vegetables are the jewels of super nutrition because they carry the vitamins, minerals, and carbohydrates necessary to thrive in the realm of health.

Ecology entails using what nature gives us to live on—an abundance of vegetation. My use of vegetables covers virtually every savory dish I create. The vegetable side dishes are designed to support entrées that don't have an abundance of vegetables in them. For example, BBQ Seitan does not have a substantial amount of vegetables and can use a vegetable side dish in order to create balance. This section was designed to support those types of recipes with creative flavors and combinations.

Breaded Vegetables

YIELD: *4 servings*
TIME: *35 minutes*

Breading

¾ cup whole wheat bread flour
¼ cup gluten flour
4 teaspoons oregano
4 teaspoons basil
2 teaspoons granulated garlic
2 teaspoons sea salt
½ teaspoon white pepper

2 cups water
*1 cup whole grain bread
   crumbs*
6 slices eggplant
*12 slices (total) zucchini,
   carrots, and/or yellow
   squash*
*2 medium portobello
   mushrooms*
½ cup olive or sesame oil

Serve with Italian Country Loaf, Smoked Mushroom Loaf, and Navy Beans Tarragon.

In a mixing bowl, combine the breading ingredients and mix well. In another bowl, pour the water. In a shallow bowl or large plate, place the whole grain bread crumbs. Dip each vegetable into the water. Drain for a few seconds, dredge in breading mixture, dip quickly back into the water, and then in bread crumbs. Make sure each piece of vegetable is completely coated with bread crumbs on all sides. Place each finished vegetable on a plate. In a 10-inch frying pan, heat the oil over medium heat until hot and fry vegetables until golden on both sides, drain on paper towels, and serve hot.

Grilled Vegetables

YIELD: *4 servings*
TIME: *24 hours marinating;*
   30 minutes cooking

Marinade

3 cups water
1½ cups apple cider vinegar
1 tablespoon chopped fresh basil
1 tablespoon chopped fresh
   oregano
2 teaspoons sea salt
1 teaspoon thyme
1 teaspoon dill weed
1 teaspoon black pepper

Vegetables

4 mushrooms, halved
2 whole plum tomatoes, halved
1 small onion, halved
1 red bell pepper, quartered
½ yellow squash, cut lengthwise
   into ½-inch thick slices
½ acorn squash, cut into ½-
   inch thick slices
½ eggplant, cut lengthwise into
   ½-inch thick slices
5 shallots (optional)

Serve with Garbanzo Bean Burger, American Bounty, and Pistachio Polenta.

In a mixing bowl, combine the marinade ingredients and mix well. Add the vegetables to the marinade, making sure that they are all submerged, and marinate for at least 24 hours. When ready to grill, drain the vegetables and grill them either under a broiler, on a stove-top grill, or on an outdoor grill until the vegetables are soft but still firm. Serve hot.

NOTE: Soft vegetables such as tomatoes and mushrooms, which cook more quickly, must be grilled separately from the firm vegetables such as the acorn squash.

VARIATION
The grilled vegetables can be cooled and served as a salad.

Eggplant Roll

YIELD: *3 servings*

TIME: *20 minutes preparation;*
25 minutes cooking

1 large eggplant (4 to 6 inches
    in diameter)
1 tablespoon extra virgin
    olive oil
1 teaspoon sea salt
1 teaspoon extra virgin olive oil
1 cup peeled carrots, cut French
    fry–style
1 cup green string beans, cut
    in half lengthwise
½ cup sliced onions
1 teaspoon chopped fresh
    rosemary
1 clove minced garlic
¼ teaspoon sea salt

Serve with Eggless Frittata, Tofu Cacciatore, and Wild Rice
and Corn Loaf.

Preheat broiler. From the widest portion of the eggplant cut
6 crosswise slices, ¼ inch thick (use remaining eggplant for
another recipe). Thinly coat eggplant slices with a small
amount of oil. Sprinkle salt on both sides and place slices on
a lightly oiled baking sheet. Place the sheet under the broiler
and broil eggplant until lightly browned. Remove from oven
and allow eggplant to cool completely. In a 10-inch frying
pan, heat the oil and sauté the carrots, string beans, onions,
rosemary, garlic, and salt over medium heat for 8 to 10 minutes, or until vegetables are tender-crisp. Remove pan from
heat. Divide vegetables evenly into 6 portions. Place each portion in the center of each eggplant slice so that the vegetables
form a line from one side to the other. Arrange green beans so
they extend slightly beyond one edge, and the carrots slightly
beyond the other. Roll up each eggplant slice and lay seam
side down on a serving plate. Serve immediately with either
Sauce Concassé or Sauce Renaissance.

NOTE: This dish can be made ahead of time and refrigerated
for later use. When ready to serve, simply heat in a covered
baking dish in a 350 degree F oven for 5 minutes or until
heated through.

Pesto String Beans

YIELD: *4 servings*
TIME: *30 minutes*

3 cups yellow wax string beans
2 teaspoons extra virgin olive oil
1 cup diced red bell pepper
1 cup diced onion
¼ teaspoon sea salt
½ cup water
6 tablespoons Spinach Basil Pesto
(page 167)

Serve with Italian Country Loaf, Tofu Cacciatore, and Italian Bistro Sandwich.

In a vegetable steamer, steam the string beans for 5 minutes or until tender-crisp. Remove beans and set aside. In a 10-inch frying pan, heat the oil and sauté the bell pepper, onions, and salt over medium heat for 5 minutes or until onions are transparent. Add the beans, water, and pesto and sauté for 5 minutes longer, stirring frequently. Remove pan from heat, transfer vegetables to a serving dish, and serve immediately.

Subji

YIELD: *5 servings*
TIME: *35 minutes preparation;*
30 minutes cooking

2 cups carrots, peeled, sliced into
half-moons
2 cups broccoli, stems and florets
2 cups cauliflower florets
1 tablespoon canola oil
2 cups chopped onions
2 cloves minced garlic
1 teaspoon coriander powder
1 teaspoon cardamom powder
1 teaspoon garam masala
(optional)
1 teaspoon curry powder
½ teaspoon sea salt
⅛ teaspoon ground white pepper

Serve with Curried Vegetable Casserole, Eggless Frittata, and Millet Burger.

In a vegetable steamer, steam carrots for 8 minutes or until tender-crisp. Remove carrots and rinse in cold water. Peel and thinly slice the broccoli stems, steam for 1 minute, then remove and rinse in cold water. Steam broccoli and cauliflower florets together for 2 minutes or until the broccoli is bright green and tender-crisp. Remove and rinse in cold water. In a 10-inch frying pan, heat the oil and sauté the onions, garlic, coriander, cardamom, garam masala, curry, salt, and pepper on medium heat for 5 to 8 minutes or until onions are transparent. Add carrots, broccoli, and cauliflower, then sauté until the vegetables are heated through and the spices infused with the vegetables. Serve hot.

Green Beans New Orleans

YIELD: *4 servings*
TIME: *20 minutes preparation; 25 minutes cooking*

2 cups green beans, ends trimmed, cut diagonally
2 teaspoons canola oil
¼ cup finely diced red bell pepper
¼ cup finely diced Spanish onion
¼ cup finely diced celery
2 cloves minced garlic
¼ teaspoon sea salt
6 drops liquid hickory smoke (optional)
¼ cup commercially prepared seitan "ham," smoked tempeh, or tofu, chopped into ½-inch pieces (optional)

Serve with Smoked Mushroom Loaf, BBQ Seitan or BBQ Tempeh, and Grilled Vegetable Sandwich.

In a vegetable steamer, steam the beans for 5 minutes or until they turn bright green and tender-crisp. Remove beans and rinse under cold water, then drain and set aside. In a 10-inch frying pan, heat the oil and sauté the bell pepper, onion, celery, garlic, and salt over medium heat for 5 minutes or until the onions are transparent. Add beans, liquid smoke, and seitan "ham" and cook another 5 minutes to thoroughly blend the seasonings. Serve hot.

Asparagus with Yellow Pepper Sauce

YIELD: *3 servings*
TIME: *20 minutes*

15 medium to small asparagus spears
½ cup warmed Yellow Pepper Sauce (page 154) or Mango Dressing (page 75)

Serve with Seafood Patties, Seitan Pine Nut Crêpes, and Seitan Reuben Sandwich.

Remove white bottom third of the asparagus spears (save for use in soup stocks). Cut away center third of spears (save for use in stir-frys); the tips alone will be used. In a vegetable steamer, steam the asparagus tips for 5 minutes or until they turn bright green and are tender-crisp. Remove asparagus and rinse under cold water, then drain. Serve with either sauce or dressing.

Green Beans with Smoked Portobello Mushrooms

YIELD: *6 servings*
TIME: *35 minutes*

2 cups fresh green beans (about ½ pound), ends trimmed
1 tablespoon canola oil
1 cup chopped Smoked Portobello Mushrooms (page 18) (or use unsmoked mushrooms and add ¼ teaspoon liquid hickory smoke to sautéed vegetables during last few minutes)
¾ cup diced red onions
2 cloves minced garlic
1 teaspoon thyme
½ teaspoon sea salt

Serve with Seitan Burger, Pecan Nut Loaf, and Tofu Carbonara.

In a vegetable steamer, steam beans for 5 minutes or until tender-crisp. In a 10-inch frying pan, heat the oil and sauté the mushrooms, onions, garlic, thyme, and salt on medium heat for 5 minutes or until the onions are transparent. Add beans (and liquid smoke if necessary), and cook until beans are heated through. Serve hot.

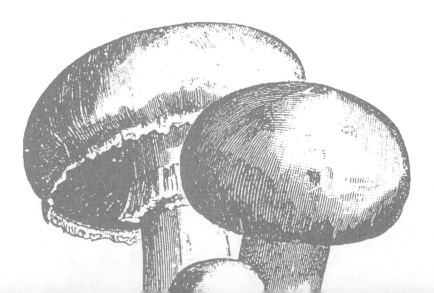

German Braised Red Cabbage

YIELD: *4 servings*
TIME: *20 minutes preparation;*
35 minutes cooking

1 tablespoon sesame oil
4 cups thinly sliced red cabbage
1 cup diced onions
½ cup peeled, shredded carrots
1 cup peeled, cored, diced
Granny Smith apples
(about 1 apple)
6 cloves minced garlic
¼ cup dark raisins
2 tablespoons apple cider
vinegar
2 tablespoons honey
1 teaspoon sea salt
¼ teaspoon liquid hickory
smoke (optional)
¹⁄₁₆ teaspoon cinnamon

Serve with Smoked Mushroom Loaf, American Bounty, and Tofu Carbonara.

In a 2-quart saucepan (with lid), heat the oil on high heat and sauté the cabbage, onions, carrots, apples, and garlic for 3 minutes. Add raisins, vinegar, honey, salt, liquid smoke, and cinnamon and reduce heat to medium. Simmer covered for about 30 minutes or until cabbage is tender but firm. Serve hot.

Traditional supermarket foods have a 4 percent annual growth while healthy foods have a 16 percent annual growth. The natural foods industry is a 20 billion dollar a year industry.

Ragoût of Winter Vegetables

YIELD: *4 servings*
TIME: *25 minutes preparation;*
35 minutes cooking

2 6-inch pieces kombu soaked
in 2 cups water
1 cup onion chunks
1 cup peeled, roll-cut carrots
1 cup peeled, roll-cut parsnips
1 cup turnip or rutabaga
chunks
½ cup peeled, butternut
squash chunks
½ teaspoon sea salt
1 tablespoon tamari
1½ teaspoons ginger juice (or
½ teaspoon ginger powder)
1 tablespoon arrowroot or corn
starch dissolved in 2
tablespoons cool water
½ cup finely chopped fresh
parsley

Serve with Wild Rice and Corn Loaf, Seitan Pine Nut Roll, and Pecan Nut Loaf.

Slice each kombu strip crosswise into ½-inch pieces. In a 2-quart saucepan (with lid), place the kombu at the bottom, then add the onions, carrots, parsnips, turnips, squash, and soaking water. Sprinkle vegetables with salt and simmer covered on medium heat for 20 to 30 minutes or until the vegetables are slightly soft and the water is reduced to one cup. When vegetables are cooked, add tamari, ginger, and arrowroot/water mixture, and continue cooking until thickened. Stir in parsley and serve hot.

Sautéed Arame and Vegetables

YIELD: *4 servings*
TIME: *40 minutes*

⅔ cup dry arame, soaked,
    drained
2 cups water
1 tablespoon sesame oil
2 cups peeled, julienned carrot
2 cups thinly sliced fresh fennel
2 cups thinly sliced fresh leeks
    (use lower ⅓ of stem only)
1 teaspoon ginger powder
1 teaspoon fennel powder
½ teaspoon sea salt
2 tablespoons mirin or
    sweet sherry

Serve with Seafood Patties, Golumpke, and Tofu Bonne Femme.

In a 1-quart saucepan, combine the arame and water and cook on medium heat for about 7 to 10 minutes. Remove from heat, drain, and set aside. In a 10-inch skillet, heat the oil and sauté the carrots on medium heat for 4 minutes. Add fennel, leeks, ginger, fennel powder, and salt, and sauté for 7 minutes. Add arame and mirin, then continue cooking another 1 to 2 minutes or until mixture is heated thoroughly. Serve hot.

Sugar Snap Peas with Carrots and Walnuts

YIELD: *4 servings*
TIME: *25 minutes*

2 tablespoons walnuts
1 cup peeled, roll-cut carrots
1 teaspoon sesame oil
1 cup sugar snap peas
4 teaspoons Sucanat
⅜ teaspoon sea salt
½ teaspoon allspice
2 tablespoons water

Serve with Beans in Red Wine Sauce, American Bounty, and Jewish Seitan Roast.

Preheat oven to 325 degrees F. Spread the walnuts on a baking sheet and roast for 15 minutes or until lightly browned and very fragrant. Remove walnuts and transfer to a container to cool slightly. When cool, chop walnuts coarsely. In a vegetable steamer, steam carrots for 5 minutes or until tender-crisp. In a 10-inch frying pan, heat the oil and sauté the walnuts, carrots, snap peas, Sucanat, salt, and allspice on medium heat for about 6 minutes. Add the water and stir well to deglaze the pan and disperse the flavors through the vegetables. Serve hot.

Sweet Potato and Carrot Tzimmes

YIELD: *5 servings*
TIME: *25 minutes*

1½ cups peeled, diced sweet
 potatoes
1½ cups peeled, diced carrots
1 tablespoon unrefined corn oil
½ cup diced onions
¾ teaspoon sea salt
¼ teaspoon clove powder
½ cup chopped prunes
¼ cup honey

Serve with Jewish Seitan Roast, American Bounty, and Smoked Mushroom Loaf.

In a vegetable steamer, steam the sweet potatoes and carrots for about 10 minutes or until tender. In a 10-inch frying pan heat the oil and sauté the onions, salt, and cloves on medium heat for about 5 minutes or until the onions are transparent. Add the steamed vegetables, prunes, and honey and sauté another 5 minutes. Transfer to a serving dish and serve hot.

Sweet Potatoes, Carrots, and Cranberries

YIELD: *6 servings*
TIME: *15 minutes preparation;*
 20 minutes cooking

3 cups peeled, coarsely chopped
 sweet potato
2 cups peeled baby carrots,
 coarsely chopped
¼ cup maple syrup or honey
¼ cup dried cranberries
¼ teaspoon allspice powder
¼ teaspoon sea salt
2 teaspoons arrowroot powder
 dissolved in 2 tablespoons
 cool water
2 tablespoons chopped fresh
 parsley

Serve with American Bounty, Smoked Mushroom Loaf, and Tofu Carbonara.

In a vegetable steamer, steam the sweet potatoes and carrots for about 10 minutes or until tender. In a 1-quart saucepan, combine the syrup, cranberries, allspice, and salt and cook on medium heat for about 5 minutes. Add the arrowroot/water mixture and gently stir in half of the parsley and vegetables. Continue cooking another 1 to 2 minutes or until mixture is heated thoroughly. Transfer to a serving dish, top with remaining parsley, and serve hot.

Side Dish Grains & Potatoes

Pilaf (also known as pilau, plaw, and pilaw) is defined as a rice dish made with herbs, meats, and vegetables in a broth. The following pilafs don't call for meats or a broth; instead the vegetables and seasonings are cooked with the grains.

Grains are the heart and soul of good nutrition and an important food in ecological cuisine since they are plant-based, high in complex carbohydrates and fiber, and low in fat and protein. These attributes make them the ideal food. Pilafs are a wonderful way to enjoy eating grains because of the limitless creativity in grain cookery. It is best to serve an entrée such as Tofu Cacciatore on a bed of plain cooked rice or other grain to avoid a clash of flavors. Regardless of how they are served, carbohydrates are an essential component of any nutritionally balanced ecological menu.

In this section, there are some splendid pilaf and potato recipes. Potato Pancakes, Pesto Mashed Potatoes, Italian Pistachio Pilaf, and Chestnut Pilaf with Black Rice are some of the recipes you will have the opportunity to savor. I often eat a pilaf as an entire meal, especially the Italian Pistachio Pilaf. Pilafs and side dishes are my favorite courses.

Bulgur Walnut Croquettes

YIELD: *8 servings*
TIME: *20 minutes preparation;*
25 minutes cooking

1½ tablespoons extra virgin
    olive oil
1 cup finely diced onions
1 cup peeled, finely diced carrot
1 tablespoon granulated garlic
    (or 6 cloves minced garlic)
1½ teaspoons ground anise
½ teaspoon black pepper
2 cups water
1 cup bulgur
1 cup chopped walnuts
3 tablespoons low-sodium
    tamari (or 2 tablespoons
    regular tamari)
6 tablespoons gluten flour
    combined with 6 tablespoons
    unbleached white flour
canola oil for deep frying

Serve with Italian Country Loaf, Smoked Mushroom Loaf, and Tofu Carbonara, or use as a filling for Savory Crêpes.

In a 10-inch frying pan (with lid), heat the oil and sauté the onions, carrot, garlic, anise, and pepper for 5 minutes or until onions are transparent. Add the water, bulgur, walnuts, and tamari and stir until evenly combined. Cover and cook until the mixture thickens, then remove from heat and stir in the gluten/flour mixture until well blended. Form the mixture into croquettes using about 2½ tablespoons per croquette. In a large pot or deep-fryer, heat the oil to 350 degrees F and deep-fry the croquettes for 2 to 3 minutes or until lightly browned. Drain on paper towels and serve hot with Spinach Basil Pesto or Carbonara Sauce.

NOTE: When deep-frying, it is important to bring the oil to 350 degrees F to avoid saturating the croquettes with oil.

Wehani Rice Pilaf

YIELD: *8 servings*
TIME: *10 minutes preparation;*
  1 hour 20 minutes cooking

1 cup wehani rice
2 cups water
$\frac{1}{16}$ teaspoon sea salt
4 dried shiitake mushrooms
1 cup hot water
1 tablespoon sesame oil
1¼ cups chopped onions
¼ cup finely diced celery
3 cloves minced garlic (or 1
  teaspoon granulated garlic)
1 teaspoon ginger powder
1 teaspoon sea salt

Serve with Tofu Bonne Femme, Eggless Frittata, and Navy Beans Tarragon.

Wash and drain the rice and combine in a 2-quart saucepan (with lid) with the water and salt. Bring to a simmer over medium heat and cover, reduce heat to low, and simmer for 45 minutes. Do not remove lid. Remove from heat and allow to sit covered for 10 minutes. Fluff with a fork and set aside. Meanwhile, soak the mushrooms in hot water for 1 hour. After soaking, drain the mushrooms (the soaking water makes an excellent soup stock) and squeeze out excess water, then thinly slice. In a 10-inch frying pan, heat the oil and sauté the mushrooms, onions, celery, garlic, ginger, and salt for 5 minutes or until onions are transparent. Add the cooked rice, stir to blend the flavors, then turn off heat and let sit covered for 10 minutes. Serve immediately.

VARIATION

To serve as an entrée, increase the portion size to 1 cup and add ¼ cup of seitan or any cooked bean to frying pan before mixing in the rice.

Southern Black-Eyed Pilaf

YIELD: *4 servings*
TIME: *20 minutes preparation;*
  20 minutes cooking

2 tablespoons unrefined corn oil
1½ cups chopped fresh fennel
1 cup sliced okra
3 tablespoons finely diced
  onions
2 tablespoons minced shallots
3 cloves minced garlic
8 sprigs fresh thyme
½ teaspoon sea salt
⅛ teaspoon white pepper
2 cups cooked short grain
  brown rice
2 cups cooked black-eyed peas
1 cup cooked or canned hominy
½ cup finely diced red bell
  peppers
½ cup finely diced yellow
  bell peppers
½ cup finely diced green
  bell peppers
chopped pecans and chopped
  parsley for garnish

Serve with BBQ Seitan and BBQ Tempeh, Anasazi Bean Sandwich Rolls, and any of the burgers.

In a 10-inch frying pan, heat the oil and sauté the fennel, okra, onions, shallots, garlic, and seasonings over medium heat for 5 minutes or until onions are transparent. Add the brown rice, peas, and hominy and heat thoroughly. Add the bell peppers and mix well. Garnish with pecans and parsley. Serve immediately.

Chestnut Pilaf with Black Rice

YIELD: *4 servings*
TIME: *30 minutes preparation;
1 hour 15 minutes cooking*

1 cup black rice
2 cups water
$1/16$ teaspoon sea salt
1 6½-ounce package frozen
    chestnuts (or 1 cup by
    volume)
1 tablespoon extra virgin
    olive oil
½ cup finely diced onions
½ cup finely diced red bell
    peppers
½ cup finely diced fresh fennel
    (or ½ cup finely diced fresh
    celery with 1 teaspoon
    fennel seed powder)
2 cloves minced garlic
½ teaspoon sea salt
2 tablespoons chopped fresh
    parsley

Serve with American Bounty, Smoked Mushroom Loaf, and any savory crêpe variation. If black rice is unavailable, use brown, wehani, wild, or white rice alone or in combination.

Wash and drain the rice and combine in a 2-quart saucepan (with lid) with the water and salt. Cover and simmer for 45 minutes. Do not remove lid. Remove from heat and allow to sit covered for 15 minutes. Fluff with fork. Preheat oven to 375 degrees F. Place the chestnuts on a baking sheet and roast for 30 minutes or until lightly browned and very fragrant. Remove chestnuts and transfer to a container to cool. Once cool, chop chestnuts into quarter pieces and set aside. In a 10-inch frying pan, heat the oil and sauté the onions, bell pepper, fennel, garlic, and salt for about 5 minutes or until the onions are transparent. When the rice is finished cooking, add the sautéed vegetables, roasted chestnuts, and chopped parsley to the saucepan, mix well, and serve.

Wild Rice and Cabbage Pilaf

YIELD: *6 servings*

TIME: *30 minutes preparation;*
2 hours 10 minutes cooking

1 tablespoon canola oil

½ cup diced onion

½ cup diced celery

3 cloves minced garlic

1 tablespoon thyme

2 teaspoons dark miso

1½ teaspoons powdered, dried
shiitake mushrooms

½ teaspoon sea salt

¼ teaspoon allspice

1¼ cups wild rice, washed
and drained

2½ cups water

⅜ cup dried apricots

¾ cup hot water

2 cups water

2 tablespoons apple cider
vinegar

1½ cups shredded red cabbage

1 tablespoon apple cider
vinegar

chopped fresh parsley for
garnish

Serve with Seitan Pine Nut Crêpes, Golumpke, and Tofu Carbonara.

In a 2-quart saucepan (with lid), heat the oil and sauté the onions, celery, garlic, thyme, miso, mushrooms, salt, and allspice over medium heat for 3 minutes. Add rice and first measure of water, bring to a simmer and cook covered about 1½ hours or until rice is soft and all the water is absorbed. Meanwhile, chop the apricots and soak in the hot water for 20 minutes, then drain and set aside. In a small saucepan, combine the third measure of water and vinegar and bring to a simmer over medium heat. Add the cabbage and blanch for about 6 seconds. Drain cabbage immediately and set aside to cool. With your hands, rub the second measure of vinegar into the cabbage until it turns a brighter red color. Set the cabbage aside. When the rice is finished cooking, add the apricots and red cabbage. Mix well and garnish with chopped parsley. Serve immediately.

Bulgur Potato Pilaf

YIELD: *4 servings*

TIME: *25 minutes preparation;
40 minutes cooking*

¼ cup walnuts

¾ cup water

½ cup bulgur

2 cups peeled, diced russet
potatoes

1 tablespoon sesame oil

1¼ cups finely diced onions

1 cup halved mushrooms

¼ cup chopped sauerkraut

6 cloves minced garlic

2 teaspoons dried thyme leaves

2 teaspoons chili powder

¾ teaspoon sea salt

¼ cup finely chopped fresh
parsley

Serve with Golumpke, Jewish Seitan Roast, and Vermont Seitan with Chestnuts.

Preheat oven to 350 degrees F. Place the walnuts on a baking sheet and roast for 20 minutes or until lightly browned and fragrant. Remove walnuts and transfer to a container to cool. Once cool, chop walnuts coarsely and set aside. In a 1-quart saucepan (with lid), combine the water and bulgur, bring to a simmer and then cover. Remove from heat and let bulgur sit to absorb water. In a vegetable steamer, steam potatoes for 15 minutes or until firm but soft, then drain and cool. In a 10-inch frying pan heat the oil and sauté the onions, mushrooms, sauerkraut, garlic, thyme, chili powder, and salt for about 5 minutes or until onions are translucent. Add the potatoes, bulgur, nuts, and parsley, then mix well. Heat thoroughly, then remove from heat and let sit for 1 minute to marry the flavors. Serve immediately.

"The body is recycled air and water, and food is recycled energy. Our bodies are one step in the process."

—DEPAK CHOPRA

Greek Pilaf

YIELD: *4 servings*

TIME: *25 minutes preparation;*
45 minutes cooking

½ cup wehani rice
1 cup water
⅟₁₆ teaspoon sea salt
½ cup white basmati rice
1 cup water
⅟₁₆ teaspoon sea salt
1 tablespoon extra virgin
    olive oil
1 cup finely diced onion
½ cup finely diced red bell
    pepper
½ cup pitted, chopped, black
    Kalamata olives
6 cloves minced garlic
1 teaspoon dried oregano
⅛ teaspoon sea salt
¼ cup finely chopped fresh
    parsley

Serve with Eggless Frittata, Mediterranean Salad, and Grilled Vegetable Sandwich.

Wash, rinse, and drain the two rices individually. Place each rice in separate 1-quart saucepans (with lids) with separate measures of water and salt, and cook covered for 45 minutes. Do not remove lids. Remove both saucepans from heat and allow to sit covered for 15 minutes. Combine the rices, fluff with a fork, and set aside. In a 10-inch frying pan, heat the oil, and sauté the onion, bell pepper, olives, garlic, oregano, and salt on medium heat for about 5 minutes or until the onions are transparent. Add the two rices to the sautéed vegetables and stir for 1 minute. Remove from heat, top with parsley and serve immediately.

VARIATION

By adding 2 cups flaked seitan, cooked beans, or diced tofu or tempeh, this side dish becomes a main course meal.

Italian Pistachio Pilaf

YIELD: *6 servings*
TIME: *45 minutes*

1 cup white basmati rice
1¾ cups water
¹⁄₁₆ teaspoon sea salt
2 tablespoons extra virgin olive oil
1 cup diced onions
6 cloves minced garlic
2 cups seitan, thinly sliced (page 112)
1 cup diced red bell pepper
2 tablespoons fennel seed powder
½ teaspoon sea salt
¼ teaspoon black pepper (optional)
1 cup sliced scallions
½ cup chopped pistachios

Serve with Italian Mixed Greens Salad, Roasted Vegetable Terrine, and Grilled Vegetable Sandwich.

Wash and drain the rice twice and combine in a 2-quart saucepan (with lid) with the water and salt. Bring to a simmer over medium heat and cover, reduce heat to low, and simmer for 15 minutes or until rice is soft and all of the water is absorbed. Remove from heat, fluff rice with a fork, and set aside. In a 10-inch frying pan, heat the oil and sauté the onions and garlic over medium heat for 5 minutes or until onions become transparent. Add the seitan, bell pepper, fennel, salt, and pepper and sauté for another 3 minutes. Add the rice, scallions, and pistachios, and mix well. Serve ½ cup of pilaf per person along with a vegetable side dish or salad.

VARIATION: *Italian Pistachio Crêpes*
Preheat oven to 375 degrees F. Prepare Savory Crêpes (page 111). Use ¼ cup filling per crêpe and roll up. Place crêpes into baking dish, brush with water, then cover with a tightly fitting lid. Bake for 20 minutes and serve with Carbonara Sauce, Fresh Basil Sauce, Sardaline Sauce, Saffron Sauce, Quick Espagnole Sauce, or Roasted Vegetable Sauce.

Harvest Pilaf

YIELD: *6 servings*
TIME: *30 minutes preparation;*
45 minutes cooking

½ cup pumpkin seeds
1 cup long grain brown rice
2 cups water
¹⁄₁₆ teaspoon sea salt
1 tablespoon canola oil
½ cup diced onion
½ cup fresh or frozen kernel
corn
2 cloves minced garlic
2 teaspoons whole savory
1 teaspoon sage
1 teaspoon cumin powder
1 teaspoon sea salt
½ cup peeled, grated carrot
½ cup diced celery

Serve with American Bounty, Smoked Mushroom Loaf, and Tofu Carbonara.

Preheat oven to 325 degrees F. Place pumpkin seeds on baking sheet and roast for 10 to 15 minutes or until they begin to pop and are lightly browned and fragrant. Remove pan and immediately transfer seeds to a container to stop the roasting. Wash and drain the rice and combine in a 2-quart saucepan (with lid) with the water and salt. Bring to a simmer over medium heat and cover, reduce heat to low, and simmer for 1 hour or until rice is soft and all of the water is absorbed. Remove from heat, fluff rice with a fork, and transfer to a casserole or large serving bowl. In a 10-inch frying pan, heat the oil and sauté the onion, corn, garlic, and seasonings over medium heat for 5 minutes or until onion is transparent. Towards the end of the sauté time, add the carrot and celery and sauté for 1 to 2 minutes. Remove pan from heat and add the sautéed vegetables and pumpkin seeds to cooked rice. Mix well and serve immediately.

Potatoes Bonne Femme

YIELD: *4 servings*

TIME: *25 minutes preparation;*
   35 minutes cooking

4 large potatoes
2 tablespoons canola oil
1½ cups diced onions
1 cup peeled, diced carrots
4 cloves minced garlic
¼ teaspoon black pepper
½ teaspoon dried thyme leaves
1 10½-ounce package firm
   silken tofu
1 cup soy milk
3 tablespoons white miso
1 tablespoon arrowroot powder
1 cup fresh or frozen peas
¼ cup each finely diced red bell
   pepper and finely chopped
   fresh parsley for garnish

Serve with any of the burgers, Vermont Seitan with Chestnuts, and Beans in Red Wine Sauce.

Preheat oven to 375 degrees F. Wash the potatoes well, then prick the skin in several places with a fork. Place potatoes on a baking sheet and bake for about 45 minutes or until soft. Remove potatoes and slice in half down the middle, more than halfway down but not through the skins. Set each potato, open side up, on a serving plate. In a 10-inch frying pan, heat the oil and sauté the onions, carrots, garlic, pepper, and thyme over medium heat for 5 minutes or until onions are transparent. In a blender, combine the tofu, soy milk, miso, and arrowroot and blend until smooth. Pour the tofu mixture into the sautéed vegetables and simmer until sauce thickens, stirring constantly to prevent burning. Add peas to sauce and cook for 5 more minutes. Remove sauce from heat and pour over the split baked potatoes. Garnish with red pepper and parsley. Serve hot.

VARIATIONS

The sauces from Garbanzos and Millet with African Peanut Sauce, Garbanzos Vesuvius, Beans in Red Wine Sauce, Navy Beans Tarragon, Tofu Bonne Femme, Tofu Cacciatore, and Tofu Fricassée all go well with these potatoes. Bake the potatoes as directed above and place open faced on a serving plate. Pour ¾ cup of sauce over each halved potato. Sprinkle with 1 tablespoon each finely chopped parsley and finely diced red bell pepper, then serve hot.

Paprika Potatoes

YIELD: *4 servings*
TIME: *10 minutes preparation;*
  40 minutes cooking

2 tablespoons canola oil
½ teaspoon paprika
¼ teaspoon sea salt
4 medium red potatoes, peeled,
  quartered

Serve with Seitan Burgers, Grilled Vegetable Sandwich, and Golumpke.

Preheat oven to 325 degrees F. In a large mixing bowl, combine oil, paprika, and salt and mix well. Toss potatoes in oil mixture until well coated. Place the potatoes into a baking pan and roast for 35 to 45 minutes, turning them over about halfway through the roasting time, until they are soft in the center and golden on the outside. Serve hot.

Pesto Mashed Potatoes

YIELD: *4 servings*
TIME: *25 minutes*

3 cups peeled, cubed russet
  potatoes
4 cups water
¹⁄₁₆ teaspoon sea salt
½ tablespoon extra virgin olive
  oil
2 tablespoons Spinach Basil
  Pesto (page 167)
½ teaspoon sea salt
¼ cup soy milk

Serve with Italian Country Loaf, Garbanzo Burgers, and Eggless Frittata.

In a 2-quart saucepan, combine potatoes, water, and salt. Bring to a simmer over medium heat and cook for 15 minutes or until they are soft. Drain and place the cooked potatoes and oil in a mixing bowl then whip with an electric mixer until potatoes are mashed. Add pesto, second measure of salt, and half of the soy milk. Mix on a slow speed for 1 minute. Add remaining soy milk and mix on a slow speed for 1 minute longer. Scrape down the sides of the bowl and mix on a high speed for 3 minutes. Transfer potatoes to a serving bowl and serve immediately.

Southwestern Mashed Potatoes

YIELD: *6 servings*
TIME: *15 minutes preparation;*
 30 minutes cooking

2 cups peeled, cubed russet
 potatoes
1 cup fresh or frozen kernel corn
2 cups water
¼ teaspoon sea salt
½ cup soy milk
¼ teaspoon cumin powder
¼ teaspoon sea salt

Serve with Anasazi Bean Sandwich Rolls, Smoked Mushroom Loaf, and Tofu Carbonara.

In a 2-quart saucepan, combine potatoes, corn, water, and first measure of salt and simmer over medium heat for 15 minutes or until the potatoes are soft. Drain potatoes and corn, then place in a mixing bowl and whip with an electric mixer until they are pasty with few or no lumps. Add the soy milk, cumin, and second measure of salt and whip on high speed for about 5 minutes or until light and fluffy. Serve immediately.

Potato Pancakes

YIELD: *4 servings*
TIME: *30 minutes*

4 cups grated potatoes, skins
 left on
½ cup finely diced leeks or
 onions
¼ cup unbleached white flour
¼ cup finely chopped fresh
 parsley
4 drops liquid hickory smoke
 (optional)
2 tablespoons Vogue Vege Base
½ teaspoon sea salt
⅛ teaspoon black pepper
2 tablespoons canola oil

Serve with Grilled Vegetable Sandwich, BBQ Seitan and BBQ Tempeh, and Golumpke.

Squeeze the grated potatoes dry in a paper towel. In a mixing bowl, combine potatoes, leeks, flour, parsley, liquid smoke, Vogue Vege Base, salt, and pepper and mix together well. Take ¼ cup of the mixture for each pancake and form into flat patties. In a 10-inch frying pan, heat the oil over medium-low heat and fry the potato pancakes until they are golden brown on both sides and cooked through to the center. Place the pancakes on paper towels to drain off any excess oil and serve.

Desserts &
Dessert Sauces

A major aspect of ecological cuisine is nutrition. Desserts are notorious for being nutrient deficient because they are generally loaded with white flour, white sugar, butter, and dairy creams which are so refined that they are lacking in even the most basic nutrients. With my desserts I use a lot of fruits and vegetables, nut butters in place of dairy butter, and silken tofu in place of regular creams. The desserts in this section are eco-friendly because they are all plant-based and have far less refined foods in them than traditional desserts.

At the 1988 International Culinary Olympics, my pastry presentation theme was "Bridging the Nutritional Gap." Every one of my desserts and pastries were created with vegetables. Though not from the International Culinary Olympics, Peach Butternut Sorbet, Kiwi Cucumber Sorbet, and Pumpkin Mousse reflect the style of dessert I presented there.

I use a lot of fruits in my desserts because they are an exciting and nutritious option to natural and traditional sugars. The key to a healthy dessert is to keep the sweetness at a moderate level. If there is too much sweetness, it can overpower the natural flavor of the dessert and raise havoc with one's blood sugar. Personally, I like semi-sweet desserts that tease my taste buds. Good examples are Chestnut Mount Bré and Biscottini di Prato. The selection of desserts in this section are well-balanced to cover a variety of occasions. Cakes, cookies, pies, and crêpes are just some of the categories covered in this section.

As for children who balk at eating their vegetables, they can easily be enticed to eat their vegetables in desserts. I define diplomacy as letting someone else have your way. Eating your vegetables for dessert is the way to do it with children.

With desserts like the Pistachio Cream in Squash Shell, a rather sweet sauce is needed to carry the dessert, for the same reason that some entrées can carry themselves without a sauce and some need the lift. My dessert sauces are lower in fat and higher in nutritional value. The Whipped Cream is an exception, but then have you ever had a great tasting low-fat whipped cream? I lean towards fruit sauces because they add a variety of flavors, natural sweetness, and nutritional value. What makes my desserts stand out is that they are attractive and have flavor and texture, along with being cholesterol free.

Dessert Crêpes

YIELD: *8 crêpes or 4 servings*
TIME: *10 minutes preparation;
50 minutes cooking*

*1¼ tablespoons unrefined
corn oil*
1 cup water
4 teaspoons Sucanat
*¼ teaspoon orange extract
(or ½ teaspoon grated
orange zest)*
*3 tablespoons whole wheat
bread flour*
*3 tablespoons whole wheat
pastry flour*
⅓ cup Ener-G Egg Replacer
*1 cup Hazelnut Whipping
Cream (optional)*

Dessert crêpes differ from savory crêpes by their sweetness. It's best to use them fresh but they can be frozen for later use.

Preheat a crêpe pan over medium-low heat. In a mixing bowl, combine the oil, water, Sucanat, and orange extract and stir well. In a separate bowl, combine the flours and egg replacer, mix well and add to liquid ingredients. Mix batter until smooth. Using a paper towel, lightly oil the preheated crêpe pan. Pour about 2½ tablespoons of batter in pan and immediately tilt and rotate to spread the batter evenly over the surface. Cook the crêpe for 3 minutes, then flip over and cook other side for 1 minute longer. Transfer each crêpe to a plate and serve 2 crêpes with ¼ cup Hazelnut Whipping Cream per serving.

Almond Dessert Crêpes

YIELD: *4 servings*
TIME: *40 minutes*

*2 pints non-dairy vanilla
   "ice cream" (Living Rightly
   Non-Dairy Frozen Dessert)*
½ cup roasted almond butter
*1 recipe Dessert Crêpes
   (page 201)*

This is an ice cream crêpe in which the almond butter is beat into the ice cream. A fruit sauce is recommended to cut the richness of this delightful dessert. Let the filled crêpe sit for about 3 minutes before serving so the ice cream will soften. For a personal touch, any flavored ice cream can be used.

In an electric mixer, beat the ice cream and almond butter together until well blended. Immediately spread the 8 crêpes with the ice cream mixture, dividing the mixture evenly between them. Quickly roll up each crêpe, folding in the sides as you roll. Individually wrap the crêpes in plastic wrap and freeze until the ice cream becomes solid. Unwrap the crêpes and arrange them 2 to a plate. Serve cold with Plum Syrup, or Quick Raspberry Sabayon Sauce.

VARIATION: *Pistachio Dessert Crêpes*
Replace the roasted almond butter with ¾ cup finely ground pistachios and ¼ cup Licor 43 or other liqueur, then proceed as directed.

Crêpes Suzette

YIELD: *4 servings*
TIME: *30 minutes*

¼ *cup cashew butter*
½ *cup frozen orange juice*
  concentrate
2 tablespoons barley malt syrup
1 tablespoon Grand Marnier
1 teaspoon pure vanilla extract
¹⁄₁₆ *teaspoon sea salt*
1 cup diced bananas
1 teaspoon grated orange zest
  (optional)
1 recipe Dessert Crêpes
  (page 201)
2 tablespoons cognac

There is no better way to end an elegant meal than with this dessert. These crêpes taste as good as their presentation.

In a blender, combine the cashew butter, juice concentrate, syrup, Grand Marnier, vanilla extract, and salt and blend until smooth. In a mixing bowl, combine the diced bananas and orange zest with ¼ of the orange juice mixture and stir until bananas are well coated. Divide banana mixture evenly between the 8 crepes. Place a small amount in center of each crêpe, fold crêpe in half, then half again into quarters. In a 10-inch frying pan, heat remaining orange juice mixture over medium heat. Lay folded crêpes in pan and heat for 1 minute, then turn them to the other side and heat for another minute. Pour the cognac into the sauce, stir, and light with a match. Serve crêpes while still flaming.

VARIATION: *Tropical Crêpes*
To the filling mixture, add ½ cup toasted coconut, ½ cup diced fresh pineapple, and ½ cup diced bananas and proceed as directed. The frozen orange juice concentrate can also be replaced with ½ cup frozen pineapple juice concentrate.

Glazed Fruit Dessert Pizza

YIELD: *6 servings*

TIME: *1 hour 15 minutes
    preparation; 30 minutes
    cooking*

Crust

1½ tablespoons Sucanat
½ cup warm water
¾ teaspoon active dry yeast
1 cup whole wheat bread flour
⅔ cup unbleached white flour
1 tablespoon canola oil
¾ teaspoon grated orange zest
¾ teaspoon grated lemon zest
¼ teaspoon sea salt

This dessert is worth trying—I surprised myself with it! To make it even more special, top each serving with a spoon of Hazelnut Whipping Cream.

CRUST

In a small mixing bowl, combine ½ teaspoon of the Sucanat with the warm water and add the yeast. Allow mixture to stand about 5 minutes, or until yeast is foamy. In a large mixing bowl, combine ½ cup of the whole wheat flour with ⅓ cup of the unbleached white flour. Add proofed yeast to flours and mix well. Cover bowl with a damp cloth, then set it in a warm place to rise for 30 minutes. After 30 minutes, mix down the sponge and add remaining Sucanat, oil, orange and lemon zest, salt, and enough of the remaining flours (using the whole wheat flour first) to make a smooth and elastic dough. Knead dough for 5 to 10 minutes. In a large mixing bowl, pour 1 teaspoon of oil into a large bowl, place the dough inside, then turn it in the oil until it is evenly coated. Cover the bowl with the damp cloth and set aside to rise for about 45 minutes or until doubled in size.

Preheat oven to 350 degrees F. Punch dough down and roll into a 12-inch diameter crust, about ½ inch thick. Turn edges up slightly. Transfer crust to a lightly oiled baking sheet or pizza pan. Brush surface with ½ tablespoon of oil. Partially bake the crust by pricking holes with the tines of a fork across the surface to prevent air bubbles from forming. Bake crust for 8 minutes or until the dough is set and does not indent when touched.

NOTE: Partially baked crusts can be frozen for later use or used immediately.

Topping

¼ cup honey

4 pitted, ripe plums, cut into
   wedges

½ cup almond butter

¼ cup FruitSource, Sucanat,
   or maple sugar granules

¼ cup arrowroot powder

2 peeled, pitted, large ripe
   peaches or nectarines, cut
   into wedges

2 peeled, pitted, cored ripe
   pears, cut into wedges

1 peeled kiwi, cut into 6 slices

Glaze

¾ cup fruit juice–sweetened
   apricot preserves

Topping

In a 2-quart saucepan, bring honey to a simmer over medium heat. Add plum wedges and simmer gently for no longer than 3 minutes. Remove saucepan from heat and immediately transfer plums to a small bowl. Spread almond butter evenly over top of the prebaked crust, leaving 1 inch uncovered around the edges. Sprinkle FruitSource evenly over the almond butter. In a mixing bowl, toss fruit slices in the arrowroot powder. Starting with pear wedges, arrange in a circular pattern close to the edge of the almond butter, overlapping them slightly. Arrange peach wedges over the bottom half of the pears, plum wedges over the bottom half of the peaches, and kiwi slices in the center (when completed, there should be no exposed areas on the surface of the pizza except for the outer edge of the crust). Bake pizza for another 20 minutes.

Glaze

In a 1-quart saucepan, bring preserves to a simmer over medium heat, stirring occasionally. Continue to simmer until the preserves thin out into a liquid. Remove saucepan from heat and set aside. When pizza is removed from the oven, brush liquefied preserves over fruits and entire surface. Allow pizza to cool to room temperature, or refrigerate until it is chilled. Slice into wedges and serve.

Sweet Almond Rice Cakes

YIELD: *4 servings*
TIME: *10 minutes preparation;*
  2 hours cooling

¾ *cup blanched almonds*
¾ *cup honey or FruitSource*
  syrup
2 *tablespoons almond butter*
1 *teaspoon pure vanilla extract*
¹⁄₁₆ *teaspoon sea salt*
2 *cups puffed brown rice*

These cakes are perfect for afternoon teas or served with a sorbet for dessert.

In a blender, grind the almonds to a medium-coarse meal. In a 2-quart saucepan, bring the honey to a simmer over medium heat, then simmer on low heat for 5 minutes. Add ground almonds, almond butter, vanilla extract, and salt. In a large mixing bowl, add the puffed rice, then pour the syrup mixture on top and mix well. Press mixture into a lightly oiled 8-inch square baking dish. Allow to set for 2 hours. Cut into portions and serve.

VARIATION

Preheat oven to 350 degrees F. Bake rice cake for 5 minutes, cool for 30 minutes, then slice and serve.

Double Pie Crust

YIELD: *2 9-inch crusts*
TIME: *40 minutes*

1½ cups whole wheat pastry
flour
1½ cups unbleached white
flour
¼ teaspoon sea salt
½ cup coconut butter or
canola oil
10 tablespoons cold water

There is no butter, lard, or hydrogenated shortening in this healthy pie crust. When it comes out of the oven, the crust is hard, then tenderizes as it cools. If you are a lactic vegetarian and want a flakier crust, substitute butter for the canola oil.

In a large bowl, combine the flours and salt. Gently blend in the butter with a fork or pastry cutter, until the flour resembles a coarse meal. Add the water and mix until the dough sticks together and pulls away from the sides of the bowl. Gently form dough into a disc shape, cover with plastic wrap, and refrigerate for 30 minutes. Remove chilled dough from the plastic wrap and divide in half. On a lightly floured surface, roll each half into a circle large enough to fit and cover a 9-inch pie plate. The crust is now ready to use or freeze for later use.

Date Cream Pie

YIELD: *8 servings*
TIME: *10 minutes preparation;*
12 hours chilling

1¼ cups water
2 8-ounce packages chopped
dates (should yield 3 cups)
2 cups rinsed, crushed, extra
firm tofu
1 tablespoon pure vanilla
extract
⅛ teaspoon cinnamon
1 cup cashew butter
½ recipe pre-baked Double Pie
Crust (page 207), shell only
mint leaves and sliced
strawberries for garnish

This simple pie filling only needs to be blended. It makes a great summer dessert because it is light, sweet, and (except for the crust) needs no baking.

In a blender, combine the water, dates, tofu, vanilla extract, and cinnamon and blend well. Add the cashew butter and blend until smooth. Pour mixture immediately into pie crust and refrigerate overnight to set. Garnish each slice with strawberry and mint leaf and serve cold.

Mince "Wheat" Pie

YIELD: *8 servings*
TIME: *1 hour 15 minutes
    cooking*

*1 recipe Double Pie Crust
    (page 207)*
1 teaspoon canola oil
½ cup diced onions
¾ teaspoon sea salt
2 cups water
*1½ cups (packed) ground
    seitan (page 112)*
*1 cup peeled, cored, chopped
    Granny Smith apples or
    quince*
½ cup diced dried apricots
½ cup currants or raisins
¼ cup chopped roasted walnuts
½ cup Sucanat
2 tablespoons pecan butter
2½ teaspoons cinnamon
1½ teaspoons allspice
1 teaspoon grated lemon zest
¼ teaspoon clove powder
*2 tablespoons arrowroot
    dissolved in 2 tablespoons
    cool water*
2 tablespoons lemon juice
2 tablespoons light rum

This is my answer to mince meat pie and is every bit as good as the original in flavor but far superior in nutrition. Mince "Wheat" Pie won a silver medal in the 1988 International Culinary Olympics.

Preheat oven to 375 degrees F. Prepare pie crusts as directed in the recipe. In a 10-inch frying pan, heat the oil and sauté onions and salt over medium heat for 5 minutes or until onions are transparent. Add water, seitan, apples, apricots, currants, walnuts, Sucanat, pecan butter, cinnamon, allspice, lemon zest, and cloves. Bring to a simmer and cook for 20 minutes. Add arrowroot/water mixture, stirring constantly. Cook for another 3 minutes or until mixture is thickened. Remove pan from heat and add lemon juice and rum. Transfer filling to a covered container and refrigerate until cool. When ready, pour filling into the prepared pie shell and cover it with the second crust, sealing the edges well and making slits in the top to allow steam to escape during baking. Bake for 45 minutes or until crust is lightly browned and filling is slightly bubbling. Remove from oven and cool on rack. Serve at room temperature.

Sugar Dough

YIELD: *6 servings*
TIME: *45 minutes*

¾ cup coconut butter
6 tablespoons Sucanat
1 tablespoon liquid lecithin
1 tablespoon pure vanilla extract
6 tablespoons cold water
1½ cups whole wheat pastry flour
1 cup unbleached white flour

Originally developed for the Fig Bars, this dough also makes a good short cookie by itself. It can be used with any fruit filling to make a variety of fruit bars.

In a mixing bowl, combine the coconut butter, Sucanat, and lecithin, and cream using an electric mixer. Mix in the vanilla and the water. Add the flours and mix to blend all of the ingredients thoroughly. Freeze dough for 30 to 90 minutes before using it or chill overnight. Use as needed for torte bases and to line pans that will hold creamy fillings. Baked as instructed in individual recipes.

Fig Bars

YIELD: *14 servings*

TIME: *30 minutes preparation;*
30 minutes cooking

2 cups water

4 cups finely chopped whole
dark figs

2 tablespoons arrowroot
dissolved in 2 tablespoons
cool water

2 tablespoons pure vanilla
extract

1 teaspoon ground cinnamon

1 recipe chilled Sugar Dough
(page 210)

These bars are ready for snacking and also make a wonderful companion to a fruit salad.

Preheat oven to 350 degrees F. In a 2-quart saucepan, simmer water over medium heat. Add figs and cook about 10 minutes or until they are almost a thick paste, stirring constantly to prevent burning. Add arrowroot/water mixture and cook until thickened. Remove saucepan from heat and add vanilla and cinnamon. Set filling aside. Lightly oil 2 loaf pans. Divide the sugar dough into 4 pieces and roll each piece out on a lightly floured surface. Lay 1 piece in each pan. Divide filling in half and spread evenly over dough in each pan. Lay remaining 2 pieces of rolled dough over the top of the filling in each pan, lightly press into filling, and bake for 30 to 40 minutes (if you are using a gas oven, place a baking sheet under the loaf pans to prevent the bottoms from burning). Remove pans and set aside to cool completely. Cut around the sides of each loaf pan, hugging the sides with the knife. With one hand covering the top of the pan, gently flip it upside down to release the loaf. Repeat with second loaf pan. Place both loaves on a cutting board and slice into 1-inch bars. Serve warm or at room temperature.

VARIATION

To increase the sweetness, add ½ cup Sucanat to figs when simmering. The figs should remain the predominant sweetener.

Papaya Fruit Bar

YIELD: *8 bars*

TIME: *20 minutes preparation;*
25 minutes cooking

2 cups coarsely chopped dried
papaya spears, naturally
sweetened

1 cup water

¼ cup stone ground whole
wheat flour

2 cups no-fat raisin cinnamon
granola

½ cup unsweetened macaroon
coconut

¼ cup stone ground whole
wheat flour

¾ cup water

½ cup almond butter

1 teaspoon pure vanilla extract

This makes a great dessert for any picnic, party, or part of a brown bag lunch because it keeps for days without refrigeration.

Preheat oven to 350 degrees F. In a food processor, process the papaya into ¼-inch pieces. Add the first measure of water and flour and process until well blended. Set aside. In a blender, grind the granola to a medium-coarse meal (this should yield 1½ cups). In a mixing bowl, combine granola, coconut, flour, second measure of water, almond butter, and vanilla extract together until evenly blended. Lightly oil a 7½ x 11½ x 1½-inch baking pan and evenly press half of the granola mixture into it. Spread papaya mixture over granola mixture, press remainder of granola mixture over fruit mixture, and bake for 25 minutes. Remove from oven and let cool for at least 10 minutes to allow the fruit bar to become firm. I prefer to serve it slightly warm in the winter or chilled during the summer.

VARIATION: *Date Fruit Bar*
Replace papaya with 4 cups chopped dates.

Peach Cobbler

YIELD: *6 servings*
TIME: *20 minutes preparation;*
   30 minutes cooking;
   30 minutes cooling

Filling

6 cups blanched, peeled,
   thickly sliced peaches
   (about 12 peaches)
½ cup Sucanat
¼ cup arrowroot powder
1 teaspoon pure lemon extract
   or 6 tablespoons fresh
   lemon juice
1 tablespoon canola oil

Topping

¼ cup whole wheat pastry flour
¼ cup unbleached white flour
½ teaspoon baking powder
⅛ teaspoon sea salt
1/16 teaspoon ground cinnamon
¼ cup water
2 tablespoons honey or
   FruitSource syrup
1½ teaspoons canola oil
½ teaspoon pure vanilla extract

½ recipe Hazelnut Whipping
   Cream (page 237)

This dessert was one of my favorites when growing up so I couldn't resist creating a natural foods version. Served with Hazelnut Whipping Cream, it is superb.

Filling

In a mixing bowl, combine peaches, Sucanat, arrowroot, and lemon extract and mix well. Pour filling into a lightly oiled 8 x 12-inch baking pan and set aside.

Topping

In a mixing bowl, combine flours, baking powder, salt, and cinnamon and mix well. In another bowl, combine water, honey, oil, and vanilla extract and mix well. Add dry ingredients to the wet and whisk together until well blended.

Assembling the Cobbler

Preheat oven to 375 degrees F. Pour the topping over filling and bake for 30 minutes or until the top is lightly browned and the cobbler seems a little springy. Remove pan and let cool. Serve with dollops of Hazelnut Whipping Cream.

Strawberry Fruit Tart

YIELD: *8 servings*

TIME: *50 minutes preparation;
50 minutes cooking*

Tart Crust

*1 cup lightly roasted whole
    almonds*

1 cup rolled oats

1 cup whole wheat flour

¼ teaspoon ground cinnamon

1/16 teaspoon sea salt

½ cup maple syrup

½ cup unrefined corn oil

1 teaspoon pure vanilla extract

Pastry Cream

*¾ cup water mixed with
    ½ cup honey*

1¾ cups soy milk

½ cup brown rice syrup

2 tablespoons agar flakes

¼ teaspoon sea salt

*2 tablespoons arrowroot
    dissolved in ¼ cup cool
    water*

*1 tablespoon pure vanilla
    extract*

Lemon Glaze

¼ cup water

1 tablespoon agar flakes

¼ cup brown rice syrup

2 teaspoons lemon juice

*1 pint washed, stemmed fresh
    strawberries*

A version of the classic French fruit tart, this makes a pleasing dessert to serve after American Bounty or Italian Country Loaf.

Tart Crust

Preheat oven to 350 degrees F. In a blender, grind the almonds into a fine meal. Transfer almonds to a mixing bowl, then grind the rolled oats into a fine meal. Add ground oats to the almonds along with flour, cinnamon, and salt, then mix well. In a separate bowl, whisk together syrup, oil, and vanilla extract. Add liquids to dry ingredients and mix until well blended. Lightly oil a 9-inch tart pan and press dough evenly into it. Bake for 15 minutes or until crust is completely baked. Remove from oven and set aside to cool.

Pastry Cream

In a 2-quart saucepan, combine the water/honey mixture, milk, syrup, agar, and salt and bring to a simmer over medium heat. Cook until agar is completely dissolved. Add the arrowroot/water mixture to the agar mixture and cook until mixture thickens. Add the vanilla and blend well. Let cream cool until not quite set, then pour into pre-baked tart shell. Spread pastry cream evenly over the crust and allow to cool completely.

Lemon Glaze

In a 1-quart saucepan, combine the water and agar and bring to a simmer over medium heat. When mixture starts to thicken and agar is completely dissolved, add the syrup and lemon juice and mix well. If glaze is too thick while still hot, add a little more rice syrup until desired consistency is reached. If glaze becomes too thick because it has cooled down, warm it in a saucepan over medium heat until it reaches the desired consistency.

Assembling the Tart

Cut the strawberries in half. Lay them on the pastry cream in an orderly fashion, then brush the entire surface of the tart with the lemon glaze. Refrigerate until well chilled and serve cold.

VARIATION
Replace strawberries with peeled and sliced kiwis.

Fresh Nectarine Crisp

YIELD: *6 servings*
TIME: *30 minutes preparation;*
30 minutes cooking; 1 hour
cooling

2 quarts (or about 2 dozen)
fresh nectarines
7 tablespoons arrowroot
powder
2 cups apple-peach juice
½ teaspoon lemon extract
¾ teaspoon cinnamon

Topping

1½ cups rolled oats
1 cup rice flour
½ cup canola oil
½ cup apple-peach juice
¼ teaspoon ginger powder
⅓ cup barley malt syrup

This dessert is both sugarless and wheatless, a terrific treat for those with food allergies.

Preheat oven to 350 degrees F. Blanch, peel, and dice the nectarines. Mix the arrowroot into 1 cup of the apple-peach juice. In a 2-quart saucepan, bring remaining juice to a simmer over medium heat and add arrowroot mixture, stirring constantly until well blended and thickened. Add the nectarines, lemon extract, and cinnamon and mix well. Pour fruit mixture into a lightly oiled 8 x 12-inch baking pan and spread out evenly.

Topping

In a mixing bowl, combine the oats, flour, oil, juice, and ginger and mix to form a crumbly mixture. Sprinkle topping evenly over fruit mix, and drizzle syrup over entire surface of topping. Bake for 30 minutes or until the top is lightly browned. Remove pan from oven and allow crisp to cool thoroughly. Cut into portions and serve.

VARIATION
Add 2 cups of finely diced unsweetened dried pineapple rings to the nectarine filling. Proceed as directed.

Chocolate Bread Pudding

YIELD: *6 servings*

TIME: *15 minutes preparation;*
4 hours soaking; 40 minutes
cooking

5 slices fresh whole wheat bread
2½ cups soy milk
1½ cups Sucanat
¼ cup pecan or other nut butter
¼ cup cocoa powder
1 tablespoon arrowroot powder
    or cornstarch
¹⁄₁₆ teaspoon clove powder
¼ cup agar flakes (or 1
    tablespoon agar powder)
1½ cups water

Served warm during winter or cold during summer, this recipe surpasses traditional bread pudding and is a good way to use leftover bread.

Cut the bread into 1-inch cubes (this should yield 4 cups). In a large mixing bowl, combine the milk, Sucanat, pecan butter, cocoa powder, arrowroot, and cloves and mix well. In a small mixing bowl, combine the agar with the water and let sit for one minute, then add to soy milk mixture. Mix well and pour over the bread cubes, cover and let sit at room temperature for 4 hours. Preheat oven to 350 degrees F. Lightly oil a 6-cup baking dish. After the 4-hour resting time, stir bread mixture with a wooden spoon, and pour into the baking dish. Cover and bake for 40 minutes. This dessert can be served hot out of the oven. However, it is best to let cool for at least 30 minutes to set up before serving. Serve with Hazelnut or regular Whipped Cream.

Carrot Cake with Orange Icing

YIELD: *15 servings*
TIME: *30 minutes preparation;*
1 hour 10 minutes cooking

Orange Icing

½ pound firm tofu
½ 10-ounce jar orange
marmalade
½ cup maple syrup
6 tablespoons tahini
½ tablespoon pure vanilla
extract

Carrot Cake

2½ cups brown rice flour or
whole wheat pastry flour
2 tablespoons cinnamon
4 teaspoons baking powder
2 teaspoons baking soda
1 teaspoon sea salt
¾ cup water
¼ cup flax seed meal (about
2 tablespoons flax seed,
finely ground)
1½ cups unrefined corn oil
1 cup maple syrup
½ cup soy or rice milk
3 cups grated carrots
1 cup chopped walnuts

My assistant Nancy Loving perfected and contributed this recipe. It's the only recipe in this book that isn't from my files. It can be used in place of the Orange Poppy Seed Cake for the Orange Cranberry Ice Cream Cake.

Orange Icing

In a vegetable steamer, place the tofu and steam for 5 minutes. In a blender, combine tofu, marmalade, syrup, tahini, and vanilla extract and blend well. Adjust sweetness to taste, then refrigerate until needed.

Carrot Cake

Preheat oven to 300 degrees F. In a large mixing bowl, combine the flour, cinnamon, baking powder, baking soda, and salt and mix well. In a blender, place the water and flax seed meal (these can be replaced by 8 ounces of soft tofu) and blend well. Add oil, syrup, and milk and blend again. To the dry ingredients, add carrots, walnuts, and blended liquids and mix well. Pour batter into a lightly oiled 9 x 13 x 2¼-inch baking pan. Bake for 1 hour and 10 minutes, then cool completely and top with Orange Icing.

VARIATION: *Apricot-Orange Icing*
In a 2-quart saucepan, combine 1 cup apple juice, 1 cup orange juice, 1 cup dried apricots, and 2½ tablespoons agar flakes, bring to a simmer, and cook for 10 minutes or until apricots are softened and agar has dissolved. Cool mixture slightly, then transfer to a blender and add 1 10-ounce jar of orange marmalade. Blend well. Add maple syrup to taste and pour icing on the cake before it cools and sets up. If icing has begun to set, blend again, then pour immediately onto the cake. Refrigerating the iced cake will cause the icing to set up quicker.

German Chocolate Cake

YIELD: *12 servings*
TIME: *15 minutes preparation;
40 minutes cooking*

1½ cups Sucanat
1½ cups unbleached white flour
1¼ cups whole wheat bread
  flour
¾ cup cocoa or carob powder
2 teaspoons baking soda
½ teaspoon sea salt
2 cups water
½ cup maple syrup
6 tablespoons canola oil
2 tablespoons apple cider
  vinegar
2 teaspoons pure vanilla extract
1 recipe Coconut Squash Cake
  Icing (page 239)

I was so fond of this cake before becoming a total vegetarian, I decided to make a plant-based version of it. It reminds me of the traditional cake and uses vegetables in the frosting.

Preheat oven to 350 degrees F. In a large mixing bowl, combine the Sucanat, flours, cocoa powder, baking soda, and salt and mix well. In another bowl, combine water, syrup, oil, vinegar, and vanilla extract. Add the wet ingredients to the dry and mix well. Pour batter into two lightly oiled and floured 9-inch round cake pans. Bake for 30 minutes, or until a toothpick inserted in the center of each comes out dry. Remove pans and cool completely. Remove cakes from pans and turn one layer onto a serving plate so the bottom of the cake is facing up. Spread ⅓ of icing over the surface. Place the other cake layer on top of the icing, and use remaining icing to cover top of the cake (do not put any icing on the sides). Cut into slices and serve.

"I began to long for a book which would demystify and reveal all the basic and classic cakes, butter creams, icings, fillings, and toppings in their simplest form and then show how to combine them to create just about any cake imaginable."

—ROSE LEVY BERANBAUM

Orange Poppy Seed Cake

YIELD: *2 8-inch cakes*
TIME: *20 minutes preparation;
25 minutes cooking*

1¼ cups whole wheat pastry
flour
1 cup unbleached white flour
2 tablespoons poppy seeds
1 tablespoon baking powder
½ teaspoon coriander powder
¼ teaspoon sea salt
1 cup honey or FruitSource
syrup
¾ cup frozen orange juice
concentrate
juice of 1 orange, plus water to
make ½ cup
5 tablespoons unrefined corn or
canola oil
2 tablespoons Ener-G Egg
Replacer mixed with ¼ cup
water
2 teaspoons pure vanilla extract

Of course this cake is terrific just as it is, but by adding crushed and whole strawberries on top along with a dollop of Hazelnut Whipping Cream, it becomes a great strawberry shortcake!

Preheat oven to 350 degrees F. In a mixing bowl, combine the flours, poppy seeds, baking powder, coriander, and salt. In another bowl, combine the honey, orange juice concentrate, orange juice, oil, **egg** replacer, and vanilla. Add dry ingredients to the wet and blend until smooth. Pour the batter into 2 lightly oiled and floured 8-inch round cake pans or a 9 x 13 x 2¼-inch baking pan and bake for 20 to 25 minutes, or until a toothpick inserted in the center comes out clean. Allow cake to cool completely, then remove from pan. Frost with either Coconut Squash or Apricot-Orange Icing and serve.

Hazelnut Cream Cake

YIELD: *1 9-inch cake*
TIME: *20 minutes preparation;*
40 minutes cooking; 1 hour
chilling

Base

2 cups water
1 cup whole wheat couscous
½ cup maple syrup
½ cup Sucanat
⅛ teaspoon sea salt
½ cup hazelnut flour or meal
(or ¼ cup hazelnut butter)
½ teaspoon pure vanilla extract

Filling

2 10½-ounce packages extra
firm silken tofu
2 tablespoons agar flakes
½ cup water
¾ cup maple syrup
½ cup hazelnut butter

This cake is a version of the Chocolate Cream Couscous Cake in my first book, *Friendly Foods*. It has a wonderful creamy texture and the flavor is mildly sweet. The rich and subtle flavors can be enjoyed to their best advantage when served with Plum Syrup.

Base

In a 2-quart saucepan (with lid), combine water, couscous, syrup, Sucanat, and salt, cover and bring to a simmer, and cook over low heat for 20 minutes. Add the flour and vanilla extract, then stir well. Pour the mixture into a lightly oiled 9-inch springform pan. Flatten and smooth with a rubber spatula. Leave base to cool and become more firm while you prepare the filling.

Filling

In a blender, place the tofu and blend until smooth. In a 1-quart saucepan, combine agar and water, then bring to a simmer over medium heat. Continue to simmer for 10 minutes or until agar has dissolved. To the blended tofu, add agar mixture, syrup, and hazelnut butter and blend well. Pour filling over base in the springform pan and refrigerate for 1 hour or until firm. Gently remove cake from pan, cut into slices and serve.

VARIATIONS

Pour a thin layer of Hazelnut Butter Sauce (page 244) over top of the cake while it's still in the pan. Place warm Chocolate Ganache (page 234) in a pastry tube and pipe a design onto the top of the cake. Pull a knife lightly over the surface, from the center to the outside edges, to create a marbled effect. Chill to set, then gently remove cake from pan. Cut into slices and serve. Or drizzle Chocolate Ganache over top of the cake while still in the pan. Chill to set ganache, then remove cake from pan as above and serve.

Ice Cream Rice Cake

YIELD: *4 servings*
TIME: *10 minutes preparation;*
60 minutes chilling

1 pint non-dairy vanilla "ice
cream" (Living Rightly Non-
Dairy Frozen Dessert)
½ cup roasted almond butter
2 cups puffed brown rice

Drizzled with Plum Syrup, Raspberry Syrup, or Hazelnut Butter Sauce, this cake is the perfect ending for any meal.

In an electric mixer, mix the ice cream with the nut butter on medium speed for about 3 minutes or until well blended. Immediately fold in the puffed rice. Press mixture into a lightly oiled pan or mold, or form it into a 3-inch diameter roll and wrap it securely with plastic wrap. Place immediately into the freezer where it should remain for at least 1 hour or until it is solid. When ready to use, unmold or unwrap the cake and cut 2 slices per person. Serve immediately with fruit or dessert sauce.

Orange Cranberry Ice Cream Cake

YIELD: *10 servings*

TIME: *30 minutes preparation; 2 hours chilling*

½ cup unsweetened sun-dried cranberries

½ cup water

¼ cup frozen orange juice concentrate

1 Orange Poppy Seed Cake (page 219), baked in a rectangular baking pan and frozen

2 pints non-dairy vanilla "ice cream" (Living Rightly Non-Dairy Frozen Dessert)

½ cup frozen orange juice concentrate

1 teaspoon grated orange zest

Most ice cream cakes are made with dairy ice cream and rich cakes. I decided to make a healthy non-dairy option with a strong fruit flavor to cut the richness. No enjoyment is sacrificed—this cake is great.

In a 2-quart saucepan, combine cranberries, water, and juice concentrate and bring to a simmer over medium heat. Reduce heat to low, then simmer until all the liquid has evaporated. Remove saucepan from heat and set aside. Remove cake from freezer, then cut it in half crosswise into 2 equal pieces. Line the bottom and sides of a square baking dish with plastic wrap. Place 1 cake half into the dish and press gently so it will fit snugly. In a large mixing bowl, combine the cranberry mixture, ice cream, second measure of orange juice concentrate, and orange zest. Using the flat beater of an electric mixer, blend together until smooth and well blended. Spread ice cream mixture evenly over the cake layer. Cover ice cream with the second cake layer and press down gently to eliminate any spaces. Cover dish with plastic wrap and place in freezer until ice cream is firm. To serve, remove the cake from the freezer and let stand for 5 minutes. Cut into pieces and serve.

Peach Butternut Sorbet

YIELD: *12 servings*
TIME: *50 minutes*

1 cup frozen fruit juice
    concentrate mixed with
    2 cups water
2 cups rice milk
1 cup peach purée
1 cup steamed butternut squash
¾ cup cooked fresh kernel corn
¼ cup FruitSource syrup or
    honey
2 tablespoons toasted coconut
1 tablespoon grated orange zest
½ teaspoon nutmeg

This sorbet may be served as an intermezzo, dessert, or complement to another dessert. Try it with cookies, fruit cobbler, Papaya Fruit Bars, Fig Bars, or any cake.

In a blender, combine all ingredients and blend until smooth. Transfer mixture to ice cream maker and process according to manufacturer's instructions. Store the resulting sorbet in the freezer in a covered container. If an ice cream maker is unavailable, pour mixture into a covered container and freeze for 30 minutes or until it is firm. In both methods, if sorbet is too hard when removed from the freezer, transfer to a food processor and process for 30 seconds or until it is smooth, then serve immediately.

Kiwi Cucumber Sorbet

YIELD: *4 servings*

TIME: *20 minutes preparation;*
12 hours chilling

1½ cups non-dairy vanilla "ice
cream" (Living Rightly Non-
Dairy Frozen Dessert)
1¼ cups peeled, diced, frozen
kiwis (about 4 kiwis)
¾ cup peeled, halved, seeded
cucumber
2 tablespoons brown rice syrup
1 tablespoon lemon juice
4 drops lime essence (optional)

This unusual sorbet can be served either as a dessert or an intermezzo. The cucumber combines with the kiwi very well, producing a cooling and satisfying treat.

In a blender, combine ice cream, kiwis, cucumber, syrup, lemon juice, and lime essence and blend until smooth. Transfer mixture to a covered container and freeze overnight. Remove frozen mixture and place in a blender. Blend for 1 minute and serve immediately.

VARIATIONS: *Kiwi Cucumber Smoothy*
Omit the lime essence, blend until smooth, and serve immediately.

Fruit Salad Sorbet
Quarter and seed 1 ripe cantaloupe. Separate rind from each quarter, then slice cantaloupe crosswise into bite-sized pieces and place back onto the rind. Chop 8 fresh mint leaves. Wash, stem, and quarter 8 large strawberries. For each serving, place a quartered cantaloupe slice onto a plate and surround with 8 strawberry quarters. Place a scoop of the sorbet on top of each melon slice, sprinkle with some of the chopped mint leaves, and serve immediately.

Mangolope Custard

YIELD: *8 servings*

TIME: *15 minutes preparation; 15 minutes cooking; 2 hours chilling*

6 tablespoons brown rice syrup

¼ cup agar flakes

1 tablespoon lemon or lime juice

1 tablespoon arrowroot powder dissolved in 2 tablespoons cool water

2¾ packed cups peeled, seeded, chopped mango

2¾ packed cups peeled, seeded, chopped cantaloupe

When I lived in Miami Beach, mango trees were very abundant. This is an excellent dessert for a hot summer day.

In a blender, combine syrup, agar, and lemon juice and blend until smooth. Pour mixture into a 1-quart saucepan and bring to a simmer over medium heat. Cook for approximately 8 minutes or until agar is dissolved. Remove saucepan from heat, add arrowroot/water mixture to hot agar, and stir with whisk to blend thoroughly. Return saucepan to heat and cook for another 3 minutes. In a large mixing bowl, combine mango and cantaloupe and pour mixture over fruits. Stir to blend everything well. Pour custard into a 4-cup mold and refrigerate for 2 hours. Serve cold.

Pears Mascarpone

YIELD: *3 servings*
TIME: *30 minutes*

*3 firm, ripe Anjou or Bartlett
    pears*

Cream

½ cup finely ground walnuts
8 ounces extra firm silken tofu
*1 tablespoon Kirschwasser
    (cherry liqueur)*
¼ cup Sucanat
*1 tablespoon minced fresh mint
    or 3 drops mint extract*
1 teaspoon lemon juice

*3 walnut halves and 3 fresh
    mint leaves for garnish*

I use the richness of silken tofu to substitute for Mascarpone cheese, and walnuts and Kirschwasser to complement the pear. The result is an extraordinary dessert.

Peel, halve, and core the pears. In a vegetable steamer, steam the pears for about 8 minutes (if pears are not as ripe as they should be, continue steaming until they are tender yet still firm). Transfer pears to a small bowl and place in the refrigerator to cool.

Cream

In a blender, combine walnuts, tofu, Kirschwasser, Sucanat, mint, and lemon juice and blend until smooth. Transfer cream to covered container and refrigerate for 30 minutes or until needed.

Assembling the Mascarpone

When ready to serve, spoon the cream onto each of 3 plates. Place 2 pear halves on top of the cream. Garnish each plate with 1 walnut half and 1 mint leaf. Serve cold.

Chestnut Mount Bré

YIELD: *6 servings*
TIME: *45 minutes*

1 cup frozen chestnuts
½ cup water
½ cup maple syrup
½ cup water
½ cup soy milk powder
½ teaspoon pure vanilla extract
1 recipe Whipped Cream
  (page 237)

While traveling southern Switzerland and northern Italy in the fall of 1992, I encountered a sweet known as *vermicelles*, puréed chestnuts topped with whipped cream. I loved the idea and created this recipe. The flavor is very delicate and sophisticated. Serve it with Plum Syrup and wait for the accolades.

In a vegetable steamer, steam the chestnuts for 20 minutes. In a 2-quart saucepan, combine the steamed chestnuts, first measure of water, and syrup, then simmer for 30 to 40 minutes or until the syrup is reduced to about ¼ cup. In a blender, combine the chestnut mixture with the second measure of water, soy milk powder, and vanilla extract and blend into a smooth paste. At this point it can be placed on a plate in a mound, or follow the traditional serving method and pipe it through a pastry tube in long strands to make a lighter pile. Top with Whipped Cream and serve.

VARIATION:

Chestnut Mount Bré on Couscous Timbale
This additional step will take another 30 minutes. In a 2-quart pot, combine 1½ cups water, ½ cup white or whole wheat couscous, ½ cup peeled and finely diced butternut squash, and ½ cup FruitSource syrup or honey and cook on medium heat until squash and couscous are soft. Lightly oil 6 cups of a standard muffin tin and evenly divide couscous mixture between them. Cover and cool in a refrigerator until ready to use. To serve, place the couscous timbale as a base for the Chestnut Mount Bré (preferably piped in long strands), then top with Whipped Cream.

Sweet Rice Dumplings

YIELD: *18 dumplings*
TIME: *20 minutes preparation;*
    70 minutes cooking

1½ cups walnuts
1½ cups sweet brown rice
2¼ cups water
1⁄16 teaspoon sea salt
¾ cup raisins
¾ teaspoon ground cinnamon

Dumplings are typically cooked after they are assembled, but in this recipe, the rice is cooked prior to assembly. These sweet rice dumplings will keep refrigerated for several days and are very nutritious.

Preheat oven to 350 degrees F. Place walnuts on a baking sheet and roast them in a 350 degree F oven for about 15 minutes or until lightly browned and very fragrant. Remove pan from oven and immediately transfer walnuts to another container to stop roasting. When cool, coarsely grind or finely chop walnuts and set aside. Wash and rinse rice, then place in a pressure cooker along with the water and salt. Seal and bring to pressure over high heat. Reduce heat to low and cook rice for 45 minutes. Remove pressure cooker from heat and let cool for 10 minutes to allow pressure to go down completely. In a food processor, combine raisins, cinnamon, and half the rice and grind into a paste. In a large mixing bowl, combine paste and remaining rice and mix well. Measure 2½ tablespoons of the mixture for each dumpling. With wet hands, shape each dumpling into a ball and roll in the walnuts until well coated. Arrange dumplings on a serving plate or cover and refrigerate for later use. Serve with Plum Syrup.

Sweet Golden Corn Polenta

YIELD: *4 servings*

TIME: *15 minutes preparation;*
   30 minutes cooking

¼ *cup pistachios*
1½ *cups water*
1 *cup yellow corn meal*
⅓ *cup fructose, Sucanat, or*
   FruitSource granules
2 *tablespoons apricot preserves*
4 *teaspoons agar flakes (or 1*
   teaspoon agar powder)
2 *teaspoons pure vanilla extract*

This is a dessert polenta that can be served with fruits or a complementary dessert sauce such as Strawberry Peach Coulis, Plum Syrup, or Whipped Cream.

Preheat oven to 300 degrees F. Place the pistachios on a baking sheet and bake for 20 minutes, or until very fragrant. Remove pistachios and chop while warm, then set aside. In a 1-quart saucepan, combine the water, corn meal, fructose, apricot preserves, and agar and bring to a simmer on medium heat while stirring in one-minute intervals to ensure even cooking. Cook until mixture is soft and thick, then add vanilla extract and pistachios. Mix well, then pour into a lightly oiled 8-inch square baking pan. Cool slightly, cut into quarters, then serve warm or cool with a dessert sauce.

Pumpkin Mousse

YIELD: *4 servings*

TIME: *30 minutes preparation;
1 hour chilling*

1 tablespoon agar flakes
½ cup water
*1 pound pumpkin purée (about
2 cups fresh, cooked and
puréed) or 1 16-ounce can*
*1 10½-ounce package extra
firm silken tofu*
¾ cup Sucanat
½ cup canola oil
¼ cup pecan or hazelnut butter
5 teaspoons pure vanilla extract
1 tablespoon ground cinnamon
2 teaspoons coriander powder
1 teaspoon ground nutmeg
½ teaspoon anise powder
½ teaspoon cardamom powder
½ teaspoon sea salt
¼ teaspoon ground cloves

This mousse is delicious served with a dollop of Hazelnut Whipping Cream.

Soak the agar flakes in the water until they are soft. In a 1-quart saucepan, add the agar/water mixture and bring to a simmer over medium heat. Cover and continue to simmer for 7 to 10 minutes or until agar is dissolved. Remove saucepan from heat. In a blender, combine pumpkin purée, tofu, Sucanat, oil, pecan butter, vanilla extract, cinnamon, coriander, nutmeg, anise, cardamom, salt, and cloves, plus the dissolved agar, and blend until smooth. Transfer mixture to a large mixing bowl. Using the whip attachment of an electric mixer, whip the mousse for 5 minutes to aerate it. Transfer the mousse to a covered container and refrigerate for 1 hour or until set. Serve cold.

Opposite: Rainbow Fruit Terrine (page 232) with Blueberry Cream Sauce (page 239)

Pistachio Cream in Squash Shell

YIELD: *4 servings*

TIME: *30 minutes preparation;
    2 hours chilling*

1 medium butternut squash

*6 tablespoons ground pistachio
    nuts*

*½ 10½-ounce package extra
    firm lite silken tofu*

*½ cup FruitSource granules or
    fructose*

1 tablespoon cognac

½ teaspoon pure vanilla extract

*1 tablespoon agar flakes (or
    1 teaspoon agar powder)*

1 teaspoon cocoa powder

This recipe presents a new possibility: eating your vegetables for dessert. A sweet fruit sauce makes it complete.

Cut the top (neck) from the butternut squash, leaving only the rounded end. Peel, slice in half, and remove the seeds. In a 3-quart saucepan, steam the squash with 1 inch of simmering salted water until the squash is tender but still firm enough to hold its shape. Transfer squash to a plate and set aside. In a blender, combine pistachios, tofu, FruitSource, cognac, vanilla extract, and agar and blend until mixture becomes coarse and pasty in texture. Dry out the cavity of the squash and roll a small amount of cocoa powder in it to create a thin coating. Transfer pistachio cream to a double boiler, cover, and heat until it reaches 150 degrees F. Turn the squash upside down and tap it to remove the excess cocoa powder, then fill it immediately with the pistachio cream while it is still hot. Press the filling in to make sure there are no air pockets. Refrigerate squash for 2 hours or until chilled, then slice and serve 3 slices per person with Plum Syrup.

Opposite: Hazelnut Cream Cake (page 220) with Strawberry Peach Coulis (page 242)—upper right; Pistachio Cream in Squash Shell (page 231) with Plum Syrup (page 241)—lower left

Rainbow Fruit Terrine

YIELD: *8 servings*

TIME: *50 minutes preparation;
2 hours chilling*

Gelatin

*4 cups Banana Casablanca
juice or other fruit juice*

*3 tablespoons frozen pineapple
juice concentrate*

*¼ cup plus 2 tablespoons agar
flakes*

*4 teaspoons arrowroot powder
dissolved in 2 tablespoons
cool water*

*2 tablespoons chopped fresh
mint*

1 cup sliced fresh strawberries
3 peeled, sliced kiwis
2 peeled, sliced peaches
¾ cup fresh blueberries
¼ seeded, sliced cantaloupe

Light, refreshing, and very colorful, this dessert is perfect for a warm summer's evening. Serve with Blueberry Cream Sauce.

Gelatin

In a 2-quart saucepan, combine the juices and agar and bring to a gentle simmer over medium heat. Cook for 10 minutes, or until all of the agar has dissolved. Add the arrowroot/water mixture and stir to thicken. Remove saucepan from heat and add chopped mint. Ladle a small amount (about ¼-inch layer) into the bottom of a lightly oiled 2-quart loaf pan. Place pan in freezer for about 5 minutes or until agar is set. Pour the remaining agar mixture into a separate container, cover, and refrigerate for a few minutes to cool slightly.

Assembling the Terrine

Remove loaf pan from the freezer and container of agar mixture from refrigerator. Working as quickly as possible, arrange sliced strawberries, overlapping if necessary, to cover the entire layer of gelatin. Leave about ⅛ inch around the edges uncovered so gelatin will surround the fruit layers. Next add a layer of sliced kiwis, followed by the peaches, blueberries, and cantaloupe. Return to the strawberries, repeating the same pattern until either all the fruit is used or you come to the top of the loaf pan. Ladle gelatin mixture over layered fruit, making sure to completely surround the fruit on the sides of the pan. Gently shake the pan back and forth to disperse the gelatin throughout the fruit, then with both hands lift up the loaf pan and gently tap the bottom on a flat surface to remove as many air bubbles as possible. Completely cover the top layer of fruit with gelatin, or else the fruit will discolor from being exposed to air. Place the terrine in the refrigerator and chill for 2 hours, or preferably overnight, until the agar is completely set.

Unmolding the Terrine

Remove terrine from refrigerator. Wipe outside of loaf pan with a hot, moist towel. Place a plate or platter as long as the pan over it, turn it upside down, and unmold terrine on the plate. Using a serrated knife, slice the terrine into 1-inch thick slices and serve cold or at room temperature.

VARIATION: *Rainbow Fruit en Gelée*

Reduce the quantities of each fruit by half, coarsely chop them, then add directly to slightly cooled agar mixture. Pour fruit/agar mixture into one lightly oiled decorative mold or several smaller molds. Chill until set, unmold, and serve.

Biscottini di Prato

YIELD: *24 small biscuits*
TIME: *40 minutes preparation;
90 minutes cooking*

1¾ cups almonds
1 cup water
½ cup canola oil
2 tablespoons warmed liquid
   lecithin
5 teaspoons pure vanilla extract
3 cups whole wheat pastry flour
1¼ cups maple sugar or
   Sucanat
1 teaspoon baking powder
¼ teaspoon sea salt

This Italian biscuit goes well with Rainbow Fruit Terrine or Mangolope Custard.

Preheat oven to 325 degrees F. Spread almonds on a baking sheet and roast for about 15 minutes or until they are lightly browned. Remove almonds and immediately transfer to a container to stop roasting. When slightly cool, place almonds in a food processor and grind to a medium-coarse meal (this should yield 1¼ cups). Increase oven temperature to 350 degrees F. In a large mixing bowl, combine the water, oil, lecithin, and vanilla extract and mix well. In another mixing bowl, combine the flour, sugar, baking powder, and salt and mix well. Add the dry ingredients to the wet and mix until well blended. Pour the batter into a lightly oiled and floured 8½ x 12 x 2-inch pan. Bake for about 45 minutes or until the top springs back when touched and a toothpick inserted in the center comes out clean. Remove cake and gently cut into four 3 x 8-inch portions. Transfer biscuits to a larger baking pan, spread them apart, and place pan in a pilot-lit oven to dry out overnight, or in a 150 to 200 degree F oven for 1½ hours (if using a heated oven, check biscuits every 30 minutes to make sure they are not overbaking). When done, remove biscuits and let cool completely. Store in a dry, airtight container until ready to use, then cut into smaller pieces and serve.

VARIATION
Soak ½ cup chopped raisins in ¼ cup warm water for 20 minutes. Drain and add to the wet ingredients, then proceed as directed.

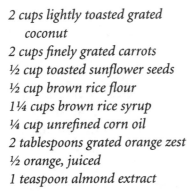

Golden Macaroons

YIELD: *4 dozen cookies*
TIME: *50 minutes*

2 cups lightly toasted grated
* coconut*
2 cups finely grated carrots
½ cup toasted sunflower seeds
½ cup brown rice flour
1¼ cups brown rice syrup
¼ cup unrefined corn oil
2 tablespoons grated orange zest
½ orange, juiced
1 teaspoon almond extract

Glaze

2 tablespoons barley malt syrup
1 tablespoon water

This macaroon combines a unique blend of flavors and textures, resulting in a mildly sweet and chewy cookie.

Preheat oven to 325 degrees F. In a large mixing bowl, combine coconut, carrots, sunflower seeds, and flour, mix well and set aside. In another bowl, combine rice syrup, oil, zest, juice, and almond extract. Add wet ingredients to the dry and mix well. Using a tablespoon, form the dough into mounds and place on a lightly oiled baking sheet. Bake for 15 to 20 minutes. In a small bowl, combine the barley malt syrup and water. After 10 minutes of baking, brush the macaroons with the glaze to give them a light golden brown color and shine (do not glaze the cookies at the beginning of the baking period or they will burn). When the macaroons are done, remove and transfer to a cookie rack to cool.

Concern for the earth is essential to compassionate action.

Cajeta Tart

YIELD: *8 servings*
TIME: *35 minutes preparation;*
35 minutes cooking

Tart Dough

*1 cup peeled, cubed butternut
    squash
1½ cups unbleached white flour
¼ cup FruitSource syrup or
    fructose
¼ cup arrowroot powder
1 teaspoon sea salt
1 tablespoon unrefined corn oil
1 teaspoon pure vanilla extract*

Custard Filling

*½ cup Sucanat
½ cup FruitSource granules
2 tablespoons lemon juice
¼ cup almond butter
1 cup soy milk powder
4 cups soy milk
½ teaspoon baking soda
2 tablespoons agar flakes mixed
    with 2 tablespoons water
2 tablespoons arrowroot powder
    or cornstarch dissolved in
    2 tablespoons cool water
1 teaspoon pure vanilla extract*

The idea for this tart came from *The Coyote Cafe Cookbook* by Mark Miller. I converted it from an egg and dairy recipe to a totally vegetarian recipe; puréed squash gives the pie crust more color. The recipe won a silver medal at the 1992 International Culinary Olympics and is my favorite custard tart.

Tart Dough

Preheat oven to 350 degrees F. In a vegetable steamer, steam the squash for 10 minutes or until soft, then drain and purée in a food processor or blender. In a mixing bowl, combine the flour, FruitSource, arrowroot, and salt and mix well. Add the oil, vanilla, and squash purée, then mix into a dough. If dough is too stiff, add a small amount of water. Flour a work surface, place dough on surface, and roll out ⅛ inch thick into a rectangle 14 x 10 inches. Lay rolled dough into a lightly oiled baking pan and press into place to cover all surface area of the baking pan. Set aside while preparing custard filling.

Custard Filling

In a 3-quart saucepan, combine Sucanat and FruitSource and cook on medium heat for 5 minutes, or until the sugars begin to brown. Stir constantly until the sugars are caramelized. Add the lemon juice and continue to cook until it becomes a smooth syrup. Add the almond butter, mix until smooth, then cover and set aside. In a mixing bowl, whip the soy powder into the soy milk. Bring the caramel to a simmer, then reduce heat to low and slowly add the soy milk/powder mixture to the warm caramel in 1-cup increments, stirring constantly after each addition until caramel is well dissolved. Add the baking soda, which will cause the mixture to foam up. Add the agar/water mixture and continue to simmer for 10 minutes. Add the arrowroot/water mixture and the vanilla and continue to stir and simmer until mixture thickens. Pour filling into dough-lined baking pan and bake for 30 minutes. Place a baking sheet or drip pan under the tart pan to catch any spillover while baking. Serve warm.

DESSERT SAUCES

Whipped Cream

YIELD: *2½ cups*
TIME: *10 minutes preparation;*
    1 hour chilling

1 10½-ounce package extra
    firm silken tofu
½ cup corn or canola oil
½ cup brown rice syrup
¼ cup maple syrup
¼ cup soy milk powder
1 teaspoon pure vanilla extract

Serve with Chocolate Bread Pudding, Dessert Crêpes, Fresh Nectarine Crisp, Pistachio Cream in Squash Shell, or with a fresh fruit salad.

In a blender, combine all the ingredients and blend until smooth. Transfer to a covered container and refrigerate for 1 hour or until well chilled. Serve cold.

Hazelnut Whipping Cream

YIELD: *3 cups*
TIME: *10 minutes preparation;*
    1 hour chilling

¼ cup hazelnut butter plus ½
    cup canola oil (or ½ cup
    hazelnut oil)
1 10½-ounce package extra
    firm silken tofu
½ cup maple syrup
1 tablespoon pure vanilla
    extract
¼ cup cooked white rice
    (optional)
½ teaspoon agar powder
    (optional)

Need a stiff cream for that special dessert? Use the optional cooked rice, and/or agar powder. For a thinner, more pourable consistency, omit both. This cream tastes great either way.

In a blender, place all the ingredients and blend until smooth. Chill for 1 hour and serve cold.

VARIATION: *Creme Glacé*
In a blender, combine 1 tablespoon Hazelnut Whipping Cream and 1 tablespoon cognac for each serving and blend until smooth. Use as a glaze for dessert crepes, fresh fruits, or pastries.

Mango Sauce

YIELD: *2 cups*
TIME: *25 minutes cooking;*
1 hour chilling

1 cup peeled, pitted ripe mango
½ cup papaya or apricot juice
concentrate
½ cup water
1 tablespoon arrowroot powder
dissolved in 3 tablespoons
cool water

Serve with Dessert Crêpes and Hazelnut Cream Cake.

In a blender, place mango, juice, and water and blend until smooth. Transfer mixture to a 2-quart saucepan and bring to a simmer over medium heat. Add the arrowroot/water mixture and stir with a whisk until sauce thickens. Remove saucepan from heat and transfer sauce to a container. When cool, cover and refrigerate for 1 hour or until well chilled. Serve cold.

Quick Raspberry Sabayon Sauce

YIELD: *2¼ cups*
TIME: *10 minutes preparation;*
1 hour chilling

2 cups frozen, unsweetened
raspberries
1 10½-ounce package soft
silken tofu
5 tablespoons FruitSource syrup
or honey
3 tablespoons sake
½ teaspoon pure vanilla extract

Serve with Dessert Crêpes, Almond Dessert Crêpes, Pistachio Cream in Squash Shell, and Chocolate Bread Pudding.

In a blender, combine the raspberries, tofu, syrup, sake, and vanilla extract and blend until smooth. Transfer sauce to a container and refrigerate for 1 hour until chilled. Serve cold.

Blueberry Cream Sauce

YIELD: *1½ cups*
TIME: *10 minutes*

1 10½-ounce package extra
    firm silken tofu
½ cup fruit juice–sweetened
    blueberry preserves
2 tablespoons mirin or sake
¼ cup honey, maple syrup or
    FruitSource syrup
2 tablespoons lemon juice
½ teaspoon pure vanilla extract

Serve with waffles, French toast, and fresh fruit salads.

In a blender, combine all the ingredients and blend until smooth. Serve chilled or at room temperature.

Coconut Squash Sauce

YIELD: *3 cups*
TIME: *20 minutes preparation;*
    1 hour chilling

2 cups almond milk
¼ cup coconut milk
1 cup dried, unsweetened
    coconut
3 tablespoons arrowroot
    powder dissolved in 3
    tablespoons cool water
1 cup Sucanat
½ teaspoon pure vanilla extract
½ cup peeled, steamed
    butternut squash

Serve with German Chocolate Cake and Chocolate Bread Pudding.

In a 2-quart saucepan, combine almond milk, coconut milk, and dried coconut and bring to a simmer over medium heat. Remove saucepan from heat, add arrowroot/water mixture, and stir vigorously with a whisk until thickened. Add Sucanat and vanilla extract, then transfer to a blender, add squash, and blend until smooth. Chill for 1 hour and serve on ice cream or as a dessert topping.

VARIATION: *Coconut Squash Cake Icing*
In a food processor, grind 2 cups chopped walnuts to a medium-coarse meal (this should yield 1½ cups). Blend walnuts into Coconut Squash Sauce and chill at least 1 hour before using.

Country Fruit Topping

YIELD: *2 cups*
TIME: *30 minutes preparation;*
  1 hour chilling

1 cup whole grain bread crumbs
½ cup Sucanat
6 tablespoons coarsely ground
  walnuts
2 tablespoons walnut or
  hazelnut oil
2 tablespoons grated orange zest
1 tablespoon pure vanilla
  extract
1 teaspoon cinnamon

Serve this topping to add excitement to any simple fruit dessert.

In a mixing bowl, place all the ingredients and mix together until well blended. Chill for 1 hour and serve cold on fresh fruit salad, puddings, ice creams, and Glazed Fruit Dessert Pizza.

Peach and Yellow Pepper Coulis

YIELD: *1½ cups*
TIME: *10 minutes preparation;*
  50 minutes cooking; 1 hour
  chilling

1 yellow bell pepper
2 teaspoons olive oil
1 cup peeled, sliced, fresh
  peaches or canned sliced
  peaches
¼ cup fruit juice–sweetened
  apricot preserves
1 tablespoon lemon juice
⅛ teaspoon coriander powder
¹⁄₁₆ teaspoon sea salt

Serve with Fresh Nectarine Crisp and Peach Cobbler.

Preheat oven to 325 degrees F. Wash, dry, halve, and seed bell pepper. Rub skins with oil. Place pepper halves on baking sheet and roast for 30 to 40 minutes or until soft and the skins begin to shrivel. Remove pepper from oven and place in brown paper bag to steam for 10 minutes. When cool, remove the loosened skins. In a blender, combine pepper, peaches, apricot preserves, lemon juice, coriander, and salt and blend until smooth. Refrigerate for 1 hour or until well chilled. Serve cold.

Plum Syrup

YIELD: *2 cups*
TIME: *15 minutes preparation;
2 hours cooking; 1 hour
chilling*

*4 cups pitted, sliced, unpeeled
plums*
*¾ cup FruitSource syrup
or honey*
1 tablespoon lemon juice
¹⁄₁₆ teaspoon sea salt

Serve with Dessert Crêpes, Ice Cream Cake, and any fruit salad.

In a 2-quart saucepan, combine plums, syrup, lemon juice, and salt and simmer over low heat for about 2 hours or until the mixture has reduced ⅓ to ¼ the original amount. Transfer mixture to a blender and blend until smooth. Refrigerate in a covered container for 1 hour or until ready to use.

Raspberry Syrup

YIELD: *1 cup*
TIME: *40 minutes cooking;
1 hour chilling*

2 cups fresh raspberries
1 cup brown rice syrup

Serve with Dessert Crêpes, Ice Cream Rice Cake, and any fruit salad.

In a 1-quart saucepan, combine the raspberries and syrup and simmer over medium to low heat until mixture is reduced to 1 cup. Strain, cool, and refrigerate sauce in a covered container for 1 hour or until chilled. Serve cold.

Red Pepper Mango Sauce

YIELD: *1½ cups*
TIME: *10 minutes preparation;*
50 minutes cooking; 1 hour
chilling

1 red bell pepper
1 teaspoon olive oil
1 cup peeled, pitted mango
¼ cup fruit juice–sweetened
  strawberry preserves

This sauce has a superb flavor and texture. The roasted red bell peppers accentuate the flavor of the mango.

Preheat oven to 325 degrees F. Wash, dry, halve, and seed bell pepper. Rub skin with oil. Place pepper halves on baking sheet and roast for 30 to 40 minutes or until soft and the skins begin to shrivel. Remove pepper from oven and place in brown paper bag to steam for 10 minutes. When cool, remove the loosened skins. In a blender, combine pepper, mango, and strawberry preserves and blend until smooth. Refrigerate for 1 hour or until well chilled. Serve cold.

Strawberry Peach Coulis

YIELD: *1½ cups*
TIME: *10 minutes preparation;*
1 hour chilling

1 cup washed, hulled, chopped
  fresh strawberries
1 cup peeled, chopped fresh
  peaches
2 tablespoons finely diced
  candied ginger
2 tablespoons brown rice syrup
⅛ teaspoon sea salt

Serve with Fresh Nectarine Crisp, Peach Cobbler, Rainbow Fruit Terrine, or Sweet Golden Corn Polenta.

In a blender, combine all the ingredients and blend until smooth. Transfer sauce to a container and refrigerate for 1 hour or until chilled. Serve cold.

Yellow Pepper Apricot Sauce

YIELD: *1⅓ cups*
TIME: *10 minutes preparation;*
1 hour chilling

2 yellow bell peppers
2 teaspoons olive oil
½ cup apricot preserves

Serve with Dessert Crêpes and Pistachio Cream in Squash Shell.

Preheat oven to 325 degrees F. Wash, dry, halve, and seed yellow bell peppers. Rub skins with oil. Place pepper halves on baking sheet and roast for 30 to 40 minutes or until soft and the skins begin to shrivel. Remove peppers from oven and place in brown paper bag to steam for 10 minutes. When cool, remove the loosened skins. In a blender, place peppers and apricot preserves and blend until smooth. Refrigerate for 1 hour or until well chilled. Serve cold.

Chocolate Ganache

YIELD: *1¼ cups*
TIME: *10 minutes*

½ cup soy milk
1½ cups chocolate chips
(preferably dairy free and
sweetened with a natural
sweetener)
1 tablespoon maple syrup

Serve with Chocolate Bread Pudding, Hazelnut Cream Cake, and Cajeta Tart.

In a 1-quart saucepan, combine milk, chocolate chips, and maple syrup and cook over low heat. Stir constantly until chocolate has completely melted and mixture is smooth. Remove from heat and use 2 tablespoons per serving.

Almond Butter Sauce

YIELD: *1 cup*
TIME: *10 minutes*

½ cup brown rice syrup or
  FruitSource syrup
¼ 10½-ounce package firm
  silken tofu
¼ cup almond butter
2 tablespoons soy milk
1 teaspoon pure vanilla extract

Serve with Chocolate Bread Pudding, Dessert Crêpes, and German Chocolate Cake.

In a blender, combine all the ingredients and blend until smooth. Transfer the sauce to a covered container and refrigerate until ready to use.

VARIATION: *Hazelnut Butter Sauce*
Replace almond butter with hazelnut butter. Proceed as directed. This sauce also works well as an icing on Hazelnut Cream Cake, over which Chocolate Ganache (page 243) may be drizzled.

Beverages

Water is essential to our survival. Natural body functions, by their very nature, consume and give off moisture. These functions depend on moisture from the internal blood supply and moisture that comes from outside sources. Just plain water is all that is necessary to survive, but as human beings, we demand more variety.

In 1985, the American population consumed more carbonated beverages than water. We like to enjoy our liquids in various forms and that is fine as long as the alternatives are nutritious. From an ecological perspective, I prefer less refined foods even though they are acceptable, especially if they are plant-based. My beverage section focuses on using whole foods combined with some refined foods to make them energy efficient (less refining is needed to produce them) and nutritionally dense (using the whole fruits or vegetables).

One would have to consume 4 oranges to get the juice of one 12-ounce glass of orange juice. Raw, freshly pressed fruit juices are an excellent source of energy and nutrition for the person who is expending a great deal of energy and needs something that will give the energy and nutritional boost at the same time. While fruit juices are a good source of energy, they should be consumed with moderation.

Mint Milk Shake

YIELD: *2 servings*
TIME: *20 minutes*

1 cup non-dairy vanilla "ice cream" (Living Rightly Non-Dairy Frozen Dessert)
8 washed, fresh mint leaves
1 tablespoon peppermint Schnapps
½ cup soy milk (or ¼ cup soy milk powder plus ½ cup water, blended until smooth)

Mint and cream make a tasty combination and the peppermint Schnapps rounds out the mint flavor in this summer delight.

Remove ice cream from freezer and let soften at room temperature for 10 minutes. In a blender, combine all the ingredients and blend until smooth. Serve immediately.

Amasake Shake

YIELD: *4 servings*
TIME: *10 minutes preparation;*
     1 hour chilling

3 cups amasake
1 cup steamed, puréed butternut squash
2 cups soy milk
1 cup brown rice syrup
2 teaspoons pure vanilla extract

While at Valentina's Corner Restaurant, I worked long days and this power drink gave me the energy to keep my body going.

In a blender, combine all the ingredients and blend until smooth. Transfer to a covered container and refrigerate for 1 hour or until chilled. Serve cold.

Blueberry Shake

YIELD: *2 servings*
TIME: *10 minutes preparation*

1 cup unsweetened apple juice
2 cups fresh or frozen
*   blueberries*
1 cup peeled, pitted, sliced fresh
*   or frozen peaches*
1 peeled ripe banana
1 strawberry, cut in ½ for
*   garnish*

As a child, I used to pick wild blueberries during the summer in northern Michigan. This shake is great for a nutritional summer cooler.

In a blender, combine all the ingredients except the strawberry and blend until smooth. Garnish with strawberry half and serve immediately.

Carrot Milk Shake

YIELD: *2 servings*
TIME: *25 minutes*

1 cup fresh carrot juice
2 cups non-dairy "ice cream"
*   (Living Rightly Non-Dairy*
*   Frozen Dessert)*
2 tablespoons lecithin granules
*   (optional)*
¼ teaspoon pure vanilla extract

This is the best way to put excitement and nutrition into ice cream and a great way to entice children (and adults) to get their vitamin A. Use the freshest carrot juice, not more than 1 day old.

In a blender, combine all the ingredients and blend until smooth. Serve immediately.

VARIATION: *Carrot-Orange Milk Shake*
Replace 1 cup of the ice cream with 1 cup of freshly squeezed orange juice and blend until smooth.

Cucumber Avocado Milk Shake

YIELD: *2 servings*
TIME: *20 minutes*

2 cups non-dairy "ice cream"
    (*Living Rightly Non-Dairy
    Frozen Dessert*)
½ cup peeled, seeded, chopped
    cucumber
½ cup peeled, seeded, mashed
    ripe avocado
¼ cup brown rice syrup (or 2
    tablespoons mild-flavored
    honey)
5 chopped large fresh mint
    leaves
2 strawberries for garnish

This vegetable shake goes well with any burger because of its savory sweet flavor.

In a blender, combine all the ingredients except the strawberries and blend until smooth. Garnish each serving with a mixture of chopped fresh mint and a strawberry and serve immediately.

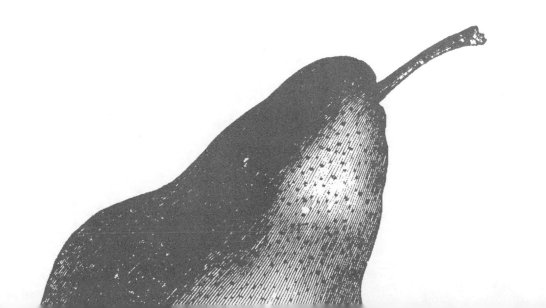

Peach Milk Shake

YIELD: *2 servings*
TIME: *10 minutes*

*2 cups peeled, pitted, sliced
    peaches (about 3 peaches)*
*1½ tablespoons fresh lemon
    juice*
*1 cup non-dairy vanilla "ice
    cream" (Living Rightly Non-
    Dairy Frozen Dessert)*

The lemon brings out the flavor of the peaches, making it perfect for an intermezzo or an after-dinner dessert. It's also good just by itself.

In a blender, combine all the ingredients and blend until smooth. Serve immediately.

VARIATIONS: *Peach Sorbet*
Pour the blended ingredients into an ice cream maker and freeze according to the manufacturer's instructions. If an ice cream maker is unavailable, pour blended mixture into a covered container and place in a freezer for several hours or overnight. Remove container from freezer, break frozen contents into chunks, and blend in a food processor for 30 seconds or until smooth. Scoop out the sorbet and serve as a dessert or an intermezzo.

Banana Milk Shake
Omit the peaches and the lemon juice. Add 2 bananas, cut into chunks, ¼ cup peach juice, and ¼ teaspoon pure vanilla extract to the ice cream and blend until smooth.

Raspberry Milk Shake

YIELD: *2 servings*
TIME: *10 minutes*

1 cup non-dairy lemon "ice cream" (Living Rightly Non-Dairy Frozen Dessert)
1 cup frozen, unsweetened raspberries
¼ cup white honey or FruitSource syrup
¼ cup water

This shake can also be served as a sorbet or intermezzo. The strong flavor of the raspberries is accented by the lemon in the ice cream.

In a blender, combine all the ingredients and blend until smooth. Serve immediately.

VARIATION: *Raspberry Sorbet*
Omit the water. In a blender, combine all ingredients and blend until smooth. Serve in a sorbet cup or in a halved and hollowed lemon or lime cup.

Mango Strawberry Smoothy

YIELD: *2 servings*
TIME: *10 minutes*

2 cups peeled, diced mangoes
2 cups stemmed, quartered strawberries
1 teaspoon lemon juice (optional)

When I lived in Miami Beach, I would rise early in the morning and pick freshly fallen mangoes from the ground. This smoothy brings back the taste of those mornings.

In a blender, combine all the ingredients and blend until smooth. Serve immediately.

Papaya Smoothy

YIELD: *2 servings*
TIME: *10 minutes preparation;*
30 minutes chilling

4 stemmed fresh strawberries
¼ peeled ripe banana
¼ cup chilled orange juice
1 seeded, cubed medium
    papaya

This smoothy is so rich and sweet that it could pass as a dessert. Served immediately after blending, it is thick enough to pass for a sorbet.

Place strawberries and banana in a freezer for 30 minutes or until frozen. In a blender, combine all the ingredients and blend until smooth. Serve immediately.

Strawberry Banana Smoothy

YIELD: *2 servings*
TIME: *15 minutes*

2 cups chilled apple cider
1 cup stemmed fresh
    strawberries
1 cup peeled banana, sliced
    ½ inch thick
⅓ cup chopped dates

This was a very popular smoothy at the Unicorn Village Restaurant in Aventura, Florida. My afternoon shift started with a glass of this smoothy.

Place strawberries and banana in a freezer for 30 minutes or until frozen. In a blender, combine all the ingredients and blend until smooth. Serve immediately.

Tropical Fruit Smoothy

YIELD: *2 servings*
TIME: *10 minutes*

1 cup coconut milk
1 cup peeled, seeded, diced
 papaya
1 cup peeled, diced fresh
 pineapple
1 cup stemmed, halved fresh
 strawberries
1 tablespoon toasted coconut
 for garnish

This smoothy is meant to be enjoyed by itself because it has such a delicate combination of fruit flavors.

In a blender, combine the milk, papaya, pineapple, and strawberries and blend until smooth. Garnish with a sprinkling of the toasted coconut and serve immediately.

Hot Pear Cider

YIELD: *6 servings*
TIME: *10 minutes preparation;*
 30 minutes cooking

1 quart pear juice
1 quart apple juice
¼ teaspoon cinnamon
¼ teaspoon clove powder
¼ teaspoon ginger powder
1 quartered lemon
1 quartered orange

This winter treat can also be served cold in the summer.

In a 3-quart saucepan, combine all the ingredients and bring to a simmer over medium heat. Simmer for 30 minutes and serve hot.

SEASONAL & HOLIDAY DINNER MENU SUGGESTIONS

How is a menu composed? In the restaurant business, the menu is the bible of the operation and must take into account labor costs, food costs, and marketability. The same is true of a family. You have limited time to cook, limited finances, and must cater to your family's taste. The menu is the bible of nutritional wellness in the family and can greatly facilitate the effective use of one's time and energy.

With ecological cuisine, while honoring the traditional approach to menu planning, the focus is on balancing the menu nutritionally and ecologically. This entails bringing different colors, textures, and tastes into focus. The menu should reflect seasonal foods and nutritional balance, and the pleasure of fine dining is combined with the purpose of nurturing the body. The menu serves as a guide and inspiration to apply the artistic and nutritional values of culinary art.

Creating an ecological menu entails the use of primarily plant-based foods. Using seasonal and locally grown organic (produced by sustainable agriculture) foods is the next guide, followed by using whole and fresh foods as much as possible. Fresh whole foods require less processing and provide more nutrition when consumed. Eco-Cuisine is the consciousness of consuming foods and looking at one's diet in relation to the planet as a whole. This cuisine marries individual and planetary health because they are one in essence.

The season and occasion for the menu determines what type of foods will be served. The balance of the menu is decided by color, flavor (sour, bitter, sweet, pungent, salty), and texture. With nutrition it entails making sure that the meal is high in complex carbohydrates, and fiber, and low in fat and protein. The soup should have a cracker served with it to add crunch to the otherwise soft vegetables in the broth. With a heavy dinner menu, a light salad should be served. All of the individual courses must be balanced in color, flavor, and texture, as does the entire meal.

I build my menus around the entrée; the selection of the entrée will determine what the rest of the savory courses will be, and they in turn determine what type of dessert will be offered. Appetizers should be light, well-seasoned, and in small quantities in order to stimulate the appetite. The soup will be lighter, given that the entrée will be substantial. Crackers or croutons add textural contrast. Salads are light, fresh, and crisp with a sweet or sour dressing, and served either before or after the entrée.

If serving a gourmet meal, an intermezzo of light, sweet citrus sorbet is served to cleanse the palate before the entrée. The entrée is the main attraction and generally the main source of protein, accompanied by a vegetable or starch side dish. At this point in the meal, the diner should feel close to satiation. The dessert should be light and sweet to cool the appetite and round out the menu. It is soft and light in texture and rich in flavor. The richness of the dessert is determined by the richness of the total menu.

Planning menus is a valuable tool for anyone who cooks a great deal at home because it can save time and money. One can shop for a week and prepare some foods such as sauces a day or two in advance if one knows that it is on the menu. Following are some menus reflecting my inspiration and passion for vegetarian gourmet food.

Spring

Collard Roll with Fresh Vegetables

San Francisco Vegetable Soup

Japanese Salad with Cilantro Vinaigrette

Grilled Vegetables and Pasta
with Thai Peanut Sauce

Smoked Portobello Mushrooms

Strawberry Fruit Tart

Florida Aspic with Orange Aioli Sauce

Yellow Pepper Cream Soup with
Confetti Corn Fritters

Tempeh Salad with
Lemon Garlic Dressing

Vegetable Paella

Asparagus with Yellow Pepper Sauce

Almond Dessert Crepes with Quick
Raspberry Sabayon Sauce

Summer

Cold Cucumber Kiwi Soup with
Mango Crackers

Arugula and Smoked Portobello
Mushroom Salad

Pistachio Polenta with Spinach Basil Pesto

Eggplant Roll with Sauce Renaissance

Rainbow Fruit Terrine with
Strawberry Peach Coulis

Carrot Aspic with Mango Dressing

Vichyssoise

Black Olive Tapenade on Pesto Bread

Roasted Vegetable Terrine with Creamy
Herb Miso Dressing

Seitan Pine Nut Crêpes with
Fresh Basil Sauce

Green Beans with Smoked
Portobello Mushrooms

Pears Mascarpone

Autumn

Wakame Quinoa Dumplings
with Wakame Au Jus

Cream of Pumpkin Soup

Italian Mixed Greens Salad with
Maple Balsamic Vinaigrette

Garbanzos Vesuvius

Harvest Pilaf

Carrot Cake with Orange Icing

Saffron Millet Soup

Mesa Verde Salad and Black Bean
Cracker Cups with Corn Relish

American Bounty with Roasted
Vegetable Sauce

Steamed Broccoli with Lima Purée Blanc

German Braised Red Cabbage

Chestnut Mount Bré

Winter

Cream of Cauliflower Soup

Andalusian Salad

Italian Shepherd's Pie

Sautéed Arame and Vegetables

German Chocolate Cake with
Coconut Squash Icing

Mushroom Duxelle Crêpes with
Burgundy Sauce Glaze

Kasha Soup

Berlin Bean Salad

Pecan Nut Loaf with
Sauce Concassé

Ragoût of Winter Vegetables

Southwestern Mashed Potatoes

Pistachio Cream in
Squash Shell

Easter

Swiss Cucumber Soup

Saffron Raisin Bread with
Onion Butter

Salad Argenteuil

Seafood Crêpes with Yellow
Pepper Sauce

Southern Black-Eyed Pilaf

Sugar Snap Peas with Carrots
and Walnuts

Orange Cranberry Ice Cream Cake
with Raspberry Syrup

Thanksgiving

Pâté Français

Roasted Vegetable Consommé

Pineapple Raisin Waldorf Salad

Vermont Seitan with Chestnuts

Millet Stuffed Squash with
Roasted Vegetables

Cranberry Relish

Pumpkin Mousse with
Whipped Cream

Hot Pear Cider

Hanukkah

Old-Fashioned Cream of Cabbage Soup

Focaccia with Walnut Applesauce Butter

Wakame Quinoa Dumplings
on Collards with Miso
Poppy Seed Dressing

Jewish Seitan Loaf with
Bulgur Potato Pilaf

Sweet Potato and Carrot Tzimmes

Chocolate Bread Pudding with
Hazelnut Whipping Cream

Christmas

Cauliflower Duxelle on Toast

Chestnut Soup

Roasted Vegetable Terrine with
Cilantro Fennel Pesto

Peach Butternut Sorbet (intermezzo)

Italian Country Loaf with
Sauce Renaissance

Green Beans New Orleans

Sweet Potatoes, Carrots,
and Cranberries

Hazelnut Cream Cake with
Plum Syrup

GLOSSARY

Technical Terms

Chop: Cut into irregularly shaped pieces.
Concassé: Roughly chopped.
Chiffonade: Cut plant leaves into thin strips or ribbons.
Dice: fine—⅛" square
small—¼" square
medium—½" square
large—¾" square

Flaking: Shave or thinly slice at a 45 degree angle about ⅛" thick.
Julienne: Cut into thin pieces ⅛" x ⅛" x 2".
Mince: Chop into very fine pieces.

Unusual Ingredients

ADUKI BEANS These small maroon-red beans are considered by the Japanese as the king of beans. They are rich in flavor, carbohydrates, amino acids, potassium, iron, calcium, and some B-complex nutrients. This bean doesn't need to be soaked before cooking and cooks in only 45 minutes.

AGAR Agar (or kanten) is derived from various red algae (gelidium). It is rich in calcium, iron, phosphorus, and vitamins A, B-complex, C, D, and K. Used mainly as a thickener, agar is an excellent vegan substitute for gelatin, an animal product. It is superior to gelatin in its health benefits and sets up at room temperature. Agar is available in three forms: powder, flake, and bar (flakes formed into a bar). Both flakes and bars need to be cooked for 10 to 15 minutes to completely dissolve. Never cook agar in any liquid that contains oil; this seems to bind the agar and prevent absorption. When foods require limited cooking, it is best to use agar powder (or Emes Kosher-Jel—see appendix) because it absorbs liquid and dissolves immediately. When adding citrus juice or zest to a recipe containing

agar, add the citrus to the hot liquid after the agar dissolves. Uncooked citrus will break down the gelatin. To make a firm gelatin, use ¾ teaspoon agar powder, 1 tablespoon agar flakes, ⅔ agar bar, or ¼ cup of Emes Kosher-Jel (see Appendix) to 2 cups of liquid.

ANASAZI BEANS Anasazi means "ancient ones" in the Navaho language. The bean holds its shape better after being cooked and has a superior flavor. Because of the romance associating it to native Southwestern foods, it sells for a higher price.

ARAME This sweet, mild-flavored sea vegetable is dark yellow-brown when growing and black when dried. After harvesting, it is shredded into thin strips and dried. Soak arame for 5 minutes, then drain and eat or cook as desired. Use it on salads and in soups, stews, or grain loaves. Arame goes well with sautéed vegetables and provides additional color, flavor, and nutritional value.

ARROWROOT   This starch is derived from the roots of the tropical arrowroot plant. It is sold as a powder and makes an excellent thickener for soups, stews, and desserts. It can also be used as a binder in grain or bean rolls and loaves when eggs are not used. Arrowroot does not work well to thicken most sauces as it tends to create a gelatinous texture. Before using, arrowroot powder should be dissolved in an equal amount of cold water (unless it is being used as a binder in a dry mix) and can replace cornstarch or kuzu in most recipes.

BARLEY MALT SYRUP   Made from sprouted whole barley, this sweetener has a caramel flavor and generally is about half as sweet as sugar or honey. Barley malt syrups that are made with corn syrup are not as desirable as pure barley malt syrup. However, in barley-corn malt syrup, the two grains have been fermented together, producing a high-quality food. Barley malt syrup is high in carbohydrates and contains some vitamins and minerals. It tends to be the least expensive of natural sweeteners. This syrup must be stored in a sanitary jar and kept in a cool, dry place. If it begins to ferment, heat the syrup to kill the active enzymes (see Eden Foods in Appendix).

BROWN RICE SYRUP   This cultured (fermented) product is made from brown rice (sometimes white rice), water, and a small amount of natural cereal enzyme. The light and delicate syrup is about half as sweet as sugar and is a complex carbohydrate. It is probably one of the most neutral-flavored natural sweeteners on the market (see Lundberg Family Farms in Appendix). In combination with other sweeteners such as Sucanat® or honey, it helps neutralize their dominant flavor. Rice syrup made with brown rice has a darker color than the syrup made from white rice, but the flavor is the same. This type of sweetener is also available in powdered form (see Devansoy Farms in Appendix).

BULGUR   Bulgur (or bulghur) is steamed, dried, and cracked whole wheat that has its origins in the Middle East. It is commonly used in the traditional dish *tabbouleh*. To cook this light grain, pour boiling water over it, cover, and let stand for a few hours or until tender.

COUSCOUS   Traditionally, couscous is made from the endosperm remnants of refined durum wheat. As a refined food, it has less nutritional value than whole wheat. A new product called whole wheat couscous is now available through natural foods stores and in some supermarkets. Darker in color than traditional couscous, it is a whole, more nutritious food. Couscous is often called "Moroccan pasta."

DAIKON   This Japanese root vegetable is a white radish that has the shape of a carrot but is much larger, usually 12 to 18 inches long with a weight of 3 to 5 pounds. It is eaten raw, cooked, pickled, or dried. Raw daikon is abundant in digestive enzymes which help transform complex carbohydrates, fats, and proteins into their readily assimilable components.

DULSE   A sea vegetable in the red algae family which was once eaten as a snack like potato chips in Western Europe and New England. Found in the waters of the North Atlantic and the Pacific Northwest, it is reddish-purple and may be eaten raw, dried, toasted or cooked. Dulse is good in salads, with cooked vegetables, and in grain dishes (I love it in my breakfast porridge). Dulse can be used in any recipe that calls for wakame.

EGG REPLACER   This powdered egg substitute is available at natural food stores and can be found near the flours, sugars, and other baking needs. Ener-G Egg Replacer is made primarily from potato starch and tapioca flour and contains no animal products, lactose, sodium, preservatives, sugar, or artificial flavorings. Although Ener-G Egg Replacer is a dry ingredient, you can use it in breads, cakes, muffins, crêpes, and other recipes that call for eggs (see Ener-G Foods in Appendix).

GLUTEN FLOUR The wheat berry is composed of bran, germ, and the endosperm (gluten and starch). Wheat gluten, which is mostly protein, is formed when the starch is removed from the endosperm. Gluten flour is derived from pure gluten; high gluten flour is bread flour or stone ground whole wheat flour that has a high gluten content relative to other flours.

HIJIKI This strong-flavored sea vegetable is a member of the brown algae family and turns black when dried. It should be soaked for 15 minutes, then rinsed and drained. Hijiki is best when sautéed with sweet vegetables and sesame oil before boiling. It will cook in 15 to 20 minutes, but a longer cooking time will help mellow out the flavor. If you are new to sea vegetables, begin with the milder arame or wakame, rather than with hijiki.

KASHA Kasha is roasted buckwheat that originates from the Volga region of the Soviet Union. Originally, it was called beech wheat because the triangular seed resembles the beech seed. The chestnut-colored kasha has a much heartier flavor than the greenish-white unroasted groats.

KOMBU The most versatile of the sea vegetables is a good source of calcium, sugar, potassium, iodine, and vitamin A. It also contains appreciable amounts of the B complexes and glutamic acid. Sold dried or in strips that measure five to eight inches, kombu is used most commonly as a flavoring. Kombu is often used in cooking beans and seitan, since it improves the flavor and digestibility. You can add a kombu strip to soup stock or use in miso soup, where it is cooked with the soup and then taken out, thinly sliced, and added back to the soup.

KUZU This powder is a concentrated starch from the kuzu (or kudzu) plant and can be used as a thickener, similar to cornstarch or arrowroot. Kuzu is sold in Asian markets and health food stores and is usually expensive. In Japan, it is also used for its medicinal properties; in the southern United States, kuzu is considered a noxious weed.

LAHVOSH Don't confuse this unleavened flat bread with crackers. It can be made of white flour (sold in Middle Eastern or mainstream stores) or of whole wheat flour (generally sold in natural food stores). It is pliable when fresh and can be steamed to make it pliable if it dries out.

LIQUID HICKORY SMOKE This product comes in natural and artificial flavors. I use only the natural flavored liquid smoke that is produced by infusing water with the essence of smoked hickory wood. Use it sparingly since it is very strong and can easily overwhelm the food that is being flavored. It is a good second choice when a smoked flavor is called for and you do not have the time or equipment to smoke the food itself (see Wright's Natural Hickory Seasoning in Appendix).

MIRIN This sweet rice wine is a flavoring agent made from sweet rice, rice koji (a natural rice culture used to convert the starches into sugars), water, and sea salt. The 13 or 14 percent alcohol solution evaporates quickly when heated. There are two types of mirin—one with salt (Eden Foods) and one without. The one with salt is appropriate in savory foods; the one without salt can be used in savory or sweet desserts. Mirin can be used in sauces, salad dressings, soups, desserts, or as a fruit liqueur.

MISO A fermented paste made from beans and/or grains and salt, miso is 10 to 12 percent protein. Because it is a predigested food, miso is a remarkable digestive aid. It is used mainly as a flavoring agent or a soup or sauce base and comes in a wide range of flavors, depending on the bean or grain from which it is made.

Shiro miso and chickpea miso are two types of light (or white) miso. These are delicately flavored and can be used in creamy sauces, salad dressings, delicate soups, and with sweet vegetables. Barley miso, brown rice miso, red miso, and hatcho miso (made from soybeans) are a few types of dark miso. These varieties of miso are stronger in flavor and have a dark, rich color. The darkest ones are great to use in strong, hearty soup stocks.

MOLÉ PASTE This seasoning originated in Pueblo Mexico. It contains chili pepper, corn oil or soy bean oil, wheat and corn flour, sesame seeds, sugar, almonds, cocoa, spices, and salt. It can be used to glaze tofu, tempeh, or seitan and in sauces and fillings with plant-based foods (see CMC Company in Appendix).

NORI Nori is a high-protein red seaweed originally called laver in English. Japanese nori is tricky to buy because it is sometimes dyed. Avoid buying nori sheets that are a uniform green; instead, choose those that are multi-hued. Asakusa nori, the most popular nori in Japan, is known as the paper thin wrapper in which sushi is rolled. Nori that grows in North American coastal waters is dried in its natural shape. Toasted, nori has a sweet, nutty, and salty taste. Sliced thin, it is a good garnish for soups. To toast nori, hold it about six inches over a medium flame, moving it at a moderate pace to prevent burning a hole through the sheet. When the nori turns from red to a light green, it is ready to use.

RICE MILK This product is derived from cooked rice that is cultured and has the liquid extracted from it. Flavorings and or emulsifiers are often added to give it more flavor and body. It is an excellent milk for breakfast and in cooking (see Eden Foods in Appendix).

RICE VINEGAR Rice vinegar has about half the acid of cider vinegar and a more delicate flavor. It is widely available at natural foods stores, Asian markets, and many supermarkets. Some rice vinegars may be made from white rice and contain additives. Those labeled Brown Rice Vinegar have greater nutritional integrity. To substitute cider vinegar for rice vinegar simply mix equal parts of water with the cider vinegar and use in the diluted state in place of the rice vinegar.

SEITAN Seitan, also know as "wheat meat," is the Japanese name for wheat gluten which has been cooked in a seasoned broth. High in protein, it is a great meat substitute in a transitional diet. It has a delicious flavor, a meaty texture, and is very filling. Several years ago, I developed Seitan Quick Mix which greatly reduces the preparation time compared to the traditional method (see Arrowhead Mills in Appendix). Pre-cooked seitan can be found in most natural foods stores.

SHOYU Shoyu, also called soy sauce, is made from soybeans, salt, and wheat. The fermentation process that creates shoyu is similar to the process used in making miso, though shoyu is not a whole food like miso. It has neither the nutritional value nor the robust flavor of miso. Shoyu is best when added after cooking or when used in marinades and cold foods because, unlike tamari, high heat destroys its delicate flavor.

SOBA Buckwheat (soba) noodles are available at Asian markets and most natural foods stores. The noodles have a brownish-gray color. Cook soba noodles in the same way as regular pasta.

SOY GRITS   Soy grits are a natural whole food made from raw or partially cooked soybeans. The texture depends on the degree they have been cracked. Soy grits come in two different sizes, small and large. I usually use the larger grits. Soy grits cook much faster than whole soybeans (see Modern Products in Appendix).

SOY MILK   To a vegan, soy milk is an important replacement for dairy milk. It has no cholesterol but about the same amount of protein, one third the fat, less calcium, and fifteen times as much iron as cow's milk. Because soy milk is lower on the food chain than dairy milk, it has fewer contaminants. The best tasting soy milk comes in aseptic containers. A good soy milk should not have an offensive flavor but may have a little chalkiness.

SUCANAT   Short for "Sugar Cane Natural," Sucanat is made by processing the juice from sugar cane. It is probably the highest quality sweetener available. 100 grams of Sucanat contains 386 calories, 389 mg of calcium, 53 mg of magnesium, 291 mg of potassium, 95.9 grams of carbohydrates, 3.41 mg of iron, and no fat. Sucanat is moist, like brown sugar, has a slight molasses taste, and can be used in place of white sugar. Because it is not a fully refined product, Sucanat cannot actually be called "sugar," according to USFDA standards.

TAHINI   Also called sesame butter, tahini is made from ground raw sesame seeds. It is popular in Middle Eastern cooking and can be found in natural foods stores and large supermarkets. Tahini has an overpowering flavor and therefore has limited use in sauces and as a flavoring agent. It is not hydrogenated, which is an asset in terms of nutrition but means that the butter must be mixed before using since the oil separates from the ground seeds. Refrigerating tahini will prevent separation and extend the life of the product (see Arrowhead Mills in Appendix).

TAMARI   Tamari is a by-product of miso. It is the liquid that rises to the surface in making hatcho (or soybean) miso. It is generally a higher quality product than shoyu (soy sauce). Tamari holds up well in intense heat, making it more appropriate to use in the cooking process, such as in a stir-fry.

TEMPEH   Tempeh is a cultured soybean product, native to Indonesia, and is rich in protein and vitamin B_{12}. In making tempeh, the cooked soybeans are incubated with a bacteria that acts as a binding agent. It has a fermented flavor and tends to compete with other ingredients. Tempeh is available at many natural foods stores (see White Wave in Appendix).

TOFU   To make tofu, the soybeans are cooked and the soy milk is extracted. Then a curdling agent such as nigari is added to the soy milk. The product is pressed to compact the curd which separates the soy whey. There are three types of regular tofu: soft, firm, and extra firm (see Nasoya Foods in Appendix). Regular tofu must be refrigerated and used within a week or so, because it will spoil. If regular tofu is being used in a cold dish, it should first be boiled for at least three minutes to kill bacteria. Silken tofu is produced within its aseptic package. It does not need to be refrigerated and will keep, unopened, for several months. Silken tofu also comes in three forms: soft, firm, and extra firm. The custard texture of silken tofu makes it excellent in desserts (see Morinaga Nutritional Foods in Appendix).

UDON   A thick, chewy, beige-colored wheat noodle from Japan, udon noodles are available at Asian markets and some natural foods stores. They are prepared in the same way as other pastas.

UMEBOSHI Umeboshi are sour, immature plums pickled in salt with red perilla leaves (beefsteak or shiso), giving them their pink color. The whole plum is used more often for its medicinal properties; umeboshi paste is usually used as a seasoning agent in cooking.

Umeboshi vinegar is the salty/sour liquid which remains after pickling umeboshi. It has a fruity flavor, a cherry aroma, and a reddish color. Because umeboshi vinegar contains salt, it is not technically a vinegar. It can be used in place of other vinegars, especially in salad dressings, and to bring up the flavor of grain and bean dishes. When using this vinegar, avoid adding salt (see Eden Foods in Appendix).

VOGUE VEGE BASE This vegetarian soup base has no chemicals or MSG. It is a vegetable-based seasoning powder and very low in salt (see Vogue Cuisine in Appendix).

WAKAME Wakame is among the most popular sea vegetables in Japan. It can be used in cooking to help soften the tough fibers of other vegetables, and adds flavor and nutrition. Wakame is available in its dry whole form, which when rehydrated looks like slippery spinach with a thick midrib, or dry chopped wakame, which is ready for instant use (see Eden Foods in Appendix). Wakame is essential to miso soup and combines well with onions, soba noodles, bamboo shoots, rice, barley, and many vegetables. You can also dry roast or fry pieces of wakame to eat as chips.

Wakame is harvested primarily in the northern seas of Japan, where it thrives in about 20 to 30 feet of water. About two thirds of Japan's 150,000-ton wakame crop is cultivated on about 19,000 sea farms. This vegetable grows quickly and needs only minimal weeding. It is ready to harvest by mid winter, when it is cut, rinsed, and sun-dried. Wakame is delicately textured. When soaking wakame, handle it gently or it will tend to fall apart.

YEAST, NUTRITIONAL This product is similar to brewer's yeast but has a less bitter taste and a gentle cheese-like flavor. Some brands of nutritional yeast use whey in the formula, so you have to read labels carefully if you want to avoid this dairy by-product.

APPENDIX

This appendix is primarily a listing of companies that produce and/or distribute high quality natural foods and culinary equipment. I frequently use products from most of these companies in my own cooking.

Natural Foods

Arrowhead Mills, Inc.
P.O. Box 2059
Hereford, Texas 79045
(806) 364-0730

A national distributor of mostly organically grown foods such as whole grains and flours (including blue corn, brown basmati rice, kamut, millet, and spelt), dried beans, seeds (including amaranth, flax, and quinoa), peanut butter, and tahini. They also sell cold and hot breakfast cereals, my Seitan Quick Mix, and various other mixes for biscuits, breads, muffins, pancakes, waffles, pasta, and soups.

CMC Company
P.O. Box 322
Avalon, New Jersey 08202
(800) 262-2780

A great source for ethnic specialty ingredients including Indian, Indonesian, Malaysian, Japanese, Mexican (my source for molé paste), Szechwan, Thai, and potpourri (miscellaneous European herbs and spices).

Cultural Survival
215 First Street
Cambridge, Massachusetts 02142
(617) 621-3818

Cultural Survival works for the human rights of indigenous peoples and ethnic minorities, helping them secure economic and social justice. The items currently available include banana chips, Brazil nuts, cashews, and honey.

Devansoy Farms
P.O. Box 885
Carroll, Iowa 51401
(800) 747-8605

Producers of Solait soy beverage powder, which can be substituted for regular soy milk. I also use this product as a dry ingredient in many of my recipes to create a rich, creamy flavor and texture. This company also produces DevanSweet, a powdered organic brown rice sweetener.

Eden Foods, Inc.
701 Tecumseh Road
Clinton, Michigan 49236
(517) 456-7424

A national distributor of mostly organically grown foods including grains, dried and pre-cooked beans (available in cans and jars), pastas (soba and udon), sea vegetables (agar flakes), barley malt, condiments (brown rice vinegar, umeboshi vinegar, shoyu, tamari, and mirin), miso, oils, specialty foods (shiso leaf powder, gomasio, umeboshi paste and plums, dried shiitake mushrooms, amasake, and kuzu powder), and beverages including rice and soy milks (or a blend), grain coffee (yannoh) and teas.

Emes Kosher Products
P.O. Box 833
Lombard, Illinois 60148
(708) 627-6204

This distributor carries Kosher-Jel, plain pareve gelatin (contains carageenan, locust bean gum, and malto-dextrin), in many forms: unflavored, unsweetened, and assorted fruit flavors. I sometimes use the plain gelatin in place of agar.

Ener-G Foods, Inc.
P.O. Box 84487
Seattle, Washington 98124-5787
(800) 331-5222

The source for Ener-G Egg Replacer and various dietary foods for people with multiple food allergies.

Equal Exchange
101 Tosca Drive
Stoughton, Massachusetts 02072
(617) 344-7227

This gourmet coffee company and alternative trade organization works towards creating fairer trade relationships between Third World farmers and North American consumers.

Fantastic Foods, Inc.
1250 North McDowell Boulevard
Petaluma, California 94954
(707) 778-7801

This company produces various instant food products, including the instant bean mix that I use in the Black Bean and Corn Roll.

Frontier Cooperative Herbs
P.O. Box 299
Norway, Iowa 52318
(319) 227-7996
For ordering call (800) 669-3275

The retail division of this company is called Herb and Spice Collection. The company also sells herbs, spices, and health care products, and are a good source of lecithin granules.

FruitSource Confections, Inc.
1803 Mission Street, Suite 401
Santa Cruz, California 95060
(408) 457-1136

An alternative to white sugar, FruitSource contains grape juice concentrate and whole rice syrup (simple and complex carbohydrates), and is available both granulated and as a syrup.

Garden of Eatin'
5300 Santa Monica Boulevard
Los Angeles, California 90029
(213) 462-5406

This company sells a wide variety of corn chips, salsa, bean dip, whole wheat pita breads, fruit bars, fruit juice–sweetened sorbets, and tempeh burgers. The chips are superb with any of the burgers or sandwiches in this book.

Grainaissance, Inc.
1580 62nd Street
Emeryville, California 94608
(800) 472-4697

This company produces mochi and amasake.

Harvest Direct
P.O. Box 4514
Decatur, Illinois 62525
(800) 835-2867

A distributor of over 600 foods which are available by mail order catalog.

Live Food Products, Inc.
P.O. Box 7
Santa Barbara, California 93102
(800) 446-1990

They sell Bragg Liquid Aminos, a liquid vegetable seasoning broth that is low in sodium and may be used in place of tamari or shoyu.

Lundberg Family Farms
P.O. Box 369
Richvale, California 95974
(916) 882-4551

The Lundbergs sell a variety of brown rices (including wehani rice), rice syrup, rice pudding mixes, and rice cakes.

Maine Coast Sea Vegetables
RR1, Box 78
Franklin, Maine 04634
(207) 565-2907

These fine people hand harvest sea vegetables off the coast of Maine (dulse, alaria, nori, kelp, and digitata), and also sell sea palm, powdered dulse and kelp, Sea Pickles, and Kelp Crunch.

Maranatha Natural Foods, Inc.
P.O. Box 1046
Ashland, Oregon 97520
(503) 488-2747

Maranatha sells nut butters (almond, hazelnut, pecan, pistachio, and cashew), trail mixes, and dry roasted nuts and seeds. I highly recommend their nut butters.

MMA Earthy Delights
4180 Keller Street, Suite B
Holt, Michigan 48842
(800) 367-4709

A good source for wild edible mushrooms, wild greens (leeks, fiddleheads, cattail, and nettles), edible flowers, baby lettuces and vegetables, fresh herbs, dried fruits, nuts, chilies, specialty grains (including hazelnut flour and chestnut flour), red and yellow sun-dried tomatoes, and saffron.

Modern Products, Inc.
6425 West Executive Drive
Mequon, Wisconsin 53092
(414) 352-3333

Producers of Fearn Natural Foods, including liquid soy lecithin, lecithin granules, soy granules (grits), and Spike, Vegit, and Veg-Sal seasonings.

Morinaga Nutritional Foods, Inc.
2050 West 190th Street, Suite 110
Torrance, California 90504
(800) 669-8638

Morinaga sells Mori-Nu Silken Tofu in 10½-ounce aseptic packages in soft, firm, and extra firm textures. They have added a "Lite" 1 percent fat version, which is also available in all three textures. This is the only silken tofu that I use.

Nasoya Foods, Inc.
23 Jytek Drive
Leominster, Massachusetts 01453
(508) 537-0713

Nasoya produces an excellent regular tofu available in soft, firm, and extra firm. They also make Nayonaise (soy mayonnaise), which is 100 percent cholesterol free.

Northern Soy, Inc.
545 West Avenue
Rochester, New York 14611
(716) 235-8970

Producers and distributors of plant-based meat analogs such as Not Dogs and soy sausage links.

Omega Nutrition U.S.A., Inc.
6505 Aldrich Road
Bellingham, Washington 98226
(604) 322-8862

This is a Canadian company which produces excellent quality organic, unrefined oils, which are sold in black plastic bottles to help retain their high quality. They sell canola, hazelnut, olive, pistachio, sesame seed, sunflower seed, and safflower oils, as well as hazelnut flour, pistachio flour, and flax seed meal.

Timber Crest Farms
4781 Dry Creek Road
Healdsburg, California 95448
(707) 433-8251

Purveyors of dried nuts and fruits, including hard-to-find blueberries, cranberries, kiwi, mango, papaya, persimmons, and star fruit. They also sell various sun-dried tomato products.

Turtle Mountain, Inc.
P.O. Box 70
Junction City, Oregon 97448
(503) 998-6778

Producers of a great low-fat ice cream substitute, Living Rightly (formerly called Living Lightly), a light, non-dairy frozen dessert that I use in many dessert and beverage recipes.

Vermont Country Maple, Inc.
P.O. Box 53
Jericho, Vermont 05465
(802) 864-7519

Vermont Country Maple produces granulated maple sugar and powdered maple sugar. These sugars have potassium, calcium, magnesium, phosphorus, manganese, and sodium, and can be used in place of rice syrup sugar, barley malt sugars, or regular sugar.

Vogue Cuisine, Inc.
437 Golden Isles Drive, Suite 15 G
Hallandale, Florida 33009
(305) 458-2915

Vogue Vege Base, produced by Vogue Cuisine, is a low-sodium vegetable-based seasoning powder that I find indispensable in my kitchen.

White Wave, Inc.
1990 North 57th Court
Boulder, Colorado 80301
(303) 443-3470

Their basic tempeh has a mild flavor and is also available in several varieties.

Wright's Natural Hickory Seasoning
Nabisco Foods
P.O. Box 1928
East Hanover, New Jersey 07936

This is the liquid hickory smoke that I use and recommend. It is completely natural with no artificial flavors.

Yves Veggie Cuisine, Inc.
1138 East Georgia Street
Vancouver, British Columbia V6A 2A8, Canada
(604) 251-1345

This company produces excellent tofu wieners, veggie wieners, chili dogs, deli slices, burgers, garden vegetable patties, garden patties with mushrooms and fine herbs, and many other fine foods.

Culinary Equipment

C M International Inc.
P.O. Box 60220
Colorado Springs, Colorado 80960
(719) 390-0505

This company sells the Stovetop Smoker Cooker that I use. They also sell alder, apple, cherry, hickory, maple, mesquite, oak, and pecan wood chips.

EdgeCraft Corporation
P.O. Box 3000
Avondale, Pennsylvania 19311-0915
(800) 342-3255

Chef's Choice kitchen knives and sharpeners are produced by the EdgeCraft Corporation. Their prices are reasonable and the quality is very high.

Lansky Sharpeners
P.O. Box 800
Buffalo, New York 14221
(716) 877-7511

This is the knife sharpening system that I use. The proper technique for using it is demonstrated in my *Friendly Foods Techniques* video.

Swiss Kitchen
228 Bon Air Center
Greenbrae, California 94904
(800) 662-5882

The major U.S. distributor for Swiss-made Kuhn-Rikon Durotherm Plus cookware (including pressure cookers), and also the Duromatic pressure cooker line. I use their quality cookware exclusively and it is the official cookware for my American Natural Foods Team.

Tilia, Inc.
568 Howard Street, 2nd floor
San Francisco, California 94105
(800) 777-5452

For those of you who like to cook ahead and freeze, can or store food airtight at room temperature, the Food$aver commercial quality vacuum packing system is designed to meet your home needs. It is USDA approved for food storage.

Spiritual practice can not be detached from practical action. One of the most practical issues is ecology.

SOURCES & SUGGESTED READINGS

Nutrition

Bailey, Covert. *Fit or Fat?* Boston, MA: Houghton Mifflin, 1989.

Ballentine, Rudolph. *Transition to Vegetarianism: An Evolutionary Step.* Honesdale, PA: Himalayan International Institute, 1987.

Ballentine, Rudolph. *Diet and Nutrition.* Honesdale, PA: Himalayan International Institute, 1978.

Barnard, Neal D. *The Power of Your Plate: A Plan for Better Living.* Summertown, TN: Book Publishing Company, 1990.

Bland, Jeffrey. *Your Health Under Siege: Using Nutrition to Fight Back.* Brattleboro, VT: Stephen Green Press, 1981.

Finnegan, John. *The Facts About Fats: A Consumer's Guide to Good Oils.* Malibu, CA: Elysian Arts, 1992.

Katahn, Martin. *The T-Factor Diet: Lose Weight Safely and Quickly Without Cutting Calories—or Even Counting Them!* New York: Bantam Books, 1990.

Koop, C. Everett. *The Surgeon General's Report on Nutrition and Health.* Public Health Service, DHHS (PHS) Publication Number 88-50210. Washington, DC: United States Department of Health and Human Services, 1988.

Ornish, Dean. *Dr. Dean Ornish's Program for Reversing Heart Disease.* New York: Random House, 1990.

Rohé, Fred. *Metabolic Ecology: A Way to Win the Cancer War.* Winfield, KS: Wedgestone Press, 1982.

Pennington, Jean A.T. *Food Values of Portions Commonly Used.* New York: Harper & Row, 1989.

Salaman, Maureen. *Foods That Heal.* Menlo Park, CA: Statford Publishing, 1989.

Food Quality

Oakley, Hugh. *The Buying Guide for Fresh Fruits, Vegetables, Herbs and Nuts.* Hagerstown, MD: Blue Goose, 1980.

Eckhardt, Linda West. *Satisfaction Guaranteed: Simply Sumptuous Mail Order Foods with Recipes and Menus for Fast and Fabulous Meals.* New York: Jeremy Tarcher, 1986.

Erasmus, Udo. *Fats and Oils.* Vancouver, BC: Alive Books, 1986.

Harrington, Geri. *Real Food, Fake Food, and Everything in Between: The Only Consumer's Guide to Modern Foods.* New York: Macmillan, 1987.

Kadans, Joseph M. *Encyclopedia of Fruits, Vegetables, Nuts and Seeds for Healthful Living.* Englewood Cliffs, NJ: Reward Books, 1975.

King, Jonathan. *Troubled Water: The Poisoning of America's Drinking Water.* Emmaus, PA: Rodale Press, 1985 (o.p.).

Lang, Jenifer Harvey. *Tastings: The Best from Ketchup to Caviar.* New York: Crown Publishers, 1986.

Moyer, Roger. *Water Treatment Handbook: A Homeowner's Guide to Safer Drinking Water.* Emmaus, PA: Rodale Press, 1985.

Walker, N.W. *Vegetarian Guide to Diet and Salad.* Phoenix, AZ: Norwalk Press, 1971.

Walker, N.W. *Fresh Vegetable and Fruit Juices: What's Missing in Your Body?* Phoenix, AZ: Norwalk Press, 1978.

Whittenberg, Margaret M. *Experiencing Quality: A Shopper's Guide to Whole Foods.* Austin, TX: Whole Foods Market, 1987.

Wood, Rebecca Theurer. *Whole Foods Encyclopedia: A Shoppers Guide.* New York: Prentice Hall, 1988.

Wood, Rebecca Theurer. *Whole Foods: A Guide for Employees of Natural Food Stores.* Hotchkiss, CO: Wood and Associates, 1983.

Diet and Ecology

Council for Economic Priorities. *Shopping for a Better World: The Quick and Easy Guide to Socially Responsible Supermarket Shopping.* San Francisco, CA: Sierra Club Books, 1994.

Duffy, William. *Sugar Blues.* New York: Warner Books, 1975.

Gore, Al. *Earth in the Balance: Ecology and the Human Spirit.* Boston, MA: Houghton Mifflin, 1992.

Lappé, Francis M. *Diet for a Small Planet.* New York: Ballantine Books, 1975.

Lerza, Catherine, and Michael Jacobson. *Food for People Not for Profit.* New York: Ballantine Books, 1975.

Rifkin, Jeremy. *Beyond Beef: The Rise and Fall of the Cattle Culture.* New York: NAL/Dutton, 1993.

Robbins, John. *Diet for a New America: How Your Food Choices Affect Your Health, Happiness, and the Future of Life on Earth.* Walpole, NH: Stillpoint Publishing, 1987.

Sale, Kirkpatrick. *Human Scale.* New York: Coward, McCann, 1980.

Simon, Arthur. *Bread for the World.* New York: Paulist Press, 1975.

Cookbooks

Devi, Yamuna. *Yamuna's Table.* New York: Dutton, 1992.

Estella, Mary. *Natural Foods Cookbook: Vegetarian Dairy-Free Cuisine.* Briarcliff Manor, NY: Japan Publications, 1985.

Famularo, Joe, and Louise Imperiale. *Vegetables: The New Main Course Cookbook.* Woodbury, NY: Barron's Educational Series, 1985.

Robertson, Laurel, Carol Flinders, and Brian Ruppenthal. *Laurel's Kitchen Recipes.* Berkeley, CA: Ten Speed Press, 1993.

Sass, Lorna J. *Recipes from an Ecological Kitchen: Healthy Meals for You and the Planet.* New York: William Morrow, 1992.

Magazines

E, The Environmental Magazine
P.O. Box 5098
Wesport, Connecticut 06881
(203) 854-5559

For subscriptions write or call: P.O. Box 699; Mt. Morris, Illinois 61054, (815) 734-1242.

Natural Health
P.O. Box 1200
Brookline Village, Massachusetts 02147
(617) 232-1000

For subscriptions write: P.O. Box 57320; Boulder, Colorado 80322-7320

Vegetarian Gourmet
2 Public Avenue
Montrose, Pennsylvania 18801-1220

For subscriptions write: P.O. Box 7641; Riverton, New Jersey 08077-7641

Vegetarian Times
P.O. Box 570
Oak Park, Illinois 60303
(800) 435-9610

Newsletters

Nutrition Action Healthletter
Center for Science in the Public Interest
1875 Connecticut Avenue N.W., Suite 300
Washington, DC 20009-5728
(202) 332-9110

University of California at Berkeley Wellness Letter
Health Letter Associates
P.O. Box 420148
Palm Coast, Florida 32142
(904) 445-6414

Tufts University Diet and Nutrition Letter
53 Park Place
New York, New York 10007
(800) 274-7581

Organizations

North American Vegetarian Society
P.O. Box 72
Dolgeville, New York 13329
(518) 568-7970

The journal *Vegetarian Voice: Perspectives on Healthy, Ecological and Compassionate Living* is published quarterly by NAVS.

American Vegan Society
501 Old Harding Highway
Malaga, New Jersey 08328

(609) 694-2887

The journal *Ahimsa* is published quarterly by AVS.
Vegetarian Resource Group
P.O. Box 1463
Baltimore, Maryland 21203
(301) 752-8348

Vegetarian Union of North America
P.O. Box 9710
Washington, DC 20016

The journal *VUNAVIEWS* is published quarterly by VUNA.

INDEX